THE SP… GUIDE FOR THE NEW MILLENNIUM

THE SPIRITUAL GUIDE FOR THE NEW MILLENNIUM

AARON JOHN BETH'EL

HILL OF CONTENT
MELBOURNE

First published in Australia by
Hill of Content Publishing Pty Ltd
86 Bourke Street, Melbourne 3000
Tel: 03 9662 2282
Fax: 03 9662 2527
Email: *hocpub@collinsbooks.com.au*

Designed by Deborah Snibson, Modern Art Production Group
Typeset by Midland Typesetters, Maryborough
Printed by Australian Print Group, Maryborough

Cataloguing-in-publication data:

Beth-el, Aaron John, date
The spiritual guide for the new millennium.

ISBN 0 85572 299 1

1. Spiritual direction. 2. Spiritual life. I. Title.

291.4

When we contemplate
we behold the direct reflection
of the temple of the divine
inside, we observe the pattern,
we worship at the altar

From the communion plate and cup provided
we eat the bread of meaning
and understanding
and drink the wine of ecstasy
and intoxication

And we are sweetly lost and found
and lost and found
and lost and found in the infinite rounds
of the eternal's memory

DEDICATION

To my Mother Pauline for her sure love

ACKNOWLEDGEMENTS

Over the years there have been many people who have knowingly or unknowingly assisted in the creation of this work, enabling me to contemplate and discover additional ways of seeing and understanding. I am grateful to you all.

In particular I heartily thank the following . . .

Phillip, my cousin, who is more like a brother, for his continuing enthusiasm and his unconventional and manifold ideas. Catherine Baker, who did an early edit and gave a wholehearted appraisal. Peter Blum, for the generous use of his computer (before I finally got my own); for his unstinting time and being ever ready to give technical help, inspired comments and philosophical discourse, as well as many a convivial coffee. Marek and Ela for their friendly technical assistance during the final stages. All the good people at Santos health foods—my second family.

The Australian Society of Authors for their constructive advice—so essential for a newly published author. Anthony Dwyer of Millennium Books, for his long-term advocacy. My editor Shelley Neller, being born on the same day, we couldn't help but have rapport. I thank her for her willingness, and for her magnificent knack of achieving the right balance.

My Mother Pauline for being my biggest fan, for her absolute positivity and her one-pointed faith in me and my work. All of my friends over the years, most of you have sparked something in the text.

Lastly I thank Michelle Anderson, the publisher at Hill of Content. For many years I prayed to have the kind of relationship with a publisher that I now have with her. Writers dream about meeting such a person, where absolute empathy and trust are able to reign.

INTRODUCTION

I have been writing 'The Spiritual Guide For The New Millennium' during the past fourteen years. It originated one night in a dream in which it actually seemed possible to enter into the mysterious workings of creation.

The next morning I excitedly began to record the impressions of my dream. This in turn led me on a quest during the next few months to discover my first 112 contemplations.

At that point I felt complete. However, my new perception of life, others, and myself, created an ongoing adventure and the contemplations continued. It soon became apparent that I was working not only with my own practical earthly experiences, but also with the inspiration of my soul, which enabled me to look more from the inside of the experiences I encountered, rather than the outside. And a redemptive kernel of understanding was nearly always to be found locked inside each.

As a student with the most to learn from this book, I respectfully offer a selection of contemplations as part of humankind's unravelling voyage to liberty.

The experiences of my daily life have taught me that life itself is our greatest teacher, if we are prepared to look and to listen. Life is eager to teach, if we open ourselves to the inherent wisdom that it flourishes upon us, unceasing and eternal . . .

with love and blessings,
Aaron John Beth'el

AUTHOR'S NOTE

The contemplations contained in The Spiritual Guide For The New Millennium are a guide to living and to understanding life in order to help achieve the ancient maxim: 'Know thyself.' However, they are not absolute, for there is always the exception to the rule.

A thesaurus may be useful for locating synonyms of a subject not listed.

Each contemplation that is one of a number on the same subject is to be considered only part of the whole matter, to be read in relationship to others of the selfsame subject.

Also, there are many crossover points between contemplations, for example; Age and Time; Emotions and Feelings; or Friends-Acquaintances and Relationships. Additionally, for a more comprehensive view, a subject such as Healing for instance, could include a look at contemplations on Body, Health, Disease, Illness, Pain, Stress, Faith and Prayer.

Where appropriate within a contemplation, key words that have their own listed contemplations may be referred to, to deepen the understanding of the primary contemplation, and for reviewing causal interrelationships between them all.

Readers may note that god or the divine (and associated expressions) are written in lower case. I have done this to detract from the ego association of entitlement with upper case lettering. My intention is to efface the idea of god possessing an ego.

Some readers may decide to spend some time focusing on a particular contemplation until they sense it is integrated into their lives. Others may want to make a list of their preferred contemplations or add to them with their own creative thoughts and experiences.

True laws are already known
they need not be learned
only realised
only recalled

A

ACCEPTANCE

1. Being accepted and the ease we experience in the presence of another are correlative, and usually established in the first moments of interaction. It is important that we approach others with a healthy self-acceptance already in place.

2. Most of us are looking for attention and acceptance from others. Essentially we are looking for others to focus their love on us that we may be recognised for the wonderful beings we are, and thereby taken into consideration, whilst freely being given permission to extend ourselves. However, until we recognise for ourselves who we are, and therefore why we are here, we will lead lives of desperate and fearful yearning for this acceptance from others.

3. We all desire to be accepted, by family, friends, co-workers, community, and so on. Through participating in the consensus of customs, dress, and language, we make ourselves acceptable to others. We give ourselves to these conventions in order to gain admittance to a group, and thereby the security it offers. This occurs in all stratas of society, from rich to poor, liberal to conservative, alternative to traditional. However, in seeking acceptance, we may be forfeiting a large degree of individuality and independence. We may find it difficult to act independently for fear of breaking the code of convention. Our internal sense of acceptance gives us the ability to truly be an individual. Ultimately it is the only place where we may find a reliable security.

4. The deeper we know ourselves, the more we can accept others, ourselves, as well as agreeably receive life. Sometimes this acceptance manifests in faith and trust. Though only the divine knows completely, and can accept entirely.

ACCUSATION

5. When we are accused by others, the danger is that the more we self-justify, the more we dig into our expression of ego. And the more we dig into our ego, the more separated we become from our accusers, and consequently their tendency would be to view us as being all the more guilty. When accused, our foremost requirement is to remember to keep faith with one's true self.

6. If we angrily accuse another, it is highly unlikely that they will admit to the crime, for our anger will likely be a catalyst to move them into their survival mode.

ACHILLES HEEL

7. The forces of balance inherent in life will sooner or later find our Achilles heel; in order that we may have awareness of it, give it attention, seek understanding, and finally bring healing.

ACKNOWLEDGEMENT

8. To truly acknowledge another human being is to acknowledge the fundamental truth of their existence. It is the supreme welcome we all seek and desire. However if others do not acknowledge us, to remember that the divine is our ongoing witness.

ACTION

9. When we act only from our ego mind there is fear, or conquest, and forgetfulness.

When we act only from our stomach, there is greed and forgetfulness.

When we act only from our genitals, there is lust and forgetfulness.

When we act from our heart, there is an awakening, a remembrance, and an invitation to love.

When we act from our soul, there is only love.

10. All movement, all action, conscious or unconscious, creates change and is change itself.

11. Action is the practising and unfolding of 'Act I On.' The force of our will in motion acts not only upon our focus but also upon ourselves, and we become that.

12. Whenever awareness contains action, the action is empowered, made more potent.

ADDICTION

13. Any addiction falsely feeds us. Addiction occurs whenever we lose touch with the fullness of present moment consciousness to the addictive substance or process outside of ourselves. Addiction appears to be a compensatory action for the loss of soul meaning. One's inner meaning, and therefore one's place here, has become doubted.

14. Our physical, mental, and emotional addictions, restrain us from truly experiencing the infinite, eternal, present moment of joy. (See Habit, Obsession.)

ADVERSITY

15. The first and most important thing to remember in the face of adversity is that one is a spark of the divine, and therefore greater than all adversity. It is an opportunity to embrace one's deeper understanding.

ADVICE

16. The more definite our advice to others, usually the more ego we have invested in our advice. Everyone is sensitive; few like to be told advice unless they are in crisis. It is preferable we only

make suggestions. Definite advice spoken from the ego, rarely sounds right to either the speaker or the listener. It makes one sound like the Teacher—superior, and the other the Student—inferior. We need to formulate our communication with greater integrity, so that there is equality of purpose in both giving and receiving. This formulation appears most possible with heart-to-heart communication.

✳

AESTHETE

17. An aesthete is a disciple of beauty, one who is intimate with beauty's laws of grace, symmetry, harmony, elegance, radiance and delight. And therefore an aesthete is not only a disciple of beauty, but also a prophet who already lives in paradise.

✳

AESTHETICS

18. Aesthetics are aligned with the will of beauty. They unashamedly gain the attention of our deep feelings and carry us with reverence into the sacred dominion of our heart and soul.

✳

AFFIRMING

19. If we are mentally forcing ourselves to instil new subconscious patterns, then our daily conscious mind (which is doing the forcing) may not fully believe in these new thoughts and create an underlying thought of rejection. The forcing may reinforce the deeper thought, that we have not got this now, and therefore such forcing is indicative of our anxiety about it. It may instead be necessary to focus on our receptivity. To feel that if these new thoughts are for our highest good, then they are truthfully ours, and therefore to gently accept, yield, and rest in this recognition.

20. It is beneficial to not only place our affirmations in the present tense, but also to place our feelings regarding them in the present tense also. This fully places the affirmation in the present, with a sense of excitement, fulfilment, and gratitude.

21. To place a time structure on affirmations, may be pandering to a never-ending round of ego expectations, and nullifying the fullness of present moment awareness where we can live already in fulfilment, already in deep knowing, regardless of the current external circumstances.

22. If we claim the qualities we seek in the moment, which is the only place we can live, this will naturally claim those qualities for the future. This is preferable to claiming for the future, and not living now. In patiently claiming now what is ours, we are not living greedily, in order to claim more in the future.

AGE

23. Identifying too strongly with chronological age shall lose us the vision and purpose for which we came here.

24. Chronological age has an imposed collection of societal beliefs attached to it, which gives us a limited view of ourselves. The age we feel has more relevance to our internal being, and according to how we govern our internal state, has more flexibility. However, the supreme truth is that of our soul, which is as old as the universe, if not older; this is our true age.

25. Asking someone their age is often an admission of not being able to take them at face value, without needing to judge them according to the beliefs and criteria of chronological age.

26. The attaching of the age belief onto the costume of our identity helps advance the idea that we are the costume, and not the ageless, blissful true self.

27. The less we live with ego, the more we live in the present, and the more ageless we become.

28. When we ask a person their age, we are asking them to identify with their conditioned sense of self, the ego, when they reply 'I am (so many) years old,' but truly the 'I am' is not this. And often what follows is a judgmental or comparing thought in our ego, which assesses how they look, and what they have

achieved in this time frame. It is all ego masquerade.

29. Chronological aging promotes the belief in limitation, but our very nature is infinite. Therefore chronological aging is a lie against the soul.

30. Children live mostly in the present, and therefore they experience long, full days. But as they develop and mature, society teaches them to move out of the present, and they spend an increasing amount of unconscious consciousness in time, both past and future. Adults usually spend most of their lives living this way, and therefore their days are fleeting, and with less content. Being rarely alive in the present makes adults prone to aging.

31. If we believe in the idea of chronological age, we will not be able to avoid measuring our lives according to the schedule of attainment, success, and limitations supposedly reached at certain ages, as laid down by the society we live in.

32. From the western point of view, there appear to be only seven years in life when we are fully socially acceptable for our age. These years are, firstly, from birth until two, when children enter a phase many call the 'terrible twos.' This discrimination continues largely unconsciously through childhood, adolescence, and teenage years, all accompanied by the passing of judgments on chronological age. And, secondly, from 25 to 29. Until one reaches 25, there is a sense of not being a full adult. However, upon reaching 30, we are considered 'over the hill.' And the more we are beyond 30, the further we are considered 'over the hill.'

33. The first 25 years of a human life are spent ripening and developing—a different concept to aging, which supposedly starts after the age of 25, if one associates oneself with the passing phenomenon of time.

34. Agism is the largest 'ism' in society for it affects everyone. And yet for the most part this 'ism' is still largely unconscious. Agism also appears to be becoming more acute in its emphasis and vigour, so that more and more people are considered unworthy or unproductive.

35. In society, the general thought is that we live to be three score years and ten. Once maturity is reached, and we continue adding years to our chronological age, we draw closer year by year to three score years and ten. The adding on of a year at birthdays then becomes a negative affirmation to one's body/mind, that one is aging and deteriorating, becoming less fit, slowing down, and preparing oneself for death.

36. The passing phenomenon of time is the background illusion imposed upon matter, but it can never be the foreground, that is, measured in the present. From the human point of view, the passing of years refers to this background illusion, not to any moment our infinite presence spends in present-moment consciousness. If we think of ourselves as being more of the background than the foreground, we are susceptible to aging.

37. According to quantum physics linear time is not the absolute we take it to be. Time is relative to the holder's outlook. From the grandiose, celestial view, of the pure unconstrained present, each of us is eternal.

38. I do not believe in chronological age as a means of measuring ability or maturity. I have met wise, able, so-called 'immature' young people, and foolish, incompetent, so-called 'mature' old people. Primarily, it is a person's awareness that measures their true maturity, not the number of years they have spent on the planet.

39. Aging predominantly mirrors the embodiment of emotional and mental negative experience. We embody our experience because we think we are a limited ego, and this limited ego carries burdens. We have forgotten our true identity—the bliss of the divine.

40. One of the causes of aging is too much external association. That is, associating with a particular era in time and with the limited perspective this gives, which makes for a great deal of our negative view of our self, others, and the world. When we internalise our association, we begin to become as one with our

true essence, so that there is less separation of self, others, places, times, or dimensions.

41. Youthfulness arises out of the aware decision to have wonder, fun, and spontaneity in life; it is not dependent upon chronological age.

42. Agism is used primarily to differentiate egos. The soul does not require such differentiation.

43. Age does not necessarily equal experience. It is consciousness that approximates to our growth. The more consciously we undergo our experience, the more we learn regardless of age.

44. Once we realise that we are more than our age, we can be creative with our expression of age. We can take a year off our birthday instead of adding one; we can feel what it would be like to live with the wisdom of a thousand years or more. We can play with it instead of taking it seriously and being victim to a number.

45. We do not grow into old age by the second, minute, hour, or day, but by seeing less, hearing less, and shortening our horizons.

46. How can we possibly be open to the unlimited and infinite in another, if we confine them to the emotional judgments that arise in ourselves, from a belief in the numeral boundaries of chronological age?

47. Our present system of time was begun from the era of Christ, a time of great transition. Whenever we as individuals experience transcendent life-changing moments, we are born again, we begin anew, and we have a new dawn from which to commence our own chronological time as an initiate on the earth.

48. When we unquestioningly take on, physically embody and personalise the passing of years as one's sense of self, we unconsciously age. However, we may see beyond the crib-like earth, to the sun, where our circumscribed perception of time first originated, and now embody the sun as our eternal, infinitely reaching source of light-time.

AGREEMENT

49. An agreement implies a union that gives equality of truth and understanding. Unless it contains these qualities its validity is annulled.

ALIVENESS

50. The energy of aliveness primarily arises from having a zestful will to love, and the awareness that one's inner being is this love. One lives on the edge where freedom, spontaneity, timing, and a higher view of beauty are seen. In the joy of this life-teeming aliveness, the security of conditioned socialised existence is dropped.

ALONENESS

51. In our aloneness we tend to come face to face with our true self, and we are full, content, and feel the expansive power of love. But when we emote loneliness, we come face to face with our ego, and we are restless, isolated, lessened, and suffer the constricting power of fear.

ANGER

52. Largely, anger results from the unexpected breakdown of the presumption that one is in control of others. However, does our anger response create what we want? Through anger do others then allow themselves to be controlled, or do they in turn attempt to control us?

53. Anger creates a covering for what we think is a deeper inadmissible need—for example: 'I want you to care and to love me.' Anger is a tool of coercion to try to get such needs met. But most attempts at using force to gain love fail. We need to ask ourselves what would be a more intelligent and loving approach.

54. When angry, of what are we fearful. Are we afraid that others' lack of understanding blinds them to the truth about us? Why are we so insecure. Do we need to convince everyone?

55. The words and emotions we use when angry are often more self-reflective than indicative of the words and emotions we say belong to others we may be entangled with. Similarly, the anger that arises because of perceived faults in another may arise because those same characteristics are unacknowledged in oneself.

56. The buildup of anger appears to weave through a pattern of . . . irritation, impatience, disappointment, frustration, annoyance, rumination, hurt, loneliness, fear, suppression, depression, resentment, anxiety, hopelessness, destructive impulses (e.g. eating, sleeping and working disorders, martyrdom and so on) stubbornness, hatred, self-righteousness, blaming and then aggression. Obviously the earlier we catch it, the less need there is to experience the subsequent deepening states of constriction before the explosion.

57. The phases of anger can be divided into three broad categories, beginning with irritation-frustration, followed by the intermediate stage of hurt-resentment, and finally detonating into blaming-aggression.

58. Anger appears to be catalysed by a sense of disappointment, fuelled by expectation. One has expectations, which are unrealised. Having many expectations can create a certain anxiety. Anxiety, however, is a closing valve on our emotional state that allows steam to build as a precursor to anger.

59. There are two broad categories of communication in anger. Blaming is the most common. And the other, far more preferable, is the conveying of a sense of one's self-frustration. Frustration also arises much earlier than the state of blaming, and therefore is closer to the truth of the original situation.

60. In a normal conversation, if we become irrationally angry, very likely our anger is arising from something previously unresolved within ourselves.

61. Our anger reveals the workings of an upset ego, threatened by a sense of separation from others, as well as a sense of a loss of power, because one's power base, the status quo, is perceived to have shifted. Anger seeks revenge for the sense of upset; it is an attempt to reclaim the status quo, and therefore it is an attempt to restore the past, and possibly not move forward.

62. Anger is characterised by . . .

(a) The interpretation that one's ego pride has been wounded.

(b) A sense of resentment, that one has not been understood.

(c) A sense of irritation, and the perception of an opposition.

(d) A sense of stubbornness.

(e) A sense of being made invalid.

(f) That one's self-worth is lowered. (Probably because one's sense of self-worth was inadequate before.)

(g) A sense of violation (one's power base is perceived to be infringed).

(h) A sense of excessive touchiness and hurt.

(i) A sense of constant and anxious checking, and eating away at oneself.

(j) A sense of blaming.

(k) A sense of revenge and sometimes violence.

(l) Uncertainty; the movement away from a calm and peaceful mind.

(m) Impatience.

(n) Disappointment, of unrealised expectations.

(o) Reactivity.

(p) Judgmentalness.

(q) Self-righteousness.

(r) Impulsiveness and hastiness, and the loss of the ability to think and act clearly.

(s) Sometimes a blind, boiling, confusing, unrestrained fit.

All of these emotions tend to disempower us. They appear to be the workings of an obsessive focus of the ego on self-righteousness. It is the ego's aggression against not only the other's ego, but in its most extreme form, against the other's total being. In this way it is an attempt to deny the other the space for existing in the world in which the angered person lives, and therefore it is the denial of their divine state, and of our divine responsibility.

63. It is unskilful to expect another to behave in an integrated and cooperative manner if we have unloaded our anger towards them. If they do behave in an integrated manner after such an outburst, it has nothing to do with our anger but more to do with their own inner harmony.

64. Anger is often an avoidance of the present for a mind full of controlling thoughts based on past expectations. It is important for us to bring our entire attention back to the present.

65. Consciously acting out anger in a non-threatening way, particularly phase three anger (see Anger contemplation No. 57), through such things as hitting pillows, using anger energy to do cleaning, having someone be a neutral sounding board and so on, can revitalise and reconnect our scattered energies so that we regain our self-power. The liver is enlivened, and we become alert, primed, and more consciously self-willed. However, our fundamental requirement is to speak the belief underlying our emotional outburst, and then to speak the truth.

ANNOYANCE

66. Annoyance over trifling, surface issues is a sign that there is something much larger bubbling underneath.

ANXIETY

67. There are two kinds of anxiety; one is generated by the fear of not fully knowing, and subsequently a fantasy of foreboding fills in the unknown part. The other is the excited fear of knowing, and of the overwhelming implications of coming close to our desire. Both are based in fear, and are lessons in trust; in neither are we fully embracing the present moment that life is offering.

APOLOGY

68. We can only apologise unreservedly and unconditionally, otherwise we seek from the other the validation for our self-justification.

69. Overly expecting an apology from someone places us in the position of 'neediness' and therefore under their power.

70. We cannot be truthfully sorry unless we have first surrendered. When we surrender, grace enters, and being sorry is swept away by love.

71. How transparent and without substance we appear to ourselves and to those around us, when we try to seek understanding, or to apologise to others with our personality ego. It seems like we are acting, and in our acting we are stepping further away from that which creates union—the uniting force of the heart.

72. There appears to be no situation in which there is any need to apologise for being true to one's true self.

APPETITES

73. Listening and acting upon the appetites of the ego will eventually overwhelm the body/mind with disease and death. When we listen with more sensitively attuned senses to our spirit, we act with mindful awareness of what we truly require.

APPRECIATION

74. When we are present in our 'being' nature (without interruption of thought from the ego mind), we appreciate life and others fully. When we appreciate, we see that all creation is vibrantly alive.

75. The things we demean today, we may appreciate tomorrow, simply because we become more conscious of their value. Appreciation is directly linked to one's conscious recognition.

76. Our ability to appreciate (both towards oneself as well as others) elevates the creative, humane, and honourable virtues. Appreciation brings these things forward, and makes us more conscious of them, that we may aspire to greater heights.

✳

APPROPRIATE

77. When someone acts in self-empowered congruence with the moment, then an appropriate action arises naturally, and its ramifications are responsibly embraced. Consistency, timing, and harmony prevail. The potency and devotion between the macrocosm of the universe and the microcosm of man are established in union.

78. There are times to be gentle and compassionate, and times to be firm and strong. The more conscious we become, the more consciously we can approach a situation as it arises, and the more we are able to choose an appropriate way and an appropriate response.

✳

APPROVAL

79. Whenever we eagerly fall into line with the thinking of others, we are also overly looking for love and approval outside of ourselves.

80. If we often look for acceptance and approval from others, we place ourselves in debt to them and under their power.

81. We cannot seek approval from another by lessening our own self-radiance, for invariably we demean ourselves in the other's view.

✳

ARGUMENT

82. During the heat of argument, if our own force of ego overshadows our heart, we have lost, even if we triumph over the other with our reasoning.

83. The greater the emotional investment we have in our

argument, the more our argument is emotionally based, not factually based. The emotion itself is then primarily used to prop our self-interest and self-centred expression, not the issue.

✳

ARMOURING

84. Armouring occurs because we desire to control the amount of sensation we are exposed to in the world. However if it is unexamined, it is often a state of avoidance. We cannot be free and at ease unless we are able to show what is in our hearts.

85. To armour ourselves we can use clothing, cosmetics, tattoos, jewellery, glasses, sunglasses, deafness, drugs, posture, set attitudes, and association with like-minded others (amongst other things). Armouring, and the setting of attitudes, usually causes a distortion in the associated part of the body. However, no one can armour themselves completely, and such attempts at armouring usually leave us highly vulnerable in at least one part of the body or emotions.

✳

ARROGANCE

86. Arrogance is the greed of the ego breeding more ego. The arrogant person thinks that ego is their true state of being. They think that this state must be vigorously upheld and sometimes inflated, particularly when threatened by what they perceive to be only the minor ego rights of others, with whom they fear they are in competition.

✳

ART

87. The application of any design can be art. However the harmonic relationship of earth, air, fire, and water in combination physically, mentally and spiritually reveals the development of the artist's inner harmony, and consequently the development of human harmony. The more pronounced the harmonic balance

between the elements, the more that art becomes aesthetically pleasing.

88. Art deeply, expresses the inquiry and revelation of the essence of life.

AS IT IS

89. The closer we get to witnessing life 'As it is,' without our compulsive need to diagnose, make interpretations and judgments of others, the less pain and self-delusion we shall create.

ASSERTION

90. The power of assertion lies in being true to one's true self.

ASSIMILATE

91. Ultimately we are all learning to assimilate each other.

ATTACHMENT

92. We attach ourselves unnecessarily when we attach to selfish and conditioned thoughts. These thoughts always have their origin outside the present, and therefore we are attempting to attach ourselves to something that no longer exists or has not come into existence.

93. Attachment to fixed thought creates all negative emotions and their consequent actions.

ATTACK

94. If someone says this is a truth and they use it to attack another, it is highly likely that it is a pseudo ego truth, based on the illusions of the separating ego.

95. When we are attacked verbally or emotionally, the ego rushes

in to defend itself, afraid that it might not somehow survive the onslaught. However if we can remember that the death of our ego occurs whenever we return to our source.

96. At the time that we are experiencing attack, we generally forget who we are, and we tend to hold and become attached to the attacker's view of ourselves. But when we truly know who we are, we are detached from that which is false.

ATTEMPT

97. If we make the attempt, we learn a little more of freedom, though it may come through trial. Not making an attempt, we deny ourselves the free will to choose, and the evolution of our consciousness that comes from making successful as well as unsuccessful attempts.

ATTENTION

98. Whenever human attention is stimulated, human consciousness endeavours to seek resolution by self-discrimination and self-integration.

99. Where we place our attention is where we also gain our awareness. Are we placing our attention in the area where we want to be aware?

ATTITUDE

100. Most states of mind are chosen. If we understand this we can allow ourselves to live more freely, happily, and be more spontaneous.

101. Old attitudes cannot create new experiences.

102. Generally attitudes are formed by a blend of opinion and fact, slanted towards the holder's viewpoint.

103. Attitude arises from the subconscious emotional state unless we consciously and actively work with it.

ATTRACTION

104. Our ability to emanate love without need, creates in us the most powerful state of magnetic attraction in ourselves towards others, and to the abundance in our environment.

105. Usually we decree our own personal level of attraction to another. It determines our openness, willingness, and our relationship to them.

106. When we know what our true nature is, then we naturally radiate love with confidence, and we attract people who want to love. Love is the foundation of our confidence of attraction.

AUTHORITY

107. The purest authority issues from the soul, because the soul makes no demands.

108. Authority is established in the belief of authority. Without a basis of belief, authority lacks power and its dominion will be difficult to uphold.

109. We can only speak with any kind of authority about our own experience.

110. Anyone, or any organisation, that presumes themselves to be an ultimate authority, and then speaks of boundaries and limitations, is not to be believed.

111. Practising authority for the sake of authority, is a futile exercise in believing that the universe revolves around one's ego.

112. If we are to be an authority, it is preferable that others grant us this status, rather than we make a claim.

113. When we make ourselves an authority, we tend to close down towards the infinite possibilities available to us, confining ourselves to those areas we view our authority covering.

114. In giving ourselves to an authority we do not respect, we constantly undermine our own will.

115. Those who have gained ascendancy and dominion over themselves command a natural authority.

AVAILABLE

116. If we are really available with all our heart, for love, happiness, work and so on, only then are we ready to serve our true purpose and to walk our true path. Only then are we accessible, able to be effective, and able to attain. We may ask 'Are we available?'

AVOIDANCE

117. Avoidance creates a background of emotional anxiety. Our lives then seem busier, but not because of things to do, rather because of the squeezing out of life from carrying this anxious, unresolved tension.

118. We cannot pretend that truth doesn't exist by avoiding it.

119. It is difficult to avoid someone or something without the impression that our own sense of wholeness has been cut off.

120. When our ego chooses avoidance of another, we are avoiding the dance of life. And we find ourselves as wallflowers, looking on from the void of our own emotional loneliness.

121. Our greatest avoidance as human beings is not the past, but the present.

122. To the extent that we are avoiding, that aspect of us is not present, or even on the planet. It is lost in a previous frame of existence elsewhere. Where are we?

AWARENESS

123. Awareness unveils the true state of a human. However as soon as this relaxed state is punctured by a thought from the egoic mind, full awareness of the infinite present is lost, and one steps

into the dimensional vestments of time, and the often emotional roller coaster ride of the ego. Our primary state of being is awareness, not egoic thought.

124. The key to all states of being, understanding, happiness, and fulfilment, is simply, awareness. Awareness is the attentive consciousness that accompanies seeing with a perpetually virgin mind, rather than the routine practice of looking through old frames of reference.

125. Full understanding of an experience often does not come until afterwards. Many of our experiences are sacrifices to our growing awareness.

126. True awareness does not create resistance to what was previously seen as being undesirable; rather it embraces all aspects in an overview of understanding.

127. To raise awareness is to raise the level of one's appreciation of oneself, and beyond this to the appreciation of others and the world.

128. The finer forces of life that animate us and surround us . . . from the spirit of this pen with which I write, to the spirit of a moth flying by, to the spirit of the air and sky, to the symphonic spirit of the evening ocean cascading in the distance . . . how rich our lives are made by this simple awareness . . . so much to see, so much to listen to, and so many with whom to speak.

129. The natural state of a soul is awareness. Being naturally aware, our souls love unquestioningly and absolutely.

130. Awareness, is the quiescent, tranquil state of love.

AWKWARDNESS

131. At those times we experience a state of awkwardness, characterised by gracelessness and incoordination, either physically or mentally, we have effectively lost balance with our inner

equilibrium. Awkwardness then becomes both an obvious sign, and a tool for regaining our inner balance and composure.

B

✳

BACK TO FRONT

132. Whenever there is excess, overindulgence, overload, exaggeration beyond the bounds of integrity, then a maxim I have named 'The Back-to-front principle' is a handy tool. It states that on such occasions, the truth will likely be found in a place completely opposite to where we think it is, or where we have been told it is.

✳

BALANCE

133. When we balance all that appears contradictory, higher or lower, then the central point from which all has arisen begins to become apparent. This reality exists without duplicity. It feels relaxed and knowing. One is at home. All is complete.

134. We are always heading towards balance, even when we sense being unbalanced. This too is part of the harmonising influence of the universe.

135. When we are not in balance, our environment reflects the fact, just as surely as it does when we are in balance. When we are not in balance, we become clumsy, the cat runs beneath our feet, things fall off the shelf. There is a correspondence, a recognition in the environment around us, even in the inanimate things that all is not well. Similarly, when we are in balance, there is an electric charge in the air, we act with harmony and confidence, everything is where it ought to be, and things run smoothly.

136. If we suspect that another is lacking balance in a particular area of their life and we exaggerate it in order to point it out (which is also an attempt to push them into that unbalanced place), at that moment we too are lacking balance in our life.

137. The keeping of balance in supreme health, seems to be in living in a state of equivalence between one's inner energy and the outer energy of the planet. It is believing and living to the ideal that one's place is here; that one is worthwhile and potent enough to live to the requirements of one's true journey, and the requirements of the earth. And also, in the breaking down of the idea of separation of self from others and the planet, so that one's life and energy are intimately and consciously linked to the life and energy here.

BARRIERS

138. When we break through our self-limiting barriers, our view is widened, and we perceive a greater sense of freedom in the world as well as ourselves.

139. Barriers between people are more easily diffused by love first, than by the sharpness of truth.

140. The one who has a love of life breaks through the barriers of separateness created by others.

141. Whenever we lower our barriers of unlove and untruth to reveal our essential nature of love and truth to each other, we find that we are not different, but similar, and union naturally begins.

BEAUTY

142. Beauty exposes the transcendent hand reaching from beyond the physical world.

143. Wherever we hear a beautiful voice, see a thing of beauty, or feel the sense of the beautiful, immediately we are transported back into ourselves, into our soul.

144. When we step upon the path of beauty, we surrender to its wonder, serenity, grace, mystery, and divinity. With these things we move in effulgent joy. Our senses constantly reach in and reach out, which in turn creates a bridge of beauty for us to walk upon the earth.

145. At the time we see a thing of beauty or a beautiful face, if instead of wanting to possess it, we praise the divine for creating such beauty and silently give thanks, our gratitude becomes an outpouring of love that adds to the appreciation of this world. The act of gratitude is magnetic, whereas the act of self-seeking is deflective.

146. It is not only beauty that is in the eye of the beholder, but ugliness also.

147. A beautiful thing or a beautiful person often has a certain innocence and fragility. Likewise, innocence and fragility help create beauty. And these states keep sublime beauty as a thing rare.

148. The admission and passage to beauty is in losing one's head to the heart's dominion; in blissfully rejoicing in the fullness of beauty inside one's heart, and in seeing its qualities shining everywhere.

149. Beauty is an entrancing symphony played not for itself but for an attentive audience, to remind us of our deep longing to return to our beatific home.

150. When we recognise beauty, we honour it and we want to pay homage, for we recognise its symmetry, grace, and harmony as being the exhilarating blossom of heaven.

151. The degree of loyalty we feel to the presence and creation of beauty, is also evidence of the loyalty to our soul.

152. Beauty carries us in a sweet hypnotic faith to the mystical shores of forever.

BEAUTY, DENY

153. If we deny the manifold qualities of our beauty, we are automatically in the process of creating something that is less than beautiful.

154. Whenever we debase beauty, we are debasing ourselves and denying our place in a natural world of beauty.

BECOMING

155. Whatever we think, whatever we emote, whatever we feel, moment by moment determines who we are, and what we are becoming.

BEGINNING

156. The more mindful we become, the more we begin. Each time we return to mindfulness, we return to the beginning. Ultimately, there are only infinite upon infinite beginnings.

157. The heart of each moment comprises innocence, love and freedom, which proclaims their immaculate beginning.

BEHAVIOUR

158. We all tend to be set by primary behaviours. Whatever we are first exposed to has a tendency for creating the future pattern.

BEING

159. Just being, without any attempt to make things happen, we regain the peace and ease of the lost world we long for.

160. When one is being, one is always at the beginning, the place of origin—refreshed and virginal.

161. A slow, still reverence is required to make us vessels to contain the energy of consciousness to be.

162. The state of full being seems to occur during those times of consciousness when we are aware of the foreground, the background, and our own ground, merging.

163. When we are not consciously 'being,' our focus is concentrated in the lesser consciousness of ego identity, ego fears, and ego desires.

164. Any state of being that is not love and joy appears to be for the purpose of learning about love and joy and for guiding us back.

165. A self-integrated, composed being lives—

Surrendered to the divine. From this surrender, a place of emptiness and no thought is entered, where we become the innocent child again.

Stillness arises from this emptiness.

From this stillness develops mindfulness. We become more mindful of the sublime and transcendent states of love, beauty, and joy.

With mindfulness we flow with life, not resisting. What we do, we do without the egoic awareness of doing.

Flowing with life, we realise that this same inner harmony we are experiencing internally is also to be seen externally. All is in its rightful place, all is present, and we are undivided from it; we are it!

166. If we are being now what we want to become, we are living now what we have already become. This unifies our future desire with our present presence.

167. The difference between not having what we know is deeply right for us, seems relative to the degree that we are not fully being who we are.

BELIEFS

168. When we have more invested in a belief or an idea than the ability to listen to our heart, we have lost.

169. No one has the authority on earth to set the parameters of ultimate belief.

170. Ego-based beliefs tend to produce ego-based results; they bring with them a degree of unconsciousness, which in turn will create disharmony, and the unhappiness of egoic disconnection. They will not produce the degree of happiness that we long for internally.

171. For the most part, conditioning beliefs become thieves of present intelligence.

172. When our beliefs are aligned with the harmonising oneness of the divine, they are no longer beliefs. Similarly, the same can be said for our experiences.

173. Because the ego is a limited state, it cannot produce more than a limited state (and often cannot produce within the limited state), therefore to believe and expect to produce an infinite state through one's ego will be difficult.

174. All beliefs are ego-based, whether we believe experience comes first or belief comes first, it is all arising in the multi-faceted play of the separated ego.

175. Both belief and experience, come second, neither comes first. We need to ask what makes the parameters of our belief, and how did we arrive at those parameters. And also, what makes the parameters of our experience, and how did we arrive at those?

176. We cannot separate belief from experience, it is all belief, and it is all experience, for who amongst us is a virginal perceiver?

177. Whenever we are put on the spot, it is so that we may look a little more deeply at our beliefs, and not for concentrating on the anxiety we may sense at the time.

178. When we look from the open-ended view of the infinite, we

have no contracting reality to defeat us, rather, we believe and know the highest of possibilities.

179. The belief in our ego largely creates the spectrum of beliefs we hold. However the awareness of our soul creates love, truth, beauty, innocence and peace.

180. The most worthwhile of beliefs seem to be the ones that reach towards an embrace of all.

BENEVOLENCE

181. At the core of every being there is a sublime benevolence. It is this we must endeavour to remember, regardless of what is said and done.

182. Unexpected benevolence, from the gift of a smile to any act of generosity, brings new life into the world.

BETRAYAL

183. Is there any greater betrayal than to betray one's soul? If we are betrayed, and we restrain our own ability to love, or we betray another and likewise have forgotten love—we are betraying our own soul.

BIGOTRY

184. Bigotry is always triggered by the narrow perception of external realities, not by the knowing of internal truths.

BINDINGS

185. Those particular bindings that may limit us, for example, family, finance, friends, work, location, and so on, can rarely be cut effectively without cutting off something of our own sense of wholeness. Rather, it seems part of our human calling that we

learn to transform our relationship to those bindings, as well as to our understanding of freedom.

BIRTHPLACE

186. To take more interest in the nationhood of one's place of birth, than the soul's decision to arrive at that place, and how that decision helped create the personal ego and nationality, is another way of elevating the ego (an effect) above the soul (cause).

BLAME

187. Blaming is often the scapegoat for our own inaction and irresponsibility. It is an attempt to enforce a stigma of guilt upon another through our self-righteousness.

188. Deep down we believe that we are innocent and therefore blameless. When someone blames us, we think that they are attacking and rejecting our very essence. Fear is often experienced, along with a loss of power. So it is not surprising that most of us respond with a stubborn, overreacting, self-righteous defence. This blaming energy is thrown back and forth between the blamed and the blamer until it culminates in a stalemate of anger and emotional hurt.

Each person demands justice by attempting to pin fault, responsibility, and guilt on the other, in order to protect their own internal state of innocence.

The more intimate the relationship, the more likelihood there is of personalised blame occurring. Each time a blaming situation arises, it is important for us to remember when we last thought, experienced, or performed the action ourselves. We then become aware that such occurrences are part of the mutual fabric of the relationship, which are to be shared and learned from, rather than to be a competition for the high moral ground, or for power.

189. A human being can only accept so much blame, and beyond this, regardless of the truth of accusation, the protective walls of the ego will arise.

190. How can we possibly apportion blame in the world? Are some to be guilty, a few to be innocent, whilst the vast majority of us are to be the judiciary? We are obliged to accept an equal share of what life and this world offers.

191. We live in a blaming society, but in reality, no soul in the history of mankind has ever been guilty. For our essential self, our soul, is always innocent. The reason it is very difficult for any of us to admit blame is that we have to deny the innocence of our soul to do so. To admit to guilt is a form of suicide, for it prematurely cuts one's vulnerable ego away from one's soul. Therefore we have to be careful when blaming another, that we speak only of their actions, and not of the person, and that we seek to rectify the situation, rather than get stuck in the blaming.

BLESSINGS

192. The declaration of blessings is initiated by calling upon one's inner divine, to bestow a sacred favour of love, through grace.

193. When we instantaneously bless others, we lay a foundation for union with them. We embrace them before the fear-filled, judgmental mind has the opportunity to create separation, that locks our energy into defensiveness, withheld emotional patterns, rigidity, and armouring.

194. How easily we forget that the creative hand of a rapturously exalted consciousness already blesses everything.

195. We seem to avoid the recognition of our blessings, because we tend to focus more on our so-called problems and obstacles. However, if we were to look closely at those too, we would see that many of them are blessings also.

196. To fully recognise, welcome and receive blessings, it is preferable we be more empty, be more present.

197. A blessing occurs wherever there is an unconditioned act of love.

BLISS

198. The divine's perpetual jubilation in creating a universe, is the sweetness of bliss.

199. Essentially, bliss is the background of the universe. All else that happens is the universal game, played upon this background of bliss. If this were not so, bliss would not exist, neither would love, truth, or innocence. Nor would these qualities feel innate.

BODY

200. The body is a condensed field of light (the sub-molecular form of the body is composed of light particles, according to science) upon which interacting frequencies are played and performed. It is an instrument that requires constant internal tuning on many vibratory levels, so that it may use its greatest potential for realising symphony with others and the divine.

201. Our body/mind speaks, listens, tastes, sees, smells, feels, loves, prays, meditates, eats, evacuates, sleeps, dreams, reproduces, breathes, thinks, remembers, cultivates, and grows, not just from the main organs or senses, but with every single cell. The body is itself alive; it is a humaniverse, it contains gods, galaxies and civilisations.

202. A human being is formed of 75% water, and the rest is composed of the elements of earth. The water has travelled far—it has touched the bottom of the ocean, circulated through the bodies of marine life, glided through underwater gardens, risen to the azure sky, created magnificent cloud sculptures, been a blanket for the sun, moon and stars, formed rainbows, taken part in storms, descended from the highest mountains, become snow and ice, rained upon land and ocean, collected in lakes and rivers both above and below the earth, irrigated wild and cultivated lands, been drunk and excreted by innumerable animals, moistened the soil and travelled through roots and trunks and branches, to finally collect in the great ocean, again and again.

The elements were once part of rock and soil, of deep valleys and tall mountains, of deserts and glaciers, of grasses, trees and flowers, of the flesh and bones of animals, birds and insects, and of the ashes of fire. Whilst the earth itself has travelled through galactic fields, and is composed of the body and soul of stars.

Thus a human being is a microcosm of earth and beyond, for all the earth and the heavens are reflected within. The ingredients of a human body have travelled from the four corners of the earth, and from the far corners of the universe, from the deepest to the highest, to take part in every branch of insentience, and every act of life. When we see the elements, waters, life and stars about us, we are also looking at the interconnecting blueprint of our future brothers and sisters, and of all other life and form.

BOLDNESS

203. Self-determination fosters boldness.

204. It is infinitely better to be bold in matters generally acknowledged to be embarrassing, than to fall in line with the norm.

205. When we are empty of selfish-thought, we can be bold without being self-conscious.

BOREDOM

206. How can we possibly be bored, when we have our own company present?

BOUNDARIES

207. Boundaries exist to protect the ego. The more rigid our boundaries, the more we are enmeshed in the illusory identity of ego. Boundary-setting can be conscious or unconscious. If conscious, it is an opportunity to find what is appropriate for the ego. If unconscious, the boundary will tend to be set reactively.

208. A boundary can be set only in ego time and space by the individuated ego mind; the soul has no need of boundaries. However, it seems part of the individuated ego's role to set boundaries, that it may have a perspective of itself, and a perspective on the rest of creation.

209. If others persistently step into our ego boundaries, it helps determine the size of our egoic bubble, and whether or not its boundaries are appropriate to the circumstance.

210. It is necessary that we be prepared to widen our self-held boundaries so we can embrace other views. And it is love that allows us to be widened, and love that allows us to embrace.

211. Most of us are doing our best within the confines of our own held boundaries. But most of us could do with expanding our boundaries somewhat.

212. When we perceive the beginnings of a hindrance or withdrawal from another, we are being given the opportunity to expand, to push through the confines of our self-created ego bubble which says we love only to this extent and no further.

213. If there is a desire to set boundaries, these ought to be viewed as guidelines rather than fences.

BOUNDLESSNESS

214. Love, truth, innocence, and beauty cannot be completely embraced; they bring with them an open window to the sky.

215. Unless we have some understanding of boundlessness, we shall likely have the limitation of narrow-mindedness.

BOUNTY

216. The bounty in our lives has come to us from many unknown and unexpected quarters. It has travelled from the far reaches of the universe.

BREATH

217. The most valuable breath is simply done with deep, slow, silent breathing. Our clear, unfeigned, inner being, gracefully comes forth. It brings centredness, peace, still mind, vitality and contentment. (See Spirit.)

BURDENS

218. It is not our responsibility to carry burdens. As soon as the innocent child within us starts to carry a burden, we begin to become serious, concerned, fearful adults.

219. When we carry a burden, we are living through the diminutive body of the ego.

220. Whatever we hide, whatever we do not speak, we tend to carry, even if our conscious mind conveniently forgets it.

221. We carry burdens when we forget to love.

C

CAPABILITY

222. The internal confidence in our self-belief is the primary key to unlock our capability.

223. Allowing our abilities to be judged upon their own merit, without self-seeking or self-destroying comment, will permit them a freer expression, as well as acceptance by others.

CARE

224. Our ability to genuinely care reveals the unrestricted active presence of love.

225. Care is the source of our self-becoming. We activate our lives and our world by where we place our care.

226. Wherever we go, we can leave seeds of caring for those who follow.

CAUSAL CHAIN

227. Love begets love, truth begets truth, fear begets fear, and hatred begets hatred.

CAUSE

228. The more conscious we become of the force of cause, the more we are able to create a known effect. For cause is both alpha and omega. It is the force of origin, purpose, belief, motivation, creation, and result.

229. When we begin to look for the cause and not just see the result, then reasons will be revealed to us as surely and as clearly as results.

CELESTIAL BEINGS

230. If we would see ourselves as celestial beings, we would naturally act with mindful awareness. We would live from the depths of stillness and peace, from where gentleness, contentment, love and compassion arise. We would live without doubt (for we realise our real nature), we would go wherever we wanted and do whatever we pleased in a state of awareness. We would live without fear, in the courage, virtue, and fortitude of the divine.

CENTRED

231. When we are centred, all other things that ordinarily seem distant are within us. For instance, love is close; it flows effortlessly from within. So are health, vitality, creativity, timing and spirituality.

232. The mindful heart is the centre between the daily conscious mind and the subconscious mind. Here a balance is found between the extremes of egoic, materialistic thinking of the daily conscious mind, and the often repetitive, illusory, and sometimes detrimental thoughts of the surfacing subconscious mind.

233. When we are centred, we are aware of our internal self, as well as our external self, which means the thoughts, feelings, and emotions of others.

234. If we are distracted from our centre through interactions with others, we are being more unconscious in our external role to them, rather than being in consciousness with ourselves.

235. The mindful heart appears to be where the inner female and male, and the outer male and female, are reconciled and balanced.

236. Being centred in mind and body, one is at the doorway to one's greatest truth, love and potency.

237. When one is centred there is no need for the ego to claim possession of life. Life just happens naturally, and the ego submits to a supporting role.

CEREMONY

238. It is the ritual and ceremony of things like weddings and passages of initiation that are more important than their legality. For the ritual and ceremony have come from within us, and we resonate with them on a deep level, where they integrate and free us on soulful terms. Whereas the legality of things seems to create separation and disunity amongst us, without any recognition of the soul.

CERTAIN

239. If we are certain, is it based on knowing or faith? And with both knowing and faith, do we have the understanding of why we are certain?

CHANGE

240. When we love greatly, we also have the flexibility to make change. When we have little love, we are not so able to make or adjust to change.

241. It is very difficult to make positive life changes if we are already too full of our own collected limiting beliefs. We may know certain beneficial ideas intellectually, but they will be difficult to be implemented in our lives unless we are empty of arrogance, addiction, self-hatred and other stuffings that deny an embrace of life.

242. The exception to the norm often produces change, but the exception itself is produced because of the need for change arising out of the norm.

243. The degree of change in the world seems proportional to the degree of disharmony in the interim, but all the time leading to ever-greater harmony and organisation.

244. We cannot force another to change, but if they do respond to our desire, the change will probably be more cosmetic than fundamental, for it is likely that resentment will obstruct their understanding, freedom and progress. Through love we allow others the space in which to make change.

245. Change in one area of life usually results in change occurring in other areas, both internally and externally.

246. It seems that in order to make change in habitual ego induced patterns, our internal energy needs to be raised from its usual tempo to one of a more powerful, more knowing, increased life-connection. And therefore from the vantage point of our

embellished energy, we can clearly see our previous limited view and its harmful effects.

To increase energy, we may for example breathe more consciously, eat only when our body indicates hunger (not the ego mind), study yoga, listen to inspired music, practise a creative art, apply energy-enhancing eastern-style sexuality, develop our humour, think to expand any limited beliefs we may hold regardless of how fixed they may at first appear, and so on.

247. In the entire earth, nothing apparently is static, and thus it is unlikely that pure stasis exists in the universe. All things seem imbued with a creative intelligence that is flowing between attraction and separation. However, paradoxically, in the pure moment, everything is constant.

CHARISMA

248. Charisma is characterised by a deep sense of knowing oneself, and of one's high worth, which exudes in confidence, with a sense of timelessness; is founded upon grace and humility, yet believes that it has a bright destiny to fulfil. One has a relaxed body with an open posture; one thinks and speaks with deliberation, and one is more in touch with the sublime states, particularly happiness and love. Overall the depth and passion of the spirit of life envelops one, making one appear larger than life.

CHARITY

249. Charity, or the love of others, for all practical purposes needs to be addressed in the present. Otherwise we are avoiding love.

CHILD

250. A child is one who listens to heaven first, and therefore acts from the spontaneity of the inner divine with a sparkling freshness.

251. Until children are consciously conceived in joy and welcomed

into the world, it will be difficult for us to create heaven on earth. For the blueprint of a soul who steps into an unconscious or unwanted choice, is founded on the constricting energies of rejection, resentment, guilt, anger, and fear. When a child is not welcome into the world, it knows it is not welcome. If it still comes, it will likely spend a lifetime adjusting to life here.

252. Our involuntary reactions to children appear to be generated from the stored subconscious experiences that we had in our own childhood.

253. The psychological wounds we receive as young children, particularly from our families, become our unique gift of healing and understanding to be embraced and then shared with the world, that we and our world may become larger and more boundless.

254. A simple psychological truth is that when the child is rejected, the child retreats. When we mature, we are responsible for inviting our inner child out to play once again.

255. Because children mostly live in the moment, the ability to relate to children is dependent upon the aliveness of our own inner child.

CHILDISHNESS

256. The negative psychological conditioning of children is often carried into adulthood, with childish and infantile behaviours being retained, though slightly modified.

The child's parental and peer group fostering of its development is usually based on a self-centred view of itself that creates a selfish orientation, whilst ambiguously combined with a need for approval and acceptance from others. If another does not give the child what it desires, the child chooses either to withdraw or to attempt an increase in closeness. In withdrawal they may decide not to play with this individual any more, or not let them into their playgroup or gang, or give them the silent treatment and no longer be their friend. With the attempt to increase closeness, they may become overly pleasing in order to acquire their needs.

The adult versions of these are seen in the ignoring of others, and the forming of closed cliques that deny other people an opportunity to interact. Or in being overly servile and becoming 'yes' people in order to gain acceptance. Overall though, what usually happens in both children and childish adults is a reactive matching of strategies, either aggressively or passively.

The child and childish adult who are denied have little real choice, for their conditioning inhibits it, and they tend to become peeved. However, a mature adult has the choice to courageously break through such conditioning and be more self-determined.

✳

CHOICE

257. 'Choice' is the testing ground of will, to self-integration. This power of choice is only available in the present. (See contemplation no. 2124)

258. Once a choice is made, virtually any state of being has the capacity to be created.

259. A multiplicity of choices can seem to give us freedom, but it can also make for confusion. A limited choice does not mean that our best choice is necessarily denied us; it can be contained within the limited. Freedom to choose does not necessarily reside in having a large choice, but more in the ability to choose the worthy.

260. A choice made purely from the excitation of hormones is often not a choice that would have rationally been made.

261. The more we choose to live consciously (rather than reactively) the more we move our frame of choice into the light of awareness, and out of the darkness of addictive subconscious choice, where most so-called choice is currently made; that is, without awareness.

262. Our ego confines us to past conditioned responses, whereas our heart and soul present us with the choice of loving now. We

are not in a place of choice if we continually react with conditioned responses.

CIVILISATION

263. Just one human, being of assistance to another, is the primary action in establishing and maintaining civilisation.

CLARITY

264. When there is clarity, we are liberated from the dimness of misunderstanding. We shine the light of awareness to gain insight and understanding of what is self-evident and what can be resolved.

265. Sometimes it seems that to have clarity of being takes great effort. However the less resistance we have, the more effortless it seems to become. Therefore the path to achieving clarity may more readily occur in a state of yielding.

CLICHES

266. It is very compelling for the automatic, cliched, conditioning judgment from the past, to become the narrow view, which precludes us from seeing the depth or intricacy now.

267. New age and old age cliches are the rigid repetitive formulas that represent the values of the time. Falling into cliches gains one community acceptance. But often there is no conscious consideration behind them, nor any of the uniqueness of individual creativity and experience.

CLOSED

268. Love exists at the core of every human being. It is to this love we are obliged to remain open and receptive, for as soon as we close down to another, we lose the opportunity to share our love and join in union with their love.

269. How can it be possible to openly love another if at the same time we have closed down part of ourselves, to protect ourselves from hurt?

270. If we purposely close down to someone, the universe seems also to shut down a similar and complementary aspect of life to us.

CO-EXTENSIVE

271. When we feel the earth, the universe, as we do ourselves, when it becomes natural to identify the 'out-there' as being co-extensive, the self enlarges in universal equanimity.

272. The more co-extensive we associate and become, the more the individual ego with all of its cares, fears, and worries becomes immersed in the omniscience of omnipresence.

273. If we stay in the right place (internally), the right place (externally) immediately becomes co-extensive on all levels.

274. The less affinity and kinship we encompass from the environment that sustains us, the less universal spirit is available to us. If we know that we are co-extensive with all, we move in a universal ocean, where sun, moon, stars, air, earth, sea and sky, give freely of their spirit.

275. Until we as souls become co-extensive, we will not feel, know, or unite with the fullness of creation and beyond.

COERCION

276. Whenever we are forced upon by others, it is often because they offer little value for what they render, and therefore the little is exaggerated.

COINCIDENCE

277. It seems that when cause is subconsciously generated through the collective mind, then we have an experience where apparently causeless effects create coincidence.

COMEUPPANCE

278. If we go into a situation looking for our own reward while outwardly appearing to be magnanimous, we usually end up having to render and pay service in some way.

COMMITMENT

279. Perhaps the highest commitment we can make to others, and ourselves, is to being fully conscious and present in the moment. Any state that is less than this soon becomes apparent. If we cannot be committed to the present, what hope is there for an ongoing commitment to the future?

280. Full commitment arises either from the deep knowing of one's heart and soul, or when one is convinced—that is, when one's resistance is overcome by the forces of love.

281. Commitment can be blind or with knowledge.

282. To be honestly committed to something or someone requires the involvement of our passion. It is passion that provides the fire, the initial force to move us, and weld us, that we may be ongoing to our commitment.

283. When we commit fully open-hearted to another, we align our souls together in loyalty and devotion to love.

284. Real commitment arises from the love that does not hold or expect. Many who feign commitment are actually operating more from a place of fear of loss, rather than being committed to love. Commitment to love appears to be the key.

285. Unless commitment is present, we will likely be operating against a background of some kind of withdrawal.

COMMUNICATION

286. For our communication to have integrity, we need moment-by-moment to communicate our present.

287. Enthusiasm, along with a warm heart, makes for contagious communication.

288. Our subconscious belief about communication is that it can give us clarity and understanding with another. However, ego-based communication runs contrary to this expectation, for all egos have their own individual experience. When we subconsciously expect perfect communication from another, we expect them to have the same kind of understanding and use of words, as we do ourselves, which is rare. Essentially we need to realise that on the ego level, language is fluctuating and inaccurate.

289. We must endeavour until our communication is received. But if we overly push, our communication will be changed from what it was originally.

290. Is it really necessary to become angry in order to communicate powerfully? A balanced communication of love and truth, communicates with utmost effectiveness.

291. It has been said that words account for 3% of our communication, tonality for 37% and body language for 60%. If we focus too greatly on words, we may be missing the essence and intention of the communication.

292. In our communication and relationship with others, on which ground do we stand? Do we solely stand on our own ground and defend our position? Do we meet on their ground and suppress our own? Or do we look for the middle ground between us?

293. Remembered lines, spouted forth, are in danger of becoming cliches in our lives, keeping us embedded in the past, and therefore unconvincing in the present.

294. In communication, everyone deserves an opening, and everyone deserves a closing.

295. Just because a communication has been offered, does not mean it has been received. Only if there is an awakened consciousness that is receptive, and then able to have understanding, can a communication have been fully received.

296. If we do not communicate clearly, we cannot communicate successfully. Similarly, if we have not clearly received a communication, we cannot respond wholly. There is no reason for pretending to be a successful receiver, other than in thinking we are being generous to the sender. But how can we be generous and ignorant simultaneously?

297. The more present we are in making our communication to others, the deeper it is received. Similarly, the more present we are in receiving communication from others, the deeper our understanding is of them.

298. To seek understanding with those who have no ears to hear or eyes to see is futile. It is more appropriate that we retain our own essential benevolence in silence. This is the most honourable and effective form of communication we can give to them.

299. Someone who is close to us, may on occasion, be more capable of giving a voice to our deeper consciousness. This is a voice that deep down we recognise, even when we ourselves have lost touch with it, or cannot articulate it.

300. Only by allowing others the space for the communication of their thoughts and emotions, without the interjection of our own self-interested thoughts and emotions, can we fully listen and be present for them.

301. Unspoken thoughts and emotions are inevitably communicated and received by others.

302. Whenever we speak judgmentally of others, we surely say something of ourselves.

303. If we become overly sensitive or critical of the words that others use, rather than the essence of what is being said, we shall

probably find plenty to be upset about, and we shall lose sight of the innocence behind communication.

304. Personal language can be used to create separation between people, as in the case of 'I' and 'you,' but can also be used to create union as in 'we.'

Insistence on singular 'I' statements may press the speaker further into their ego. Singular 'I' statements come from the ego and not from the true 'I,' the soul, which uses 'I' plurally.

'You' statements tend to refer to the ego only.

As we grow in understanding, the use of 'you' will probably fade and 'we' shall become commonplace, until ultimately the plural 'I' will dawn upon us and we shall know the collective oneness of our 'I.'

305. When people who speak different languages communicate using their own language, it is not the words that are listened to so much as the essence. It is this essence that is at the heart of all communication.

306. Whenever terminology and phraseology assume priority in everyday conversation, the heart and soul of communication are terminated.

307. Many of our most descriptive words can be translated directly into love, truth, unlove and untruth. But to use them so directly in our everyday language would expose the charade of our present communication.

308. If we can contact the personal in our communication, we open the doorway to friendship.

309. To speak disparagingly of another in order to distance ourselves from them, so that others may think better of us, always seems to backfire.

310. The more we can express of our understanding, the greater the perceived clarity of our expression.

311. To be able to speak with a loving conviction, it is necessary to relax and be at home with ourselves, that our heart's voice may be communicated.

312. In our communications with others, are we more concerned with settling upon our comfortable ego points of reference, or are we truly aware of what has been said and what has not been said?

313. If we persist in having the last word, we shall also be the last one remaining.

314. Language is neutral, however, our use of it and the meaning we extract from it tends to be personal.

COMPARISON

315. Comparing others and ourselves is an exercise in futility. We may aspire to the heights we see in others, but the only true comparison we can make is an internal one, in which our conscience will reveal to us whether we are reaching for the highest potential within.

COMPASSION

316. Compassion is not the display of sentimental emotionalism; it is the realisation of our oneness, it is absolute intelligence, it arises from the love of humanitarian justice.

317. The meaning of compassion lies in the knowledge that all beings are highborn, and therefore noble and worthy.

318. Compassion reaches in, touches us, and outflows to where it is needed. Compassion is the collective great spirit of humanity.

COMPLETION

319. Unless a relationship or situation is brought to fulfilment or a close in some way, there will likely be an unfulfilled need pressing on the psyche.

COMPLIMENT

320. When we receive a compliment, to where do we direct it, to the ego or the soul? The soul allows it to flow; the ego either resists or becomes inflated.

321. A true compliment arises when we intuitively feel that a soul is expressing its potential. Our compliment assists in magnifying the soul's pathway, and indicates to the ego where its supporting role lies.

COMPROMISE

322. It is not advantageous to compromise our position if it entails renouncing our conscience.

COMPULSIVE

323. Largely, it is the thoughts of being abandoned as a baby, as a child, or even as an adult that finally translate into our obsessive, compulsive behaviour.

CONCEIT

324. Conceit arises from the self-inflated ego, not from the self-evident love of the soul.

CONCEPTS

325. With a new concept, a light is turned on, and a new path is revealed.

CONDEMN

326. If we speak ill of someone without their presence, we become liars. And if we speak ill of someone in their presence, we

are still liars. At most we can only speak of another's actions or non-actions, not the state of being of another.

327. To condemn another without listening to their viewpoint is more than narrow-minded, it is an injustice based on one's own self-aggrandisement.

328. If we delight in others being condemned, it shows how far removed we are from our own sense of innocence and humanity.

CONDESCEND

329. We are all capable of the negative, of selfishness, deceit, irresponsibility, and crime. Anyone who says that this is not so for them will likely be practising self-righteousness in their judgment and condemnation of others, whom they regard as doing these things. This very self-righteousness is itself a crime, a deceit, an irresponsibility and an act of selfishness towards one's fellow human beings.

CONDITIONING

330. Conditioning occurs when we fail to risk stepping outside of the security we know, to the possible insecurity, but also greater possible freedom, that deep down we do know exists.

331. All emotions produce self-image conditioning and resultant behaviours.

CONDUCT

332. When speaking of an example of conduct with another, we retain our virtue by not placing the example upon their shoulders, but by carrying it ourselves. This leaves the other free to interpret, and we keep faith with ourselves for shouldering the responsibility.

CONFIDENCE

333. Confidence arises largely from confiding with the inner-self. From this develops the foundation of trusting in one's own abilities.

334. The confidence that comes from an open heart is usually accommodated in the world.

335. Confidence springs from the love of one's innate freedom.

336. The opposing force of confidence is the unresolved stress of anxiety that creates doubt.

337. Confidence occurs when we love strongly. We can only love strongly when we are fully present in the moment.

CONFIDENTIALITY

338. If someone confides in us, then it is our obligation to see it as confidential. However if a confidence becomes a burden, it is best released to the divine.

339. A truth told in confidence is generally regarded as being sacred. But an untruth told in confidence has nothing sacred about it.

340. The more separated we are from others, the more important that confidentiality becomes to us, until eventually our activities become covert in order to preserve our false sense of confidentiality.

341. In a society where truth is ignored and falsehood is used maliciously, confidentiality assumes greater importance.

342. Does the truth really need to be spoken in confidence. For how can we be covetous about truth and reality?

CONFLICT

343. Conflict can only happen between opposing egos, not between hearts or souls.

344. Very few of us are able to listen effectively or to communicate a sense of love and truth in a situation of conflict. It is most important to deal first with our own internal dialogue before making the decision to externalise it.

345. In a conflict there is no need to attack others in order to vindicate the good in oneself. It is worthier to verbalise and affirm one's inner beliefs.

346. Conflict arises because we fail to see unity, and this results in division and separation.

347. If we do not give energy to what is expected of us in conflict, how can the conflict continue?

348. Whilst in a conflict, it is essential to keep one's own integrity, for its loss is what we grieve most of all—not so much what the other person has said or done.

CONFORMITY

349. For the most part we agree to conform to what is expected of us because of our deep fear of rejection, loneliness, and our need to be accepted. We acquiesce our uniqueness and autonomy by playing a role that we have been groomed for, and to which we continue to groom ourselves, with the hope of gaining ever-greater credence. Every vocation becomes a role to play, as do states of mind which can become predominant such as shyness, cynicism, humour, niceness, intellectualism, depression, domination, self-righteousness, worry and so on. Families, societies and even nations are coerced by role-playing conformity. This largely arises from a lack of gnosis, which in turn generates the isolation that seeks resolution in compliance, self-satisfaction, and conformity.

350. When we break through our own conforming barrier, we enter a zone of discovery, delight, and freedom.

CONFRONTATION

351. Regardless of the apparent situation, it is important to try and imagine the other person as innocent. For premeditated blame and the consequent highly charged emotional turmoil of reciprocating blame between parties, only intensifies the confrontation. When we approach the other calmly, with inquiry, rather than blame, we can then more fully ascertain the truth of the situation. Emotionally charged blame and counter-blame has been the biggest cause of upset, conflict, and war in the world.

CONFUSION

352. Confusion occurs when we reach an overwhelming state of mental input, or the things around us look chaotic, particularly in our home or workplace. Both require a return to the fundamental elements that comprise harmony in the mental and physical reality. By creating order, simplicity, consistency, and coherent information, we can re-orientate ourselves to a position of clarity, for our next step.

CONGRUENCE

353. The greater the congruence of things, the more they tend to embrace universal union.

CONSCIENCE

354. Conscience voices the truth of our soul, simply, directly, and gently without demanding. The voice of conscience does not speak in terms of blame or guilt. If such a voice does speak, it is the pseudo conscience of the ego.

355. All have a conscience, but if we deny it, we deny ourselves the right to justice and freedom in the world.

356. We are all inherently mindful of our conscience. And so in relationship with another who has wronged us, it may be preferable to give time to the workings of their conscience, rather than attempt to preach to them what their own conscience has the ability to point out on a much deeper level.

357. If we do not listen to our conscience, it can become replaced with self-justification, which is characterised by excuse rather than a knowing heart.

358. Instead of waiting for pangs of conscience to awaken us to truth, can we not ask ourselves 'Am I true?'

CONSCIOUSNESS

359. Consciousness is the innate intelligence of the universe; all things are imbued with it and move according to the true specifications of their design. The building blocks of consciousness appear to be creating a synthesis that engenders awareness. This awareness is love. When we as human beings are fully congruent with our design in the truth of the moment, our consciousness is this love awareness.

360. Every act done with consciousness becomes a sacred offering to the victorious unfolding of life.

361. When we become aware of all that enters into our life, of all that we give out, of all that we transmit, in a state of loving detachment, we are living consciously.

362. All things are, by degree, conscious. Consciousness is the presence and state of the divine. Therefore all is divine.

363. When we breathe, speak, see, listen, think, pray, eat, drink, and act more consciously, love and truth become more apparent.

364. It is preferable we learn to be consciously aware during an event rather than after it.

365. Enlightened consciousness arises out of the ability to be self-reflective.

366. The speed of our environment and our reaction to it will determine how much of an impression the environment will make upon our consciousness. For example, the ambience of a country environment will be slower than that of a city. Our response will be different. In the country we will tend to be more open, relaxed, more wide-eyed, in fact all of our senses may become keener. However, in the city, the huge sensory input tends to make us reactively pull in our senses. When we realise how we open and close our senses, we may open and pull them back more consciously.

367. Generally, positivity has equivalence to being conscious. Whereas negativity has equivalence to being unconscious.

368. Consciousness appears to operate like a continuous wellspring arising from deep within the unconscious to reach the subconscious, where faint glimmers are perceived in the conscious mind, until it emerges into the knowing of conscious realisation.

369. Ultimately, consciousness that is less than super-consciousness, is a form of emerging consciousness.

CONSECRATION

370. Our life is our gift to the divine. If we consciously consecrate it to the divine, the resulting gratitude we feel manifests in an enlarging sense of our being, and therefore in the more consciously attuned presence of the divine.

CONSEQUENCES

371. Sometimes we must be prepared to suffer the consequences of our speech and actions, even when we are misperceived. Our ability to suffer consequences is the sign of our capacity to be fully interactive with life, and not just to share the good times.

372. When we choose not to face the consequences, we face instead the failure of our own inaction, which is usually a bitterer pill to swallow.

373. The consequences of our thoughts and feelings, speech and action, travel much further than we imagine.

CONSIDERATION

374. When we truly consider, we look from afar. We look from the other's viewpoint; and if that does not create synthesis, we look from the mountaintop of humanity; if that does not create synthesis, we look at earth from beyond, from the synthesis of the universe.

CONSTRAINT

375. Whenever we begin to experience psychological constraint, we are reaching the outer limits of our previous psychological conditioning. It is an opportunity to break through the past and into the present.

376. The constraints of our personality makeup are the built-in developmental tools for our greater understanding, that we may become more whole.

CONSUMPTION

377. If we eat and drink to worship the divine, we are no longer worshipping the hungry ego.

378. Food eaten consciously becomes medicine, and heals and uplifts the body/mind. Food eaten without consciousness can become a toxic burden.

379. All acts of consumption mould us. We need to deeply inquire, what are we consuming, and whether these acts of consuming serve how we wish to become?

380. It seems that the more we consume food and material goods, the more heavy and earthbound we become in body and emotions. Similarly, the less we consume, the lighter, more soulful.

381. Generally our intake of food, drink and so on, is in proportion to our connection to soul. The greater our lack of soul connection, and therefore the deeper our hurt, the more we either indulge or withhold. Without this connection we invariably focus on a compensatory need for ego survival.

382. Mindfulness during consumption leads to increased awareness, and thus the digestion of our experience as well as our heightened assimilation. Accordingly it is having trust in the divine's providence, rather than living in fear that one is not getting enough.

CONTEMPT

383. The mind that has contempt for another always needs a mask to hide behind, for if it stood naked in the light of the sun, its own frailty of belief would be exposed.

CONTENTMENT

384. Contentment arises from the sense of being embraced by one's soul, from where all life is deeply beheld.

CONTINUUM

385. The soul encompasses the continuum that was before alpha, and beyond omega, and therefore enfolds all the universes, and all they contain.

CONTRADICTION

386. Contradiction (also hypocrisy) is sometimes useful in exposing a deeper layer of belief that was previously hidden.

387. Generally it is not possible to be fully conscious while at the same time contradicting truth.

✳

CONTROL

388. Many of us want to control our lives and the lives of others. We want to stay ahead of what we regard as the forces of chaos in the world. Or is it really the force of grace, of letting go and surrender? Have we really given ourselves the opportunity to relax more into life?

389. If we get caught in wanting to change others, and wanting to correct them, we also want to be in control. This control may or may not have a benevolent aim, however our raison d'etre will be found in our own ego incompleteness. Awareness of this incompleteness helps to resolve our need for changing and correcting others, as well as revealing our interior path to wholeness.

✳

CONVENTION

390. The rules of social convention in our society leave little space for the individual human heart.

391. How often do we allow our spontaneity, desire, and freedom to be cramped by convention? When this happens, we are allowing egoic, material forces to stunt the expression of our spirit.

✳

CONVERSATION

392. The art of conversation lies in the ability to adjoin the presence of stillness with concordant notes of inspiration and insight, to create our part in the symphony. From out of the formless void and silence arise the notes and colours of our perception. By thinking, speaking and acting, we translate them into the vitality of the moment's communion.

393. The highest art of conversation conveys love, because one is being love.

CORRECTION

394. If possible, the immediate correcting of our own injustice releases us from the bonds of uncertainty, lies, guilt, regret, worry, hurt, sickness, re-balancing of the scales of justice, and the wheel of karma.

395. When we find ourselves constantly correcting others, we have become bound to leading them in accordance with our own views. But such views are from the top of the head; they leave out the view from the heart.

COUNSEL

396. Counselling can be done not just with words, but with the breath, with touching, feeling, seeing, hearing, and more. For our souls are constantly in counsel with us through every aspect of life.

397. Self-counselling is having an awareness of the divine's presence in one's action, thought, and feeling, as we make the universe our personal home.

COURAGE

398. The greatest courage of all is the courage to be true to one's true self in the moment.

COURTESY

399. Being courteous shows that we respect and value our interactions with another, and that we are prepared to accommodate them as a fellow human being. It is not, as some assume, a submissive posture, but a humane one.

CREATION

400. Our privilege to create, to call something forth, arises from our ability to conceive a reality that we imagine and determine is greater, or for the better. The power to begin manifestation is stored in our generative force, guided by our mental focus and attitude, balanced by conscience and virtue, nourished by our love and devotion, and persisted with until completion by our faith and will.

401. The world is a magical setting for imaginative acts. Each of us is a creator. We are continually creating the world in our image, trillions of times each moment.

402. Whenever we create we need to hold firmly and lovingly to our intention, and only allow changes if they add to the creation. If negative energy interferes, our lesson is in how steadfast we are to our original intention.

403. Creation is the self-objectifying act of being. The more honour we create with, the more coherent our creation, and the more we become who we truly are.

404. Seemingly the quickest way to materialise a creation is to know, believe, and feel we already have it. For example, many of us are very good at materialising the negative because we affirm it. Many of us are also very good at stating to others the degree to which we have achieved a certain understanding in our life, and very quickly within hours or days, the universe will give us precisely an opportunity to demonstrate to ourselves the validity of our spoken words. Is it not then a reasonable assumption to use this same power to achieve our desires?

405. We are all a causative force in creation, as well as being creation existing and creation potential. And thus the energy of a human being is a constantly circling spiral of creation.

406. Essentially, if we desire to affirm fault or find fault in another, we shall. Similarly, if we desire to affirm perfection or find perfection in another, we shall.

407. The more love and happiness we generate, the more we open to the realms of inspiration, creativity, and wisdom.

408. Unless creative energy has a direction, it runs chaotically without purpose.

409. The within creates the without. We can see the forces of within in the without, through the effects created.

410. If we do not remain conscious in creating our lives as we would wish, then it is likely that we will create through our subconscious fears and beliefs.

411. Creation from the point of view of a human being is rather like a jigsaw puzzle. When we get close to joining together the part of our understanding to the pieces of life's teaching, the synchronicity of union becomes more apparent.

412. The increasing of understanding, and thereby the knowledge of perfection, are signs of the wholeness of creation.

413. The soul's gift is that of creativity. All other things come out of this. It is all that anyone has been, done, or experienced. We are all creators, we are all creative, and we all create, for better or worse we create every moment. On earth the soul creates an inspirational lesson, and the ego creates a role to embody that lesson. None of us has ever lost the gift of creativity.

CREDIBILITY

414. To inordinately stress an apology, a point of view, an ability, stretches one's credibility a little too far. In our attempt to impress ourselves upon another, we instead impress them with our own obsessiveness.

415. We have come, we are here, and the truth of our presence is astonishingly credible. At the core of our being there are divine virtues, and consequently we already have the credibility of heaven. Therefore we have the innate ability to trust and be trusted in our own credibility on earth.

CRISIS

416. Whenever a crisis of any kind occurs, the fundamental lesson is that along the way we have lost our attention to the real. Because of this, the winds of change that have been restrained are now blowing unhindered; they are demanding we transform, make decisions, and embrace new openings. Now is the time.

417. The divine apparently takes a greater part in life during crisis and we soon become more aware of its presence. Our lessons are dramatically speeded up. Ideally, if we could allow more involvement with the divine in our day to day lives, there would be less need for crisis.

CRITICISM

418. Most of us are acutely and reactively sensitive to criticism of what we think to be our identity (our ego), even though many of us profess to be able to listen to, accept, and learn from criticism. However, when criticism does occur we invariably respond with emotions of hurt, and often attack our critic.

We need to ask; does criticism make change, does it bear fruit, or does it simply make the criticised sense inadequacy, hurt, and anger, and the critic more self-empowered, more superior?

419. Criticism of others or oneself is usually the overflow of the ego mind's accumulated toxins. It is an expression of self-dissatisfaction and incapacity for change. Where there is a driven need to criticise, there is a deeper unacknowledged need in the critic to look at their own application of these very issues that have now come to light. This is evidenced in those who criticise and judge the most as often being highly sensitive to receiving criticism from others.

420. If we criticise another, are we really trying to improve their situation, or are we trying to convert them to our own point of view, to show that we have a superior comprehension of their life? Unless criticism is a conscious love offering to another, enabling

them to broaden their self-understanding, most of the time it is subconscious self-projection.

421. When we criticise another, we are criticising ourselves. We are criticising the larger body of which we are all a part.

CRUELTY

422. We permit cruelty if we have not allowed or had empathy with life, beyond our own selfish bodily and mental confines.

CURE

423. Cure primarily brings the individuated sense of ego back into harmony with the soul, for the soul is always in a state of wholeness. Love is the primary force of bringing together, upon which all successful cures and remedies are based.

CYNICAL

424. The driving force of an excessively cynical attitude arises in the character that has unsuccessfully attempted to selfishly dominate the world in which they live. It is a form of egomania, the desire of wanting to place oneself above others. Their failure results in a self-perpetuating, distrusting, contemptuous, pessimistic, disbelieving, and sarcastic view of the world.

D

DANGER

425. In an environment where there is danger, a mindful, still reverence places us in the eye of the danger, where there is calm awareness of oneself and one's environment, along with a deep knowing where to go and what to do, without an emphasis into a transformation of fear.

DARK SECRETS

426. What if another discovers our darkest secrets? It says only that we are human. And what is a human but a god in training.

DARKNESS

427. Darkness is the shadow of light, it is the necessary mirror for inner reflection, to give depth, meaning and potency to the experience of light.

428. When the outer manifestations of the world seem to darken the realm of our understanding and cause us heartache, it is time to focus on the inner light of our truth.

429. Through the states of narrow-mindedness, intolerance, and dogma, we turn out the light in our mind. Forgetting that we are all divine turns off the mind's light.

430. At the darkest hour, the furthest star is made visible. And during the darkest moments of our lives, the lights of inspiration and grace may be made more visible.

431. The validity of darkness is its ability as a catalyst to cause human beings to search their souls for meaning, in order to allow a deepening process for alignment with universal unity.

432. According to our science, energy is never lost, thus the forces of darkness, whilst appearing to be becoming more widespread in the world will at the same time be allowing (in a reactionary sense) the forces of lightness to become more concentrated and potent. Now, perhaps more than at any other time in history, we have the opportunity to be more spiritually focused.

433. Darkness appears to be the unfathomable hard wiring for the revelation of light. The unconscious power which is transformed into conscious reality. It is unmanifest potential; a chaos before order. It is currently as necessary as night is to day. At night we return to our source by way of this darkness. It is the negative film of creation, that when viewed appears secret, mysterious, or threatening. It is the unillumined void of universal unconscious. We are here to return to it its own power as the bold light of truth and awareness.

DAYS

434. The light and sunlight of this day's stillness, thoughts, ideas, feelings and actions are carried and projected into the eternal reaches of the universe; they live ever more.

435. If we go to the same place to do exactly the same thing, at the same time, what is the purpose in having a new day?

436. When our whole day and night is seen to be filled with love, then we can claim to have lived a full day, being fully conscious and aware.

DEATH

437. The constricting, fearful, habitual, worrying, burdensome conditions created and prolonged by the ego induce sickness and aging, and eventually overwhelm the defences of the body/mind, to cause death.

438. In death and dying we dissociate so much from our whole self that we literally kill off, through denial, large parts of ourselves.

Eventually we flee from the body, it becomes too uncomfortable, and we have to escape the pain of our separated self.

439. Death passes us from one vibration to another. Whenever we daydream, nightdream, become creatively involved, or love greatly, we pass into another vibration. The previous vibration is left behind, we die to it. We die consciously or unconsciously—either way that which dies is no longer a required focus.

DEBT

440. Debts are a claim and an obligation between egos. Debt arises where the ego is relied and extended upon. The current banking system is founded upon the furtherance of the egoic principles of selfishness, claim, and obligation, and the forgetting of our true nature.

DEBUT

441. As an ego, we are continually making our debut, for the ego is invariably in change, it has no firm foundation. Yet the soul is one with all, and therefore has no sense of separateness to require a debut in illusory aloneness.

DECEIT

442. Whenever we practise deceit, we are also practising self-deceit.

443. If we encourage others to deceive, especially children, we are denying the forces of truth that have been transmitted from the beginning of creation, in which we all have our life and strength.

444. We deceive ourselves first when we mask our intentions.

DECISION

445. When we make decisions, we are asserting our own authority and independence, we are believing in our self-determination. Otherwise, barring lack of information, when we are indecisive, we are still subconsciously wanting to be dependent, afraid of our own power, and afraid of striking out.

446. Once we make a decision, we begin a journey. Without a decision, we cannot begin.

447. To make a balanced decision, we need to be emotionally clear. If we are not emotionally clear, it is highly likely that we will make a reactive decision. If we are in an emotionally charged state, what is the underlying belief driving it, the belief leading us to make the reactive decision?

448. A decision made because of societal, religious, or cultural beliefs that counter one's own deepest truth, is a pseudo-decision, and therefore a form of self-betrayal. We are denying our spirit the opportunity to break free; disallowing ourselves a greater voice, and a larger, boundless place to dance with freedom in the world.

449. We must somehow allow ourselves the ability to make decisions that will move us beyond our limited conceptions.

450. The energy of right decision works from greater consciousness upon the substance of accepting consciousness.

451. Do we allow outer circumstance to make our decisions, or do we allow inner insight to discern and create the path of our choosing?

452. The ability and quality of our decision/indecision appears to rest on our ability to love, and therefore how aligned we are with the discriminating forces of soul or ego.

453. Once we have made a decision in a particular area, it seems preferable then to return our awareness to the larger picture, rather than to keep focusing on the particular and risk becoming narrowly focused and obsessed.

454. Primarily our decisions need to be based on honour. We keep aligned in honour with the joy and integrity of our hearts, otherwise we undermine and betray ourselves.

455. Decisions for one's life path always have a deep resonance at the moment of choosing.

DECREE MAKING

456. All of our thoughts, speech, emotions, and feelings, have the potential to become our decree.

457. The price of making a selfish decree, or being dictatorial about something, is that the object then becomes the responsibility of the one that decrees.

458. When we make a judgmental decree, we are issuing it through the veils of our ego. Most often it reaches out to become larger than the ability of one's ego to deal with its ramifications.

DEFENSIVENESS

459. We keep intimacy at bay with our defences. We carry a stagnating, anxious, constantly guarded, uncommitted, distrusting and self-justifying shield of security that opposes and attacks others, whilst giving us a false sense of self-preservation and superiority.

460. Our defences are the citadels of our ego; the separated, walled edifices that deny the normal intimacy found in a true home.

DEFLATED

461. If we are deflated, it is a sign for us to align with our larger self that is inflated to the size of the universe. Love is our personal inflatory gas.

DELUSION

462. Delusion inevitably occurs when we interpret an ego-led perspective as being ultimate. It is usually well preceded by a loss of faith to one's inner truth.

DEMANDS

463. In order to assimilate the everyday demands of life, rather than continually compete with them mentally and emotionally, we learn more to observe—allows the blend of data and experience to find its own flow of implementation and expression from within us.

DEMOCRACY

464. Democracy will occur when the avenues to power are truly open to the people, where the ability to make change is available to the people, where truth is sovereign, and where the interest of humanity, in symbiosis with nature and earth, are paramount.

465. The democratic process requires that issues be broken down into their constituent parts, and then publicly aired, and not for them to be presented already formulated, as the formulators are then presenting a fait accompli.

DENIAL

466. If we continually deny ourselves, we shall be denying others as well as ourselves the fruits of our truth and our happier experiences. Similarly, if we deny others, we may be denying our own happiness and truth.

467. When we disengage from someone or something, the danger is that we may go too far and become cut off, out of a sense of our own insecurity, rather than having a sense of equanimity, where we can be open to all responses.

DEPRESSION

468. Whenever we are depressed, rather than condemn ourselves for it, we could be gentle and ask 'Why am I depressed?' The question then starts to work as a solution. We expose our depression for what it is—that largely it is because our ego wants to be loved, and the ego is powerless to bring about this love.

469. Depression is the act of devaluing oneself into solely experiencing the stress of rejection and isolation. This depreciation of one's true identity causes the spirit of life to be lowered, one's vitality and motivation are reduced and therefore activity is lessened; one enters a black and gloomy world where pessimism, loneliness, and unhappiness are prevalent.

Realigning with one's true nature may turn around depression. It can also be assisted by the companionship of friends and the reconnection to one's goals and activities.

470. When one is depressed, one's spirits are low, and one is devitalised. The application of conscious deep breathing invigorates and increases one's spirit and joy for life.

471. Depression is both physical and mental; both states require movement and right application.

472. When the force of depression is at its strongest, sometimes attempting to coerce positive change upon oneself can create more tension, helplessness, and further depression. However, when we accept the depression and treat it gently, we automatically love it from the higher vantage of the soul from where it can begin to softly lift. The compressed consciousness of depression cannot continue to be embodied from such a view.

473. Depression tends to occur when we have become overly obsessed with wanting to be fulfilled within a narrow focus that is not coming to pass.

474. The cause of depression is not knowing who one really is—the manifestation of the divine. If there is no active ego-self there is no other but the divine.

475. What are we choosing when we are down? At those times we tend to overlook the alternative choices that are available.

476. The cause of our depression is the sensation that we have been cut off from the umbilical cord of life's abundance, whether it is spiritually, sympathetically, or materially. But while there is life, we are always connected to its exuberant bounty, and we are part of it, we are part of it! And the earth is our street corner, and the universe is the playground of our dreams. And we are it; we are all of it!

DESIGN

477. The structure and form of something is usually indicative not only of its essence, but also of the mind in which it was conceived. The greater the harmony, symmetry, and beauty of design, the greater the awareness of mind that created it.

478. True design reflects and portrays the inspiration, beauty, and love of eternal purpose.

DESIRE

479. Approaching our primary desires from a lower position, a hoping or beseeching place; or head on, a wilful, forcing place; we approach instead from a higher, relaxed, embracing, knowing, already complete place where the desire is seen to be part of a larger vision that we have; we give ourselves the potency of power to complete, rather than if we work with the possibility of failure that comes from hoping, forcing, or fearing. And we confirm the bible's words: 'To him that hath shall be given.'

480. How can we possibly hope to fulfil our innermost dreams and desires if we follow the dreams and desires of others, or of society, in contradiction to our own?

481. Assuming we have done all we can to create the fulfilment of our desires but they still elude us, then very likely the action we need to implement more is that of gratitude. Gratitude for who we

already are, what we already have, and for those things we seek.

482. If we take time to really look at our honourable desires, usually the path of fulfilment that first led us to desire to come to earth will become apparent from amongst them.

483. Desire has two faces—that of temptation and that of inner truth.

484. Eastern mystics tell us that hope and desire are the cause of unhappiness. That if we leave them alone we will immediately be at peace. However we may be at peace in ourselves, but there is also work to be done in the world, say the western intellectuals. Perhaps living somewhere between the two philosophies will enable us to live a more authentic life. To live with a certain observable detachment from hope and desire so that we live with one foot in the realm of desire and the other in the realm of presence.

485. Desire may lead us as we rush after it, attempting to force our way to the goals we seek. Or desire may walk with us hand-in-hand and surround us with noble offerings when we walk our true path.

486. The pursuit of desires that seem external to oneself, helps perpetuate the sense of separation of oneself from the object of one's desire. If however, all desires are internalised, then already they are held in faith, close to one's bosom, from a perspective already united.

487. Whenever there is a desire, there is a looking for change, and the setting of a new balance in one's life.

488. When a decision is made in the moment, there is no separation between what one desires at that moment and the objectives of the desire. When we move out of the moment and into time, a sense of separation and often struggle becomes apparent.

489. Conflicting desires are often a sign of a conflict between an earth journey and a sacred heavenly journey.

DESTINY

490. Our original destiny, the reason why we came here, is greater than all other circumstances.

491. Destiny has a divine origin. It propels us unrelentingly throughout our lives, across the earth, through all experience, reaping and sowing, that we may deepen our knowing and our intimacy with the infinite within and its dynamic force arrayed about us. Each individual journey is forged by how we value ourselves and our direction, and is revealed by what we think, believe, feel, imagine and undertake; by what we carry, what we discard, how we greet and inspire others, and how far our vision extends.

Our destiny is enriched when we focus on the larger vision of the unity of souls and of the universe. From this vision we become sensitive to our soul and to all other souls. Accordingly we can be grateful to life, knowing that we are soulfully nurtured. We can love and appreciate the essence in others, as well as assist and encourage them on their journey, for we know of the greater vision veiled behind all antipathy, that wants to be revealed through bold and courageous acts of love. As a result, compassion and forgiveness become evident to us, since even mistakes are considered to be revelatory, whilst guilt is observed to be denying of both the vision and the love. Consequently our most prevailing individual and common destiny arises out of the confines of self-centredness, and into the clarity of luminous consciousness, where we shine its blessings to all, knowing that we have incarnated to express and increase its qualities on earth.

492. All the actions of our ego are like chaff in the wind, they will eventually pass away, whilst that which is left behind will be the state of the divine . . . . love.

493. If we align ourselves with the forces of love and truth, then our destiny is fated to be one with the universe.

DETACHMENT

494. When one is detached, one is principally detached from ego, and therefore detached from the largely self-created pain and uncertainty outside of the inherent love state of the soul. Thus one is not swayed by the demands of one's ego or the egos of others.

495. A good sign of the state of our detachment is that we can present our view without the need to convert others to it.

496. Detachment allows us to journey from the singular sense of 'I' to the universal sense of 'I.'

DETERMINED

497. When we are determined, what are the determining factors that define our purpose, and are these factors open or closed to other input?

DEVOTION

498. Whenever we fully surrender, we naturally enter the soul's realm of devotion where all things become sacred, and we worship without attachment.

DICHOTOMY

499. A human being is fundamentally a dichotomy of soul and ego, and therefore by the power of the dictum 'As above, so below,' the universe itself may be the reflection of the illusory ego of the divine.

DIFFERENCES

500. We cannot expect others to conform to our standards. Always there will be differences amongst us all. Rather we can rejoice in life's variety.

DIFFICULTY

501. On those occasions when we are beset by difficulties, it is timely to remember that we are here for an immense and sacred purpose.

502. The quickest way to change the complexion of any difficult situation or relationship is to render service.

503. With every difficulty, every problem, every sensitive condition, disease, confrontation, negativity and so on, we are being given the neophyte's doorway to the soul. It is up to us to open the door. If we can get past our own pretence, short sightedness, and imprudent behaviour, we can open ourselves to greater love and understanding.

DIRECTION

504. When we become more inner-directed, we naturally direct outer things in more logical, organised, and fulfilling ways.

505. Energy follows direction. Direction follows attraction. And attraction is drawn to the source of energy.

DISAGREEMENT

506. The elements of disagreement, if allowed to open can lead to understanding. To be overly critical at this point is to close down to the possible broadening of our own view.

DISAPPOINTED

507. Whenever we sense disappointment, the first thing to be mindful of is to keep our appointment with our breath, our deep breath of serenity.

DISCERNMENT

508. Discernment is our moment-by-moment holy adjudicator, the insightful guide on how to proceed through life. Conscious discernment creates wisdom, by awareness of one's sense perceptions, thoughts, and actions.

509. We all have the ability to discern, both high and low. Low discernment leads to bias, prejudice, division, and separation. High discernment leads to sensitivity, insight, clarity, and union.

DISCIPLINE

510. Discipline helps create self-control of the ego, and our energy can then be directed towards skill, fulfilment, and realisation.

DISCOMFORT

511. The level of discomfort we allow in our minds, bodies and surroundings is an indication of our self-esteem, and therefore our willingness to take action and make change.

512. All discomfort, be it physical, mental or emotional is the prompting of one's soul to a higher, unclouded, transparent clarity of one's being.

DISCORD

513. When there is discord of mind, speech and action, of oneself or others, in its rippling wake we are learning more of concordance.

DISCOURAGEMENT

514. Discouragement strengthens us by balancing our approach to the intended goal.

DISCOVERY

515. How much wonder, joy, and excitement of discovery of the world can we take in?

516. If we do not allow ourselves to dream and imagine beyond the confines of our present conditioning, knowledge or science, we will not be in the forefront, or be open to new discoveries.

DISCUSSION

517. Amongst those who are free (principally of their own mental and emotional limitations) any subject may be discussed with ease.

DISEASE

518. Disease appears to be a disturbance of the ego or of the animating spirit, or a combination of both, that impacts on the body/mind. The disturbance seems to result from forgetting one's true self, or from living in an environment where this is reflected, and one's susceptibility to absorbing it. However, all disease points towards the wholeness of our soul, and therefore is itself a path to health.

519. If we focus on our disease, our focus can tend to become narrow and self-obsessed. If we focus on the larger view of humanity, nature, the earth, sun, moon and stars, we enter the heavenly spaces where lies our healing, our peace, and our redemption.

520. I do not see the wisdom in being tested for disease if one's belief system is still in victim consciousness. For the confirmation of disease and the ensuing fear generated, will most likely create another victim. Surely the uplifting into insightful consciousness is the key.

521. The forces of love primarily heal disease. And therefore the manifestation of disease largely occurs because of our subduing of love.

DISHONESTY

522. Without self-love, and consequently without love of others, there is no trust and therefore no truth, and dishonesty becomes established.

DISILLUSION

523. The state of disillusionment—that is, no longer being prepared to accept the illusion—can be the igniting of the flame that leads to enlightenment.

524. When we sense disillusionment with another, we need to ask ourselves 'Am I living up to my own highest ideals?'

DISLIKE

525. If we dislike someone, it is because our ego dislikes them. The soul is always in a state of love.

DISPUTE

526. In any dispute we have with another, if we know that we are fundamentally all right with ourselves, then the burden to prove this is dissolved and we live innocently.

DISSATISFACTION

527. Dissatisfaction is not a place to take rest in, instead it is a place from which to propel oneself onward.

DISTRACTION

528. All distractions from the true self eventually point the way to the transcendental.

DIVERSITY

529. It is preferable to welcome the diversity of the choices of others, for such diversity also allows us the freedom to explore our own individual choice.

DIVINE

530. The divine is an infinite ocean of purely reflective, omniscient, omnipresent consciousness. The ecstasy of occupying such consciousness is cloaked throughout all of the elements, dimensions and life of the universe.

531. All things originate in the divine, dwell only in the divine, and have their completion in the divine.

532. The divine presence is infinitely present now, no less anywhere, anywhere, anywhere. When we know the divine is present, we too are present. We supplicate, we worship, and we love.

533. If the part of us that pretends to be all-knowing, realises that it does not know, we begin to create a place for the divine to come forth from within us.

534. The divine creates constantly, like the sun. It is so constant that the sun itself appears changeless.

535. Until we realise that we are soul, that we are divine, then we will not be able to be fully true to love, or to truth, or to our infinite power and magnificence, and therefore not fully on the earth as a universal being.

536. The divine is hidden visibility. In the clouds, in the rain, and the sun and the stars. In the earth, and in the sky. And by all things is the divine made visible.

537. The energy and power of the divine is infinite, always present, constant, yet transmutable throughout creation. It abides and nourishes every particle of matter, every flash of thought, every germ of creativity, and every dimensional reality. It embraces

trillions of stars in trillions of galaxies, and all spaces in between with ultimate cohesion, so that even the tiniest one celled creature is sustained.

And we as human beings are connected to this infinite source of energy, and at our height, we are one with it. Yet we deny and separate ourselves from it all by simply forgetting that we are divine.

538. The divine is here. So often we expect a larger than life event, but the divine is already in attendance.

539. If we truly realised who we are (divine) we would no longer be embroiled in limited, useless, negative play while here on earth.

540. The more removed we are from our divine self, the less magnetically attractive or radiant we are in our environment, and the more difficulty we seem to experience in life.

541. If god created the universe, and is omniscient, omnipotent and omnipresent, then all of the arguing, worrying, fighting, depression, drunkenness, lostness, dying and birth are god. It is god. What have we got to do with it, unless we are . . .

542. Every moment the divine is on offer. Divine union is always present, regardless of anything at all.

543. Our agreement is firm with the divine. The divine has obviously respected our desire for our own experience on earth, regardless of the times we have floundered and asked for divine intervention.

544. The less we fail to see and act with love and beauty in the world, the less we feel the presence of the divine.

545. We are one in the divine; all actions, thoughts and feelings are a sharing.

546. Whenever we desire to see the divine, it is good to see ourselves. Whenever we desire to see ourselves, it is good to see the divine.

547. If we can be grateful for everything that happens in our lives (even the 'negative' lessons, for there are positive things to be learned here) it shows ultimate trust in the divine.

548. The inner voice of the divine appears not to lead, does not condemn, is not complex, or overly praising. Its hallmarks are comfort, simplicity, inspiration and insight.

549. If we live our lives aware of the divine within, then we live powerfully with certainty and confidence. And we discover that this is it, this is the sacred life!

550. When we realise that we exist through the divine, then our anxiety about making our own way in the world as a separate entity is removed. We live and work for the divine. We are confident in our love of self and others, confident to be who we are, and to work in our area of passion.

551. If we put the divine first in our lives, we are not pushed into second place. If we place the divine second, we place ourselves second also. Therefore, when the divine is placed first the enduring love and company of the divine embraces us, and thus we are strengthened and elevated whilst living in grace.

552. When we see with the eyes of the divine, there is nothing contrary. When the conditioned mind looks, there is division and separation. The divine becomes forgotten whenever division arises.

553. At those times that we realise our divinity, we love unconditionally.

554. Is it really necessary to say 'I am God'? For the ego easily arises. There is just the experience of the divine's presence; there is no need to make a claim.

555. We may give thanks to the divine for all things. We feel divine thanks through the ecstasy of our revelations.

556. In wanting to feel connected to the divine, it is necessary to realise that we are always connected to the divine, even at those times when we sense being disconnected. It is a matter of closeness, of intimacy. We can view the divine as we would a beloved, by enlarging our sense of loving awareness.

557. It is the divine in us that attracts us to union, and the seemingly godless egoic mind that makes for separation. There is

however only the divine. Separation and attraction are the two poles that create a dynamic for the operation and understanding of free will.

558. Attention and remembrance, are sovereign buttons for reactivating and keeping tuned to the presence of the divine.

559. If the divine is omnipresent, then the divine is no more nor less present in any part of the universe, thus all things are perfectly in place. If the divine is omniscient, then the divine knows all, and knows what is required. If the divine is omnipotent, then the divine has the ultimate power to fulfil. All of our vexations about the apparent incompleteness of things can only arise from a lack of faith and communion with the divine.

560. There is only one concern, one duty—to radiate divine love.

561. The image of the divine is self-created. We can create this image from anything; all is the divine.

562. We are still in divine presence, love and beauty. We are still in the divine, we have never left.

563. With the increasing revelation of one's divinity, comes the realisation that this divinity created the universe.

DOCTRINE

564. There seems to be no such thing as a black and white situation that is free of doctrine, and the polarised opinions such doctrine generates.

DOGMATIC

565. We are all guilty of being dogmatic sometimes. When we find ourselves in the presence of someone dogmatic, we may recall our own dogma, and laugh silently to ourselves at how opinionated and domineering we were.

DOMINATION

566. Generally we only attempt to impose a domineering attitude over another when we are not in touch with our own heart, and therefore we fail to see the heart in the other.

567. In dominating another, one assumes that one has the power and the right, that one is in a higher position. But from where does the right to such authority originate? Most will be found to reside in self-interest.

DOUBT

568. Our self-doubt creates uncertainty, confusion, vacillation, fear, and lack of faith, confidence and security. Our doubt of others creates scepticism, indecision, suspicion, and distrust. However most doubt is based on an inability to see the full truth, and therefore our vision requires to be expanded.

569. If there is any intuitive doubt, of even the slightest nature, then it is best expressed, so that all the threads of truth may be gathered from the widest net and pulled together.

DREAM, THE

570. It is essential that we believe and follow our dreams, though not all dreams become a reality. Some merely, though meaningfully, lead us onward.

571. How can we not believe in our original dream, our true love, and our true work, when we haven't been truly honest or committed fully to attaining it?

DRIVE

572. A drive that arises from love is uplifting and already fulfilling, contrasted with a drive that arises from temptation, anxiety or

anger, which are all emoting forces that we tend to be driven by and subject to.

DRIVEN

573. To renounce one's driven tendencies seems a sacrifice at first, but in the process this action allows a deeper seed of integrity to bloom through the cleared space.

574. When we are driven, there is something underlying driving us. Is it what we would consciously desire and choose? Is our desire as compelling as it appears to be? Can we reclaim our freedom and power of choice by making it more simple, or more of a preference, rather than a perfectionism or an absolutism?

DRUGS

575. It appears that the main reason people take narcotics is to numb their deep-seated pains of loneliness and separation, with the hope of producing a state of union through an ecstatic or soothing experience.

576. Most of the popular recreational drugs produce a soporific or ecstatic effect by opening the individual's ego, allowing a receptive state of being from which the various frames of perception are experienced. However, if we allow ourselves to be naturally open and more receptive to the radiant earth and to the vital spark of life, we experience the love, ecstasy and harmony that comes from being sensitively attuned and co-extensively merged.

DUALITY

577. It appears that a duality of experience is currently required in order to experience free will and freedom.

DUES

578. If we become over-mindful of what we think is our due, constantly checking it, then we deny the universe the joyful energy of gifting us the spontaneous and the unexpected.

DYNAMICS

579. The dynamics of our lives indicate the areas of our evolving lessons in realisation.

E

EARTH

580. The earth is a living house and garden—a place where every species learns particular ways of self-cultivation. Whilst the earth cultivates itself through the galactic furrows of the fields of space.

581. What have we said 'Yes' to since arriving on earth? Have we said 'Yes' to life and to love? Or are we still behaving like strangers here?

582. Let us not forget we came here in love.

583. All people are currently considered native and indigenous to the earth. Animals migrate and colonise, birds migrate and colonise, fish migrate and colonise, so do insects, and seeds. Humankind also follows this same instinctive exploring pattern bequeathed by nature. This instinctive pattern may yet be discovered to have brought us to earth in the first place, and will also lead us back to the stars.

584. If we were to live as though we had just arrived on the planet, we would live without judgments, inhibitions, opinions, fears, guilts, worries, regrets, hurts, and angers, without expectation of death, without the need to fit into the constraints of a society. We would be free to live in the truth of the earth's abundance and beauty, in the timeless present.

585. Each of us brought a message to earth, if we do not deliver it, we deny the earth a fuller voice.

586. The earth is in a constant state of finely balancing her equilibrium. Every cloud, every human being, every insect, every atom, every thought, every feeling, takes part knowingly/ unknowingly in her supreme order.

587. We came to mother earth for our nurturing and our development. One day we shall have to leave her, just as we leave our human mothers, and explore the milky way.

ECSTASY

588. Whenever we feel the ecstatic, shuddering, rising, wavelike, pins and needles of connection—to life, nature, or another being, we can be sure that we are feeling the truth of our soul's connection to the unfolding of life.

589. Ecstasy is the ambrosia of home. It is the intoxicating love call of the divine.

EFFECT

590. The greater our insight and awareness of causes, the deeper our understanding of effects. From this we can take more responsibility for ourselves, and develop appreciation, understanding and compassion for others.

EFFICIENCY

591. Efficiency is a concentrating focus of our energy and purpose, whether mentally, physically, or spiritually.

EGO

592. The ego is the cloak of concealment of the divine, though somewhat imperfectly. Without it there would be no separation of the one into the many, no infinite play of forms, no ongoing process of revelation.

593. Our ego is a pseudo-living entity, in that we give life to a set of character tendencies and traits, and in living through them they become the embodiment of our personality. As long as we require a personality, we require also the ego.

594. In order to stay alive, the ego constricts itself into the experiencing of emotions, such as depression, sadness, guilt, and so on, or into overly expanded states such as bragging, selfishness and vanity. It does this to bring our attention away from what it fears most—its own annihilation through union with our soul.

595. As soon as we are in the company of another, the personal ego tends to become more active. And it operates the traits, personality, and even astrological characteristics endowed by others, as well as those formulated by one's ego since birth. The ego seems to have been produced to create the necessary sense of separation between us all, to allow the formulation of different characters in order to have maximum variation and challenge. Yet paradoxically, from out of this challenge we are learning the lessons of integration.

596. Unless there is an opening of consciousness to what is really occurring, and what we are thinking, saying and doing, then our busy, chattering, worrisome, egoic mind will rob our lives of peace and meaning.

597. Only an ego can really react to another ego in performance.

598. The ego operates by comparison, division, judgmentalness, resistance, hostility, rivalry, and opposition. The soul embraces unity, service, truth and love.

599. When we see another, our ego often identifies them as an objective entity. The more we begin to see others as subjectively in union with ourselves, the more we help remove the sense of 'other' from where our separating tendencies create our emotional pain. With those we love there is often a greater subjective base to the relationship.

600. The ego observes the dual and often antagonistic states of subject and object. Beyond these, the pure 'I' has awareness only of oneness.

601. If we are being mentally and emotionally stretched, our ego is being pulled out of its small home of complacency and being extended to fit a more spacious, more challenging residence.

602. A healthy ego depends on knowing where its home is. An unhealthy ego does not know where home is. High self-esteem is dependent upon the ego knowing where home is. (See contemplation no. 661)

603. The stress of the separated ego has a tendency to create tensions, which are usually released through emotional states, altercations, and in commiseration with others. It can also be released by the more enlightened ways of prayer, meditation, being in nature, and self-realisation.

604. The 'I' that seems separate from the rest of creation carries an enormous load. And for the most part it carries its load very well, for it is highly protective of its fragile treasure, seeking to keep alive its wonderful and peculiar individuality.

605. When approaching another, usually the ego starts to surface, and the personality with all of its characteristics and phobias comes out to play. Though if we are in the consciousness of our heart, we can remain integrated in the love realm of the present. Here we feel unhindered, expansive, at one with life all around, at home with ourselves, and free of the constraints of the ego self, and ego

dominated society. And we can also observe the sometimes uncertain and awkward parts of ego-led speech and actions of others, without reaction.

606. The parameters of the ego are learned and set, whereas the parameters of the true self are constantly experienced as forever widening.

607. An egocentric view cannot yield truth; at best it can only shadow it.

608. Egocentric viewpoints create separating tendencies amongst us all, which can often cause tension. If these viewpoints are realised as being an aspect of our creative diversity, we can lighten up and be more accepting of them.

609. We can find only separation, judgment, and comparison between each other when the ego dominates our thinking, and takes us away from the wholeness of the present, and into the rupturing, and schism-making process of ego-minded time.

610. If our ego rushes in to protect us from the unwanted thoughts and words of others, we have an opportunity to see that which it wishes to hide from us, in its own benign though clumsy way.

611. Only the ego is hard on the ego. The ego cannot be hard on the soul.

612. In clinging to our desire to be liked, if we question: 'What is it that desires to be liked,' we come to the realisation that it is the ego personality. The dilemma for the ego is, how can it be both a separate self and in union with others, and therefore liked by others? However, at the core of one's true self there is union with all, and the question or the desire to be liked does not arise.

613. The hopes and fears of the ego personality form the passing images and dialogue of the mind. This is how the ego fleshes out its sense of self.

614. If we refer to our ego in the first person, we have a case of mistaken identity. The ego more rightly ought to be referred to in the second or third person, so that the true 'I am' (soul) recovers its first place.

615. It is the ego that tends to keep the attitudinal stance and bearing of the body, which manifests in inequalities of one's deportment, such as slouching, poor posture and so on. The less ego we carry, the more our position reflects an internal nobleness.

616. There appears to be only one thing that we are required to give up—the anxiety of the ego mind, which results in all of its associated stresses, emotions, and habits. When we begin to relax and release the distress of the ego-mind, we make ourselves freely available to love.

617. The ego senses itself as being separate from all others, through which a character is created to occupy a particular territory, mindfully and emotionally.

618. Our ego is like a veil that covers our quintessential innocence. It is thickest over our most emotionally wounded parts, for example the face, chest, stomach, buttocks, and genitals. It is thin or absent on those areas where we are clear and not possessed. We can peer above our ego veil whenever we look to the horizon and above to the heavens. We can peer underneath it whenever we are in communion with the earth. And it disappears entirely when we are in a co-extensive state of being.

619. Ego thoughts are basically built upon foundational images and beliefs embedded in the subconscious.

620. If we are driven to speak of how perfect or imperfect we are, we are speaking from ego.

621. The ego seems to grow by association, whenever we imbue something or an activity with it.

622. When the ego is sufficiently inflated it often results in the ridiculing of others or oneself, and afterwards in a sense of self-remorse. The lesson to be learnt is to be mindful of the path of the true and greater self.

623. The state of no ego is the state of selflessness, without even consciousness of this selflessness.

624. If we speak or act from the heart/soul, we behold a heightened sense of our own innocence, for which the heart/soul needs no

acknowledgment or approval. However, the ego often wants to step in and take credit for these efforts. If this occurs, we are allowing our ego to infringe upon the state of our loving innocence.

625. When one lives with less ego, the egos of others become more apparent not only to oneself, but also to themselves. They are made more conscious of their egos when faced with someone who is not so ego-centred.

626. It is the ego that makes the body sick. It is the ego that ages the body. And it is the height of the ego's power, (creating separation and a memory loss towards the divine) in its struggle with the pure 'I,' that kills the body. The soul is innocent of these charges.

627. In the presence of the divine we are egoless. Whenever we are in ego, we are not in the divine's presence.

628. If we see others through a filter of limitation, we are viewing their egos through our own judgmental ego.

629. To use the vacillating ego mind in order to understand oneself, others, life, and the universe, is an exercise in attachment to false impressions, and an avoidance of the soul.

630. The ego inherently thinks of itself firstly and selfishly, and in this selfishness attempts to decree the whole state of one's being.

631. Sometimes the ego likes to think it can mimic the divine, but when it does, the wine soon runs out, it falls down, and finally it bows to the all-inclusive power of love.

632. The ego tends to think in terms of lack, which is often then expressed in bouts of depression, or acts of bravado.

633. Time is necessary for the illusion of ego. Without time, there can be no separation of the one-present into the multifaceted, egoic many.

634. It is mostly the ego that carries and experiences suffering, that it may undergo a transformative experience to reach towards the divine.

635. The ego is always right. It can never accept blame or apologise fully. Only the conscience can see clearly, and be

accepting and acknowledging, seeking forgiveness and rendering forgiveness.

636. Both introversion and extroversion are ego-based if the natural impulse of the true self is forgotten.

637. It seems impossible to find lasting happiness through the unsure foundations of the ego personality.

638. Because of the very nature of the ego, even if we were able to put the entire world into its hungry emptiness, it would not be enough. There would still be a sense of spiritual hollowness.

639. An excessively validating ego-speak in one's mind is the flip side of the excessively invalidating ego-speak. Both are founded upon highly vulnerable, illusory premises—that one is mostly an ego, and that this ego is greater or lesser than others. The middle path of harmony, stillness, and peace is where we find the balancing reality of our soul.

640. The ego seems to have been caused primarily as a means of producing memory loss of our true nature. But also it is largely created out of the awkward, constricting, inflationary and suffering emotional states, and so therefore it seems to have been made with an in-built self-dismantling capability.

641. Ego can be subconscious as well as semi-conscious. Sometimes we may have a subconscious hair trigger reaction such as embarrassment, anger, jealousy, and so on, that arises from a subconscious back-load of unresolved issues, which then propels from our expression before we have conscious thought.

642. To speak of what we do not know, as though we know, is for the mistaken purpose of inflating the ego. It has nothing to do with knowledge.

643. Essentially, we cannot convince another of our individual greatness by speaking of it in the singular, for ego-centred words never ring true.

644. It is the ego that demands to be fed, that is the glutton, that raids the fridge, that wants to fill the hunger of emotional emptiness with food and pacifying addictions. For the ego is like an

empty shell. It has nothing inside it, no substance, no within, and we find ourselves in this fear-filled emptiness. The ego does not contain the sweetness of the supreme.

645. We all appear to have at least two egos. One being fairly benevolent or validating, and the other being opposed or invalidating. Both arose from our childhood, where we were sometimes told we were good, and sometimes told we were bad. These voices now speak to us within the ego mind. Classically, it is the internalised battle of good and evil within each of us, while the observer, our soul, witnesses.

646. The validating ego seems to live more in the heart, the invalidating ego appears to live more in the mind.

647. The chattering mind and its concomitant actions are all part of ego play.

648. Our ego desires to show others as quickly as possible that it knows. It seems to be in a hurry to want to impress, because if it acted more slowly and with deliberation, a deeper consciousness would rise to the surface and become more apparent.

649. The ego has its own self-limiting, self-balancing mode called self-consciousness.

650. If the ego acquires what it thinks it needs, it creates an egoic, limited based happiness. If it doesn't get what it needs, it tends to create depression. As long as we live our lives led by ego desires, we shall experience an emotionally chaotic life. The lesson in all of this seems to be predominantly about surrender—becoming peacefully detached from our egoic needs whilst learning to place our faith in the larger co-extensive reality of our soul.

651. When we live with less ego, nothing seems so dramatic. We are no longer subject to the roller coaster ride of ego-centred life, but rather we flow freely with life, and feel at ease.

652. Only the separated ego suffers. Whenever we experience suffering, we are symbolically stepping outside of creation, in order to look back.

653. The world appears egoic in the human microcosm, but without

ego in the universal macrocosm. When we associate more with the macrocosm, we are inclined to refine and lose our egoic tendencies.

654. Joy, fulfilment or ecstasy are often drawn back from or not fully realised, because the ego draws us back from what it considers to be its own death during these experiences of soulful reunion in the pure present.

655. I have never met anyone who has been able to kill their ego. We cannot kill the ego by using the ego to kill the ego; it will simply multiply, and become schizophrenic. However, through witnessing with awareness, without conditioned thought, the ego quietens, and we move back into our hearts.

656. If we are relying upon the ego to evolve; if we are using our senses egoically; if we are measuring our progress with ego values; indeed, if we are even measuring our progress; we are operating on the inoperable channel, we are driving a vehicle that can only go in circles.

657. The ego by its very nature can never be fully conscious. For it is based on a finite set of beliefs and conditions, and cannot know or experience the infinite. Therefore, to a large extent the ego could be termed unconscious.

658. We cannot teach the ego to be pure in any direction; it cannot hold the capacity for boundlessness. We can only invite the divine to enter more consciously into our existence.

659. The introspective self-ego is primarily for times spent alone. The humanitarian ego is primarily for times spent with others.

660. If we quell our ego, we do not necessarily lose identity. Instead the personal-universal nature of our embodiment is expressed.

EGO'S HOME

661. The contained yet radiant joy of some people appears to be because they have embraced and encompassed their egos into their

hearts, and therefore they live with surety from the foundations of their soul.

✳

ELEGANCE

662. Mindfulness creates elegance.

In elegance we live in stillness.

We polish our senses.

We move with grace and dignity.

We speak what is appropriate.

We do what is simple and effective.

We choose to cultivate gentleness, harmony, and beauty.

And therefore, elegance is the practice of aligning with the virtues of one's soul.

✳

EMBARRASSMENT

663. When we are awkward or embarrassed, fundamentally we are not fully facing the immediate situation. We are only half-turned towards it, and therefore not fully self-empowered, we turn away in fear at the perceived opposition.

664. If we are true to our essence, how can we possibly be embarrassed?

665. Embarrassment seems to be caused by inordinately separatist thinking; we think that we are an island. Embarrassment exists to help correct this, by bringing us humbly back to communion with others.

✳

EMOTIONS

666. Emotions, both of those we label positive and negative, are generated from the unresolved turmoil or conditioning of the subconscious ego, or from conditioned thought. So-called positive emotions are always temporal; they arise from the ego expectation that things are going in one's favour, but things change and positive

emotions become dashed. This view of emotions, and the differentiation I place on feelings, may cause some readers to have a reactive emotional response—please read the entire contemplations on emotions with as clear and open a mind as possible.

667. Emotional energy is energy attempting to be transmuted into love. However it mistakenly thinks it needs to have something first (that is, to be loved by another) before it can undergo transmutation. With this need unmet, it tends to get stuck in whirlpools of unresolved negativity. The subconscious wanting of this need becomes the driving force and self-justification for having an emotion; that others are not doing what they are supposed to be doing—loving me without condition. Essentially we cannot depend on others to provide this love, we have to provide it for ourselves.

668. Our emotions encourage the desire for control, both of oneself and of others. They create the illusion that our individual ego has the right to direct the play of life around it; that its truth and well being are more important than those in its sphere. When others support its reality it becomes happy; when others do not uphold it, the ego becomes blaming, angry, rejected, lonely, hurt, fearful, depressed, hateful and so on.

669. Emotions result when the ego does not acquire its needs. Emotions are therefore a fabricated catalyst, with a specific intended motion, and a specific purpose. They are self-oriented and therefore often reactively needy, demanding, manipulative and thus blind to others. Ultimately they are self-defeating, whilst vainly attempting to elicit sympathy, support, and comfort.

670. We all seem to carry the longing and the wound of separation from the divine lover. It seems that whenever we are distressed, it is this wound that is stimulated to form the basis of our needy emotions. When our needy ego tries to control another in order to reclaim a sense of wholeness, we inevitably become controlled by our own unfulfilled emotions. Essentially we have forgotten that we are the lover as well as the beloved.

671. Beneath all emotional states lies the fear of abandonment and separation. The individual ego thinks that others may view it as being unworthy, and that it may become marooned to an existence of unending loneliness.

672. When we stand on a beach watching the sunrise, experiencing a sense of oneness and joy with life, we know that we are not emoting joy, we are feeling joy! There is no driven need to explain this state to others, to be selfish, demanding or judgmental with it, to unload it on anyone, to justify it or seek sympathy. When we contrast this with the forceful, emoting, state of anger for example, where there is a sense of wanting to unload it and justify, to make demands or to seek sympathy with others. Why then do we continue to believe that two entirely different states of being, that of separating emotions and transcendent feelings, are the same?

673. Our deepest desire appears to be to experience the love and peace that arises from heart-to-heart and soul-to-soul communion. This will not be able to be fully achieved until we understand what emotions are and what feelings are.

674. Whenever there is an investment in emotions, the account is opened and operated by the ego. It is not possible to have any kind of investment in love or feelings. If there is an investment in love or feelings, then the feeling is a so-called positive emotion, for example happiness, masquerading as a feeling. This happiness is generated by an investment in outside factors, which are apparently going in one's favour. However, as soon as the external situation changes, this emotive based happiness departs. Whereas feeling-based happiness, is the soul happiness that is happy for its own sake, it is not dependent on outside factors.

675. Emotions and feelings (not taking into account purely physical sensations) whilst considered to be the same in this society, I believe are very different states. They are similar only in that they can both be intense, passionate, and responsive.

The original meaning of feel, is to touch and caress, while emotion, is to shake and upheave. Primarily, feelings tend to reflect from the unconditional heart and soul and are therefore sensitively tuned to aware and intuitive states. Whereas emotions tend to reflect from the conditioned ego mind that can be either inflated or deflated, selfishly oriented and based on agitated, subconscious ego neediness.

Feelings	*Emotions*
* Arise from the heart and soul.	* Arise from the ego mind.
* Are the expression of love.	* Are the expression of a needy ego symptomatology, and are sensitive to selfish thought and interests, and therefore goal directed.
* Affection is freely given.	* Affection is expressed conditionally.
* See others subjectively.	* See others objectively.
* Are consciously active, aware and intuitive.	* Are largely subconscious, reactive, and judgmental.
* Are understanding and freeing.	* Are demanding and oppressive.
* Are compassionate.	* Are agitated, overly sentimental or aggressive.
* Are empathic.	* Are looking for someone to join in sympathy.
* See beauty and are aware of an abiding interrelationship to the greater reality.	* Do not take beauty in, or are aware of the greater reality, and are isolated and separated. The world appears different according to each agitated emotion.
* Are self-empowering. One partakes in a unified field of feeling that is both internally and externally, co-extensively generated.	* Are based on one's neediness being met outside of oneself. This can only happen at best partially and temporarily by others, and is eventually self-defeating. Others are therefore seen to be the cause of one having an emotion.

* Are consciously discerning.	* Are helpless, manipulative, and suspicious.
* Are appreciative.	* Are selfish and therefore find it difficult to be appreciative.
* Are easily shared.	* Are either suppressed or want others to take notice and be supportive to one's neediness.
* Are not interested in appealing to reason, there is no driving need.	*Sometimes attempt to appeal to reason, but their self-reasoning usually fails miserably. There is a subconsciously originating self-drivenness about them which is largely self-defeating.
* Are karma free.	* Are stirring the karmic pot with attacking and upsetting.
* Are peaceful and harmonious.	* Are troubled, fearful, anxious, annoyed and suffering.
* Are based in the pure present and have a joyful affinity to the eternal.	* Are founded on the beliefs of the conditioned ego mind and are therefore generally based on the past. One is usually caught in the stodge of time—one has to bide one's way through it.
* Are remembered without any need for tension.	* If not consciously dealt with, are stored in the subconscious whilst building tension.
* Self love and esteem are a natural consequence.	* There is either a loss of self love and esteem or an inflation of ego.

676. Because emotions and feelings are currently considered the same, it allows us to have an emotion (which is primarily sourced from unresolved childhood needs, now manifesting as neediness) under the mistaken legitimacy that emotions are our true 'feeling,' and therefore the state of our heart (or love), when in fact emotions arise from an ego conditioned belief state. Thus we have

many adults in our society currently emoting unresolved childhood emotions in order to be succoured by others, and thinking that they are expressing a feeling state.

677. We rise in feeling, and fall in emotion.

678. All negative emotions are failed attempts to acquire, possess, or secure love in some form. We have forgotten that our very being is love.

679. Are we to be perpetual slaves to our emotional woundedness? To an ongoing round of obsessive desire that passes unfulfilled before us masquerading as love?

680. When we emote, we are losing aware consciousness, we are slipping into the darkness of subconsciously reactive, primitive, fear based, survival responses. During or after, we are aware of a loss of our peace, love, wisdom and centred presence.

681. Whatever we emote is teaching us the lesson of opposition; that we need to come authentically from the opposite place of integrity.

682. Fear followed by anger appears to be the primary driving forces for all other emotions. When we examine the problems of the world, fear and anger may be seen conspicuously or concealed within other emotions.

The violent anger of war; the self-righteousness of one's own view, and the fear of another's differences. The greed of exploitation—both of people and resources. The hatred that breeds prejudice, and the resentment and jealousy of another's fortune. The culture of impatience and instant gratification. The avoidance of responsibility, and the apathy in not desiring to be a source for positive change . . . As long as we continue to believe that emotions are our primary state of being, then the problems of the world will continue.

683. Emotions have a front and a back. We may aggressively react with them front on, or passively react to them from the rear.

684. The self-seeking emotional current that manoeuvres around

our thoughts, judgments and beliefs prevents us from knowing the ever-present conjunction of truth and love.

685. Many of our emotions are the expression of the non-observed narcissism of the ego, which judges—why cannot others think like me; act like me; and emote like I do, in order that I can be fully loved without condition? Because of this we tend to compare behaviours, and keep an emotional score in our friendships and relationships, so that the hypothetical aim of the narcissist is achieved—the domination of one's emotional rule upon others. This unfulfilled need continually attempts to find fulfilment through controlling them. It is necessary to step back from our emotional demands, and lighten and let go the burden of emotive rules we live our lives by, for others will not live by such rules, and consequently we shall find plenty to make ourselves emotionally upset.

686. If one person is emotional and the other is feeling-based, the emotional person often views the other as coldly unemotional; they do not readily see the depth of feelings of love; rather they are more interested in an emotional display. Particularly in conflict the emotive one wants more than the mere agreement of the other, they want emotional alignment as well.

687. When an emotional altercation occurs, the one who perceives being attacked often instantly goes into a state of fear and panic, misperceives what is said, overreacts, senses being blamed, overemphasises and brings in additional often unrelated topics with which they are aggrieved, in order to return a counter attack of blame with a heightened emotional display of indignation, self-righteousness and anger. This creates the self-justification needed to attempt an avoidance of the possibility of emotional pain, whether the accusation is true or not. Overall there is a sense of a loss of one's power, and the urgent need to reclaim it, as well as a sense of rejection from another human being which creates separation and hurt. Generally, such a response is based on misperception because of emotional vulnerability, and ends up being a competition for power. We must learn that such reactive responses do not create

understanding or relatedness, and that they are fundamentally a denial of the wholeness of the primary intimacy of souls.

688. If we discharge emotionally without there being any conscious insight, we are reinforcing unconscious behaviour.

689. In an emotional conflict, the other person is definitely viewed as being wrong, and therefore the views become polarised. However, such polarisation will begin to be healed when one or both sides see that redemptive qualities are more important than the polarising of ego-led beliefs.

690. Emotions arise from a black and white view of oneself, others, and the world. The shades of grey between them, and of the rainbow colours are generally forgotten.

691. During or after an emotional conflict, if we ask the other 'What are you feeling?'—we are actually asking 'What emotions are you holding?'

692. Whenever we suffer depression, anxiety, confusion, guilt, boredom, contempt, worry, sadness, resentment, apathy, fear, jealousy, rejection, shyness, loneliness, hurt, anger, hatred, regret, judgmentalness, or any other emotion, the primary cause is that we are emoting impotence, we have lost power, we have lost sight of our own majesty and virtuosity.

693. We cannot witness the greater truth in any form of emotion. Instead we witness a selfish, microscopic distorted reality, where we tend to find only temporary pleasures, or things that upset and annoy us.

694. When there is emotional upset there is also a fixation on the conditioned, reactive, ego-mind. In order to see this clearly, we need to re-centre ourselves on the open, all-embracing divine mind emanating from within. Deep, calm, silent breathing will usually open the way.

695. Our regrets, frustrations, fears, hurts and jealousies from yesterday are with us in the form of memory. This memory is a recollection of a situation; it is not the situation itself. At the very best we can recall it as factually as possible, but at present we

cannot physically intervene in yesterday to make changes there. We can however make changes today, now. The more we are able to live as though the emotional traumas from yesterday are not what matter most today, but rather the evolution of our understanding is what counts, the more we will be able to live where we are most effective, that is, in the present.

Perhaps with this in mind we will eventually be able to live as though there is no emotional yesterday, and from this to live as if there is no morning today, no noon, and no evening, until only this minute, then this moment is finally left.

696. From inside each emotional costume we put on, the world appears to us to be an alien place. However in the feeling state there are no costumes and the world is always, obviously beautiful.

697. If we say 'I am feeling angry' (or any other emotion), the anger is plainly anger, but the 'I am feeling' is suspect. The 'I am' calls for defining the 'I' responsible, which in the end we discover to be the ego, not the true 'I am.' The 'feeling' we find to be not from the unconditioned heart and soul, but an emoting from the conditioned, self-oriented ego mind.

The statement when expressed truthfully becomes 'My ego is emoting anger.' However, for the most part this would not be acceptable to most, for it puts the cause back into one's own hands, and away from the self-justifying, pseudo honoured, 'feeling' state.

698. We can never hurt another's feelings, though we can say something hurtful that they may react to which upsets their emotional ego.

699. To live despairingly in any of the constricted emotional states because of unfulfilled expectations, is to deny the power we possess now, the power to love.

700. When one's emotions are upset, they are in a state of confusion, and therefore cannot be trusted for decision making. So that if we are emotionally needy and led to act, it is probably best to wait. And if we are led to be still, it is probably best to

act, for our actions will likely not bear the result we desire if we act from an emotional urgency.

701. Eating and drinking without consciousness becomes a reactive, habitual, emoting experience. Before and during our eating and drinking we lose consciousness, in order to satisfy the emotion we are holding. These emotions may be obvious, such as eating chocolate to ease depression, or drinking alcohol to numb emotional pain; or not be so obvious, such as deep-seated, subconscious inadequacy, which may create eating away at oneself and constantly snacking.

702. The state of emotional emptiness is primarily the illusion that we are contained within an empty fear-filled ego.

703. When we allow ourselves to simply experience our emotions, we automatically do it consciously as an observer, and we experience an opening to a larger view, a larger sense, where grace enters alongside.

704. Honesty around constricting internal emotions is a swift way to freedom, when communicated with love. Sometimes, the expression of emotion in this way portrays our vulnerability, and reveals the fragility of our humanness. It can be a gift that opens us to our soul, and opens those who witness, to their soul.

705. Sometimes to consciously shout one's anger, inhibitions, fears, hurts and worries before they unconsciously explode, give the ability to regain one's potency.

706. All emotional states, once consciously grasped, can be transmuted into one, two or all three of the states of (a), Right action; (b), Right assertion; or (c), Love.

707. When we emotionally cut off from someone, the emoting continues internally for us until we discharge it, usually explosively. However if we diffuse the emotion by seeing the underlying conditioned belief upon which it is based, the emoting may then be internally resolved.

708. Emotions usually occur when our beliefs are threatened. The more deep-rooted and stubborn our beliefs the more we tend to

become emotive in protecting them. We need to realise that we are not our beliefs, and to step back and loosen our grip a little. We can then have a response which is more detached, whilst remaining true to our essential nature.

709. Ignorance of our true state causes constricting emotions. If we are experiencing constriction we are in subjugation to the unstructured mind. We need to reclaim and develop the structured, creative, intuitive and meditative mind.

710. Emotions carry the ego to different depths of unconscious psychological constriction. Some of these emotions can lift locked in deeper emotional states, such as; anger has the capacity to lift us out of rejection, worry, hurt, grief, pain and fear. Embarrassment can lift displays of public anger, self-righteousness or stuck pride. Regret can lift hate. And self-righteousness can lift hurt or rejection. But fundamentally we are still isolated from our own inner truth, and from communion with others.

711. Often when we want to reprimand someone, we initially close off to them, which creates a build-up of emotional tension within us. This, in turn, creates a sense that the other, through their ignorance and thoughtlessness is somehow attacking us.

We then release this tension explosively, or mollify it in an attempt to protect them as well as ourselves from the emotion, or carry it unexpressed as a burden. This situation really calls for us to first speak our truth, openly and with love, without the necessity of constricting ourselves into such a tightened emotional space.

712. Issues regularly arise. To see them as issues rather than create battles out of them will free us from creating emotional burdens.

713. In our relationships with others, rather than express one's long suffering, hyper-needy emotions, we express the truth of what we would like, we are then in empowered cause, rather than the effects of our own victim-hood. This truth is spoken and heard more clearly when it is spoken with love, unattached to wounded emotion.

714. When we speak the truth of what we prefer, emotions are then seen to be the expression of a withholding pattern of what one thinks one needs for survival. Emotions place our focus on the desperation of what we consider to be our absolutist needs, rather than simply focusing on the possible fulfilment of what we would like. Emotions whilst largely considered to be the expression of one's truth in this society, are thus seen to be the result of avoidance of it.

715. To say that one uses emotions as a means of true self-understanding and as a path to freedom and enlightenment seems somewhat questionable. For during the time of the emotion, one thinks that one is the emotion, and not the soul's abiding love.

716. Emotions are not to be taken seriously; they are not the truth. They are a fabricated, contracted illusion of our ego; they are not our true nature of being.

717. When experiencing emotions, if we own these ego creations and say 'My ego is doing this,' then we gain perspective from which to take self-responsibility for them.

718. It does not seem possible to be fully conscious in the present moment with an emotion, on account that:

(a). Emotions all carry a large past conditioning content that precludes us being fully conscious now.

(b). Emotions reside in the ego mind; the ego mind cannot live wholly in the moment because of its conditioned makeup.

(c). Emotions are not our natural state. We generally want to be rid of them, and therefore we cannot be ourselves inside them, there is always a sense of wanting to get away from them, but we are caught in a time warp that is painfully slow.

(d). When we are in an emotion, we are subconsciously driven by it, and therefore not consciously in command of ourselves. We are conscious only of a narrow focus, which is characterised by a sense of constriction, victim-hood, and powerlessness. We are not conscious of the uniqueness of others, or the boundlessness of the earth and beyond.

(e). The 'I am' is the soul, which is constantly in love, truth, bliss, joy, innocence, nobility, creativity and so on. These states of the soul can only be experienced in the full consciousness of the present moment. The soul is not defined by any of the emotions, such as anger, sadness, depression, worry, confusion, hatred, boredom, and so on, these are all founded in the sense of one's separation from others in the ego mind, and are thus not our true state. And so we continually mislabel our true identity if we refer to the 'I am' as being anything less than divine. We seem to create for ourselves a recurring problem of mistaken identity, locked in time outside of the present moment, particularly with the emotions.

(f). When we do become fully conscious of an emotion, we are no longer in the emotion, but are a witness to it from the greater reality and perspective of our heart and soul.

719. Emotions are there to point towards the positive, for in themselves they cannot give us what we want. They point out our own ego-based negative belief on which they are founded.

720. The ego is largely made of conditioned thought and emotion—many believe that the expression of these is being true to oneself. Rather it is the truth that needs to be expressed.

721. Emotions do not arise from a feeling state; they issue from the past conditioning beliefs that damaged the foundations of our subconscious ego. These emotions, which can be either constricting, or apparently positive emotions which are hyper-inflated, drive us to self-protect our vulnerable foundation. However, this self-protection is masking the presence of a self-defeating negative foundational belief about ourselves. The emotion is not the truth. The belief is the truth of the emotion, but the belief is not the truth. The belief needs to be exposed in order for the truth to be revealed, which is the inherent sanguine nature of our being.

722. When we do not have an ongoing intimate relationship with the divine, the basis of our thinking becomes singular, we think we are a lonely entity, and thus we dwell in fear and experience

the spectrum of emotions, from despair, through conditioned happiness, to anger.

723. Primarily, if we are to grow out of our childhood emotional wounds, our self-awareness must triumph over our impulsive emoting, where present-moment consciousness is lost in emotional trauma. Or if this is not immediately possible, to focus on an intermediate level of awareness to change the emoting state. For example, with activity or rest, depending on whether the emotion is constricting or explosive. The result is that by not being so bound up in the emotion, our awareness increases, and we are more able to deal with the issue.

724. If we take responsibility for our self-created emotions, we are also taking the larger responsibility for our love and happiness.

725. When we are in an emotion we become locked into the structure of the subconscious depths of the ego. When we truly experience a being state of love, the ego vanishes but the emptiness it leaves behind contains something. It contains a receptive, intuitive, all-embracing, unruffled knowing, that gives birth to a gentle contentment and a pervasive peace. Deeply we realise, we become conscious that our being is sourced from the vast expanse of universal love.

726. Through the constricting experience of both active and passive emotions, we discover that the state of love is our only full state of being. At those times when we return to this state of love with ourselves, we return to a state of connection with all things, and we lose the separating and confronting emotional ego.

727. Each possible emotional situation requires our discernment, our ongoing commitment to be conscious, rather than reactive. We need to ask 'Is this situation worth the loss of my soul's presence and the gaining of so much emotional anguish, heartache and physical suffering?' If at first we decide it is not worth it, are we instead avoiding? If it is still worth it, it calls for us to ask 'What is happening with my senses and the general situation? What does this mean? What is driving me? From where does this

arise? And finally, are we ready to receive the serenity of our soul?'

EMPATHY

728. The experience of empathy is similar to the loving detachment we experience when we align ourselves with our inner nature. There is a mindful appreciation of all that comes to pass.

EMPTINESS

729. Largely we grow up believing we are empty and lacking. We constantly look to fill ourselves with food, vitamins, sex, addictions, money, fame, power and so on. However, from the divine view we are essentially supreme fullness, seeking expression.

ENCOURAGE

730. To encourage and be enthusiastic towards others is the unselfish sign of an open-hearted being, living in awareness of unity.

END

731. The last extremity, is always an edge where we meet the threshold of an immense, incalculable beginning.

ENEMY

732. The enemy is created by ego, not by soul. Opposing forces are always created by ego. Hatred and violence are created by ego. But the soul is the embracer of all such ignorance.

733. If we can think of our enemies in a positive light, living under the same sun that we do, we help create a new matrix for the relationship to move into.

ENERGY

734. Energy is intrinsically spirit. If we define energy without a spiritual definition, we define the universe as merely a material manifestation.

735. The amount of energy that passes through us has great equivalence to our joy for living.

736. The positive and negative forces we experience in our lives are essentially a play of energies. These energies are either resisting or affirming. To unduly emphasise the mental/emotional states that these energies manifest into, can be to lose track of their origin as being the play of primordial energy.

737. The more we leave undone, the more our energy becomes locked, and the less freely we move in life. The more up to date we are, the more energy we have to flow with life, and life is then able to offer us its spontaneous, serendipitous wonders, discoveries and opportunities.

738. All energy is intelligent, it acts and responds to universal principles based in incorruptible truth.

739. The natural consciousness of energy wants to go forward. It does not want to stop and remain stuck in negative emotions, uncleared spaces, and unresolved situations.

740. When truth is not spoken there is a loss of energy. When love is spoken there is a gain of energy. When there is understanding, energy is harmonised. When we are emotional we lose energy, even though emotions such as anger may appear to produce more energy, it is the survival energy of adrenalin.

741. The practice of a discipline enhances internal energy.

742. With an increased energy level, we have to be vigilant that we do not move into an increased ego state. Often when we are less active, we are more internally directed, and therefore more spiritually motivated.

743. The world's energy, the energy of its inhabitants, is not used directly. If it were, there would be no process called life. All would already be in a state of absolute being.

ENHANCEMENT

744. Any consciousness that enhances opens us to greater realisation.

ENLIGHTENMENT

745. Enlightenment occurs when we take full cognisance of the moment. Enlightenment becomes a continuing process when we bring this cognisance to each moment. Enlightenment can be both of the moment, and a continuing process of moments. Those deemed enlightened are living a continuing process of conscious moments.

746. In each moment, trusting, letting go of all conditioning, we are aware, we become what we have always been—love.

747. The light that exists around earth is only visible in the moment. Light's instant presence is demonstrated by our only being able to cast a shadow within its eternal, continuous current in the present. And thus enlightenment may be the awakening to the illumination of lights' infinite presence in the present moment.

748. The ego cannot be enlightened, although at times it has a sense of progress and sometimes of going backwards. Slightly beyond ego, one's unbound observing awareness is already free, already enlightened.

749. Enlightenment cannot happen in only one hemisphere of the brain. Creative and reasoning, male and female—enlightenment unites us, for in essence we are asexual.

750. When we begin to acknowledge our true 'I,' the 'I' that was before and beyond ego, the co-extensive 'I,' enlightenment

simultaneously begins to dawn, whilst also placing us within the everlasting blessedness of now.

751. In a universe that appears infinite, enlightenment radiates infinitely, and therefore if we are preaching the bliss of enlightenment as an end point, we may have reached the boundaries of our own small universe.

752. Detached from ego mind, just being, there is a love awareness of things as they are, all is light.

753. When the ego is at rest in the heart, our impressions are stilled, the eternal 'now' becomes available, we become receptive to life's felicity, to the constantly creating ecstatic love call of the divine, all is integrated, this is heaven.

754. Sending the ego home, eternity becomes conscious, time fades, the love realm of the pure present arrives, we love, for all things are innocent.

755. The composed mind is timeless, at peace, co-extensively omnipresent.

756. In the uncorrupted virginal moment, we naturally love, it is our state of being, we are opened, the universe is seen to be a manifestation of love.

757. With 'no thought,' the calm of our inner peace ascends, we devotedly perceive the world, we see with the eye of the divine, we breathe the divine in, we breathe the divine out—all is provided.

758. From internal silence there is rest and potential, our senses become holy instruments of the divine, all that our senses touch, touch the unified field of creation, we love strongly, there is no separation.

759. Witnessing with awareness, without judging good or bad, we see the preciousness of the divine incarnated into all things, we worship naturally, we feel our universal state.

760. Alive in the moment without conditioned thought or emotion, we live in love, in the divine, we are co-extensive and we are at peace.

761. Entering the doorway of the beginning, the light of the divine shines in the self-happiness of the moment, all mystery is swallowed in the infinity of our being.

762. Loving without duality, we are present, the truth is revealed, the pure 'I' is infinite, the eternal is 'I.'

763. Just being, the ego naturally journeys homeward. Thought disappears, stillness and calm arrive, all is apparent now as it innocently exists, we open to it, we fully receive it, we see the divine in all things, we love in gratitude, what is loved is loving, what loves is being loved, all is integrated, all creation is heavenly being.

ENTHUSIASM

764. To be enthusiastic demonstrates an eagerness of love and devotion to the cultivation and blossoming of the bounty of life.

765. Enthusiasm is generated by an inspired reason and by having faith in the outcome. This inspiration and faith impels us and drives us toward our goal. Love is the highest reason for the generation of enthusiasm.

ENVY

766. Envy closes down one's vivacity. It is a focusing of resentment on another's success and a comparing of one's limitations. One has forgotten to bring close the joys of existence and of one's own uniqueness.

EQUALITY

767. Full equality occurs in the recognition of our original, all embracing identity.

ESP

768. Extra sensory perception is more valid in relationship and communion with the universal self than with the selfish self.

ESSENCE

769. The vital essence of a human being is love. It is what gives us life, and gives our lives meaning, purpose, and joy.

770. The quality of something is much more meaningful in terms of its essence rather than to the more common view of how 'good' or 'bad' it is.

771. To pay more attention to the outer form of things rather than their inner essence is to lose sight of causal power.

ETERNITY

772. Eternity is the background of all that appears to be passing, and is the true present of the conscious foreground.

773. We enter the presence of eternity whenever our impressions are stilled. It is raising the consciousness of now.

774. All of eternity is in love with us, for here on this spinning pearl she has provided flowers and trees, and wind and ocean, clouds and valleys, and lakes and mountains. And all of these things love us, love us, love us.

775. Eternity was, is, and will be, before, now and after, alpha and omega, and therefore eternity is the presence of the eternal.

EUTHANASIA

776. Euthanasia is not suicide. If we look at the circumstances surrounding euthanasia and suicide we see a difference prior to the intent and in the means and support of both final acts.

777. The decision for euthanasia ought not to be a daily, conscious-minded decision. It is a decision made through the inner divine, by contemplation, prayer, and meditation, of the one it affects. If this person is unable to decide because of the nature of the injury or sickness, then the decision is for the inner divine of those who are close. Perhaps now more than any other, it is time to listen to the spontaneous and unusual revelations of intuition rather than continue to be swayed by convention.

EVASION

778. Our level of personal evasion appears equivalent to our level of frustration, anxiety, and purposelessness.

779. Whenever we evade stating what needs to be stated, or doing what needs to be done, we lose a little personal energy, we become less who we are.

EVIL

780. Evil, or the denial of life through ignorance of the divine, is not so much to be feared, as to be an appeal in mercy and compassion.

EVOLUTION

781. If we believe in what our science tells us, that life originated on earth because of a chance combination of elements in the primordial oceans, we may ask 'How was it that the elemental ingredients for life were present in the first place?'

782. There are times in mankind's spiritual evolution when our essence has more opportunity to be defined and revealed through deep struggle than through high inspiration.

783. We are part of an ongoing chain of reaction, which was unfolding before us, and which we now influence into the future. Every one of our actions produces a reaction.

784. If our focus is largely through ego, then we are still in the childhood of our evolution, and we ought to allow ourselves the same tolerance that we allow children. Whether child or adult, we came here to experience.

785. The current evolution of humanity appears to be a process of undergoing ego trial, in order to reveal the nature of soul.

786. Pre-eminently, evolution is the unfolding of all beings to the state of love.

EXAGGERATION

787. It is our own internalised preoccupation that builds exaggeration.

788. If we exaggerate in order to bolster our allegation or story, in reality we are embellishing our description for some sort of self-gain. Such exaggerations are a fabrication of the truth and thus issue from the domain of dishonesty and deceit.

EXCESS

789. Every overindulgence, every immoderation, or in other words, every betrayal to ourselves, leads us away from the centre within.

790. Only the ego is capable of carrying excesses.

EXCUSE

791. An excuse is often a polite substitute for a deeper inadmissible reason; as an ego-distancing statement to place us as far as possible from fault or blame; or because we are not taking responsibility.

EXERCISE

792. Unless there is an upliftment of the spirit, before, during, and/or after physical exercise, the exercise is largely useless. The body will soon lose the benefit if the spirit is not moved to embody the joy of movement.

EXPECTATION

793. If we prepare with confidence, we help create an attitude of trust to fulfil our expectation.

794. The energy of expectation is difficult to focus through the ego mind, for it seems like one is forcing. However, when it naturally wells up from one's heart, it brings with it its own loving confidence.

795. Negative expectation creates hesitant energy.

796. We live largely according to our expectation. We anticipate love and gain, fear and loss, and their occurrence depends upon our confidence or anxiety.

797. The unfulfilled expectations we have of others are often due to our lack of knowledge or understanding of their situation.

798. If others hold expectations of us, their expectations can only be granted if they fall within our inner determination.

799. In the intuitive realms, to expect the unexpected doesn't seem to work quite as well as to unexpect the expected. Thus the unexpected becomes more readily assimilated.

800. To unduly have expectations of one's personal advantage helps to inflate the selfish ego. But to have expectation or hope, tempered with grace and gratitude, opens one to the sanctifying favour of the inner divine.

801. When we have an expectation of another person, we often assume that we have already integrated this quality in some way in ourselves. If we have not, then life usually responds quickly with an opportunity for us to do so.

802. It is our needs and expectations that prevent us from loving others, and frequently, the perception of our needs and expectations by others that prevent them from loving us.

803. Many of us seem to live with the idea to expect and anticipate the worst in life, and it surely comes to pass. But how different life is lived when we expect the wonderful, and live in wonder.

EXPERIENCE

804. Experience is the participation in life by one's ego, in order to gain insight into one's soul.

805. Unless we truly know something through experience, we can only convey a shallow imitation and relate conventional and habitual platitudes.

806. When we experience something, we can meet it blow for blow, become possessed by it, allow it to pass through without attachment, or suffuse it with love.

807. No one can teach anyone else the lessons of life. It is only by our individual practical experience that we can know life. But in some measure we all take responsibility for one another.

808. As beings who strive to understand ourselves, it is preferable we attempt to learn from our experiences in a self-reflective way rather than be dictated to by them.

809. When we are one with our experience, there is no holding back, nor impatient scrambling.

810. Speaking of a past experience will often create a similar strand of experience in the present. This is more than just a passive synchronicity, it is an indication of the active principles of the power of the mind and spirit, the interconnectedness of all things, and the unified nature of life.

811. Experiences of an upsetting nature occur in order to stir the ego to seek communion and union with the soul. Experiences of an

uplifting nature occur in order to inspire the ego to seek communion and union with the soul.

812. Our experience can mould us in new and more beautiful ways. It does not exist to defeat us.

813. Each of us is an intermediary. We are all passing our experiences between each other, and therein we are enriched.

814. The nature of earthly life requires that any intellectual or emotional reality be fully understood and integrated through a practical experience, though there are probably many experiences we would rather not choose.

815. Primarily, only by the integration of our experience can we move on to full integration.

816. The sum total of human experience points to us simply gaining an intimate understanding of truth and love.

817. The desires of the personal ego largely determine the direction and extent of our knowledge, and therefore the beliefs we hold. Thus our desires, knowledge, and beliefs, both conscious and subconscious, will be instrumental in creating our experiences.

818. Most of what we experience is experienced by the gradations of ego, from the strong and narrow experiences of the dense ego, to the light and almost universal experiences of the refined ego. For on the level of soul, all appears to be already arranged.

EXPERT

819. True experts step beyond the egoic extroversion of their own expertness.

820. We currently live in a society where we trust too quickly in those identified as experts, even to the extent of believing more in experts, than our own intuition and wisdom.

EXPLANATION

821. If we cannot explain with the rational mind, or our explanation is not understood, we may use other ways such as humour, acting, storytelling, art, and so on. It is more important to have symphony and union with others, it is not so important how we achieve it.

EXPLORATION

822. Have we not come here to explore? To probe the heights and depths of this earth, whilst at the same time probing our own heights and depths, and all to thoroughly trial our meaning, understanding, and purpose, of love and truth.

823. We are all explorers, who are moved by heaven and touched by earth. Heaven and earth are undeniably connected. And therefore there must be a little of each in the other. Accordingly, as explorers, we will undoubtedly discover heaven. In this exploration, our own pace would seem to be the heavenly given.

EXPOSE

824. When something is exposed, it is brought into the light of revelation. We may examine its surface, or we may investigate its depths. Similarly, when someone is exposed, we may examine their surface (ego), or investigate their true depths (soul).

EXPRESSION

825. The conditioned ego mind expresses itself with selfish conditioning judgments. The soul expresses understanding with loving detachment.

826. The true self allows ultimate space for freedom of expression, whereas the ego wants to divide and conquer.

827. All elements are within us, from the depths to the heights. Therefore our expression can be one of great bounty.

EXTRAORDINARY

828. If we are looking for the extraordinary, we are likely missing what is already extraordinary before us.

F

FACE

829. Every face is the divine beloved's face. It is how we perceive that face which decides our relationship to them.

FACT

830. All undiscovered facts are currently in existence in the collective unconscious. They will eternally bubble through into the collective subconscious, and finally into the collective conscious mind.

However, a fact can only be quantified by its existence value to the partaker. Its usability and therefore the awareness of it determines the value of its existence by the user. Thus, facts exist across the range of unconscious, subconscious, conscious subjective and conscious objective minds.

831. A becoming objective fact is currently gauged and reasoned by its association to already established, agreed upon facts, until it is superseded by a higher, more embracing subjective/objective fact. Therefore the facts that we currently deem to know of creation are largely subjective, when compared to the vastness of the collective unconscious of the universe.

832. How many facts are really facts without our being and making them factitious?

833. Spiritual reality embraces all physical reality. Whatever we consent to bring into our reality is the expression of our own personal spiritual creativity. However, the greater the congruence of our personal facts of reality, the more universal its fact of application.

FAILURE

834. The ego may appear to fail, but the soul never fails. Being a victim to the dramas of life is another play of the ego.

835. There are no 'Failures,' only 'Learners.'

836. Whenever we think we are a failure in any way, we are believing that the divine is impotent in our lives rather than being omnipotent. We believe that accomplishing certain standards in society is more important than the essence of our being.

837. Nobody has the authority, judgment, or intimate soul knowledge to call another's life a failure.

838. What may appear as a failure in life, is on some level always a success. Through failure we tend to discover and understand more deeply.

839. Anytime we wilfully fail another, we also fail ourselves from belonging to humanity.

FAITH

840. Faith inherently relies upon the resolving and unifying action of love. Therefore faith is love in action.

841. Deep down faith is primarily a self-promise, even though it may involve others. And therefore it creates confidence in one's belief.

842. Faith occurs when we really see and believe in the deeper

truth. And it is good to ask ourselves 'Am I really seeing and believing in what I aspire to?'

843. If we can become what we yearn for, before it materialises, if we can live it now, then our faith is made entire. When we live with such a sense of completeness, we live as though we are already immensely rich in all areas, as well as loved, healthy, intelligent, wise, and so on. This state produces particular frames of mind that help create the state we desire.

844. Faith is a decision, an act of will, not a hope.

845. We cannot bank on a hope or a wish; we can bank only on our faith, which may be the continuing revelation of precise reality.

846. When the object of our faith is known, we can secure our faith upon it. But when the means of its manifestation are unknown, then the more we can materialise the circumstances of the object, the more fervent our faith.

847. Open faith, not blind faith, is a divine cleanser and enhancer of mind and body.

848. Fear-based faith is grasping and possessive and tends to be intolerant of other faiths. Love based faith lets go and is free. Fear-based faith is actually not faith at all, but rather the belief that one's salvation, security and wholeness are external to one's divinity.

849. Whatever occurs in our lives is a test of our faith in love and in truth. If we believe in the negative, in others, life, or ourselves we are in opposition to love and truth. We are misusing our faith and being faithful to the negative.

850. In our divinity we are complete. Witnessing and calling forth from divinity is already a completed act of faith.

✳

FALSE

851. Falsity is a delusion pretending to be real. Real has no delusion, nor does it imitate or pretend to be anything other than what it is.

FAMILY

852. Whenever we minister to another, we are bringing to life the quiescent relationship of the family of humanity.

853. Certain economic, political, technological, experimental, migratory, sexual, religious and social forces in our society have directly or indirectly helped create the breakdown of the traditional family unit. Many have separated themselves or been made outcast from these units, but in the process some have discovered new families of like-minded people. This process, whilst appearing disruptive to the traditional family unit, may lead to a quickening of the evolution of humanity, enabling us to experience and acknowledge our broader-based human family.

854. The contemporary family appears to be breaking away from the unity, loyalty, and limitations of the blood connections of the past, to form a new broader-based family, of clans, circles and associations. These families are drawn together by similar ideals, aspirations and loves. However each of us internally carries a cast of characters inherited from our original family, that may continue to seek resolution in our new families.

FAULT FINDING

855. If we are prone to condemn, disapprove, criticise or blame, we are instituting ourselves as an authority. A judging authority who chooses to pull on various threads of behaviour and pick them apart, in order to emphasise faults, as though they were a permanent condition and not a passing experience. But a number of questions need to be asked—

Do we want our primary form of communication to be as a fault-finder?

Can we expect to have a relationship with someone where we are emphasising their faults?

Will emphasising faults, without any acknowledgment of the good, keep communication open?

Are we prone to finding fault in others because of the proximity of our own?

And do we want to live in a world where faults and fault finding are emphasised?

FEAR

856. The cause of fear, and fear of failure, is forgetting that we are eternal beings living in an eternal universe.

857. If we are experiencing fear, we are experiencing the conditioned ego. We are attempting to place trust in this ego as being who we truly are, but intuitively we sense that such trust has no wisdom in it, nor is it able to show a history of success based on such trust.

858. Primarily we fear that we are not a chosen being worthy of the love of the divine or of other human beings. However, fear is a fantasy of the future, the act we fear is not now.

859. If fear is a survival instinct, what is it that is catalysing our fear beneath the requirements of our already established survival? After all we are alive now.

860. When we fully bear in mind our objective and purpose, then fear and doubt become more incidental, they tend to move further behind in our consciousness than our purpose.

861. Our fears are largely the projected creations of our own minds, and therefore they require to be faced internally by their creator.

862. Self-created fears are often an indication of the areas of life where our perceptions are too narrow and need enlarging.

863. If we inspire fear into ourselves, we are breathing fear and we are embodying it. We may instead choose to breathe and inspire affirmative and beneficial states other than fear.

864. Fear can be generated by the consumption of excess food, drugs, and material goods. The need to consume excess occurs

because of the movement away from one's centre, and the loss of one's true identity.

865. Action wins over the largely hallucinatory process of fear.

866. Whenever we break through the fear barrier, we become larger than our previous self-conceptions, and we embrace more of life.

867. Where there is fear, there is always a need. Where there is no need, there is no fear. Therefore, is our need a valid reaction to the situation? And can our need be satisfied in another way?

868. Fear arises partly out of having expectations. True love lets go of all expectations.

869. The more conscious we become, the less fear we experience in life. The more objective we can make our subjective fears, the more conscious we become.

870. When we are fearful (outside of the bounds of the survival instinct), on some level we are interpreting that we are not worthy, or deserve to feel the fullness of life's expression.

871. The purpose of fear appears to be for learning of our supreme potency through the forces of limitation, that we may learn to have grace with potency rather than unbridled power. If we are experiencing fear, we have not yet realised the fullness of our universal potency that is above and beyond all fears, we are still learning grace.

872. Underneath fear is a sense of separation, or an impending sense of separation of the ego from one's soul, others, life, and the earth. The basic belief is that this sundering will be our final death into oblivion. However, on the soul level we are always in love's union. It is the illusion of ego that creates the sense of separation. Fear then appears to be a trial by experience of where we place our faith—in ego, or in soul. Do we have the courage to choose love above fear and pain?

873. If we make friends with our fears, we become larger than them, they begin to transmute into balance and we can move beyond.

874. Fear is created and sustained in the mind; it is not created in the heart. The more phobias and fears we have in our lives, the more we are being urged to move into our hearts.

875. Because fear is the most ancient, most primary of emotions upon which all other emotions are based, when we experience fear we are only one door, one hair's breadth from the divine. Being so close to the divine, it is time to celebrate and embrace our fear!

FEELINGS

876. Our feelings are the expression of a light heart. They are innocent, there is no sense of deceit or contraction to them. The ability to feel creates an openness for empathy with oneself, others and nature.

877. True positive feelings are actually the natural state of our being. We can be happy without a reason, yet many believe that they can only experience happiness when something in the outside world appears to go in their favour.

878. With the experience of love, happiness, bliss, compassion, beauty, joy, nobility and innocence, we are feeling the bubbling fullness of our potential, and the dynamic, commanding presence of the divine.

879. When we are in a feeling state, our tendency is to find things in the outer world that are a joy to us.

880. Apart from the conveying of sensation, most of the time the phrase 'I feel' is used, it is actually a facade for the use of 'I think,' because 'I feel' is generally regarded as being a deeper, more meaningful communication. When 'I feel' is said, it is often used to explain or justify something, and therefore it is supporting a conditioned expression of need. When 'I feel' is truly experienced there is no necessity for an explanation.

881. Popular psychology encourages us to 'Own our feelings.' For example: 'When you make a mess in the kitchen, I feel angry.' The underlying truth of this statement is really 'When you make a mess in the kitchen, my ego emotes anger,' the feeling state is not

involved. The ego can then be observed for what it is—the expression of a conditioned persona. It is not essentially who we are.

882. We become self-determining when we have the awareness to consciously choose feelings rather than react with our subconsciously programmed emotions. This brings us the ability to live in love in the present. One regains one's innocence; emotional guile is no longer necessary. From the greater perspective of love, one sees things as they truly are, and thus there can be attention, appreciation, understanding and compassion.

883. All deeply unconditioned feelings arise from the soul.

884. Whenever we witness a feeling, either in oneself or others, we are witnessing the greater reality, we are witnessing the opening of the veils to heaven. (See emotions.)

FERTILITY

885. Happiness and love create the foundation of health for potency and fertility.

FLEXIBILITY

886. If we are flexible, we are openly giving our love. Love makes us receptive, adaptable, and responsive.

FLOWING

887. When there is an ease of action in our everyday life, it feels like we are flowing with a much larger force . . . with life, and with all of creation. The earth itself sings in harmony, our sense of self-consciousness is absent, and we are one.

888. A flowing stream of mind/body energy is ours if we choose to feed it from the mountains of inspiration, radiance, love, happiness, gratitude, excitement, optimism, generosity, enthusiasm, service, will, creativity, and so on. But if we divert

the stream into the valleys of depression, sadness, boredom, confusion, apathy, loneliness, guilt, regret, worry, and so on, we find that the stream becomes dammed inside a closed valley, and the energy of our body/mind becomes stagnant.

FOCUS

889. Whatever we focus on seems to begin the process of materialisation. However the time, timing and the re-routing of our beliefs usually change the outcome to most things we focus upon. Generally though, if we focus on problems we make them more ingrained, deeper, and more troublesome. If we focus on what we truly want we begin our journey towards consummation.

890. When we focus our mind our thoughts become more sharply defined. All information attempts to become integrated, and we tend to create a picture of possibility. In this form it is like a film negative, awaiting a sufficiently powerful source of illumination.

891. The paradox of the creative life, any life (for every life is creative), is that of remaining focused on doing one thing at a time, from the place of inner peace. So that one's natural desire to be creative does not become selfishly attached to the achievement oriented, time-obsessed, personality ego.

892. How much focus do we put on what we truly want, compared to what we do not want?

FORCING

893. If we are overly forcing ourselves, we are locked in ego struggle, we are associating our state of self with the ego-mind. Awareness of our state of watchful omnipresence, embraces all seemingly forceful energies.

FOREBODING

894. To live with foreboding means we are not living that moment in consciousness of the divine.

FORGETFULNESS

895. There are two kinds of forgetfulness, the mediocre and the supreme. Mediocre forgetfulness concerns the forgetting of worldly affairs. Supreme forgetfulness is the sweetness of forgetting the ego.

896. The most fundamental truth/state that we forget about ourselves is that we are soul, we are divine.

FORGIVENESS

897. Forgiveness issues from our hearts, it arises from the unconditional love of our soul. Attempting to find forgiveness through the ego mind is a tortuous exercise revolving around condemnation, guilt, and obligation. The ego mind lacks the depth of compassion and wisdom to lovingly forgive.

898. We are practising forgiveness when we let go of our own resistance in favour of giving love.

899. All the forgiveness we have applied to ourselves, we can equally apply to others.

900. Leaving behind the past is necessary in order for forgiveness. We cannot forgive if we keep dwelling in the past.

901. We seem to have been created with a need to both forgive and seek forgiveness as quickly as possible. Otherwise we carry enormous life-denying burdens.

902. The ability to forgive comes from anyone who realises ultimately that they are here not only for themselves, but for others also.

903. Inability to forgive, is the inability to see and understand that we are all students on this earth.

904. Forgiveness allows the ever-present love in one's heart to shine forth, without the resisting, holding back action of the ego. The heart naturally wants to be open, however the ego may close the gate.

FORM

905. The form and shape of something largely determines the state of its being, the conceptions it will have, and therefore its evolution, purpose and consequence.

FORMALITY

906. The further removed we become from the essential, the more we develop the outer form until it solidifies into formality, procedure, strict observance, perverse rule making, and aligning with others similarly minded, to create the conventional.

FOUND

907. If one decides that one is found, then one is not searching or overly seeking approval, or things, from others.

FREE WILL

908. One reason why the universe (at first) seems to operate impersonally, is that if it operated personally we would lack our fundamental human right of free will and choice. And so we have measures of good and evil, beauty and danger. To have only a narrowed form of creation, for example, only evil, would deny us free will. Free will is conditional upon having a multiplicity of conditions and choices. The conditions and choices seem to say to us 'Look for the honourable and the sublime.' Therefore the

universe has the appearance of a neutral page, impersonal, that we may fill it with honourable and sublime realisations.

909. Free will may not be the absolute we take it to be, for we are constantly and subtly influenced by our internal and external environment, and therefore it is somewhat tempered. However, free will may have greater autonomy when it is more intuitive.

910. Part of our gift of free will is the choosing of our spiritual inheritance. It is our right to declare it, and enjoy it, for the ego is eventually unsuccessful with the expression of free will.

911. If we have been given paramount free will, then perhaps it is only our ego doubts and fears, and our lack of trust that prevents us from bearing it.

912. Our potency of belief seems to determine our level of free will.

913. The free will we have is the choice whether to remain in ego or to merge with the truth of our inner being. This is a continuous choice.

FREEDOM

914. The highest freedom appears to be the self-liberation to love autonomously.

915. Primarily, the quality of our freedom depends upon *allowing* ourselves to be free. Our perceptions of constraint are usually far greater.

916. It seems that the forces of life, the processes, experiments, altercations, inspirations and thoughts, are guiding and teaching us to seek an ever-growing freedom through the discarding of narrow beliefs. This freedom awaits us on the other side of a number of portals. Every major area of life experience such as relationships, sexuality, health, wealth, and so on, is a portal. The attendant who opens the door of each portal and who shows the way onward, is unmistakably the spirit of love.

917. A degree of organisation is one of the elements that give us

the freedom to be free. However, an excess of organisation can kill freedom and its associated levels of creativity, initiative and productivity.

918. When we are ready to bare our souls, perhaps only then are we ready to experience true freedom.

919. The freer we are from ego, the more that truth and love reveal themselves.

920. The spirit is forever seeking freedom from the confines of an overly ordered physical life; it is its natural inclination. In order for us to live in harmony with the spirit, it is our responsibility to keep freedom alive and continue to seek the freedom that allows us to be true to the spirit, and therefore true to ourselves.

921. Love, truth, joy, and their concomitant states, appear to be the only states that contain freedom.

922. To feel the full import of our freedom, it is essential to *act* free, to dance freely, embrace freedom, sing it, love it, play free, that its cultivation may be a constant joy.

923. The more we have stored in the mind, and material stored in our possession, the less spontaneous, the less free we appear to be. But of the two, mind storage appears to be the greater prison.

924. In society it is a common belief that money gives freedom. But really, time is much more important. We can have lots of money, but still not give ourselves time to be free.

925. Freedom is present always. It is the universal background upon which all action and thought operates, though to most it is not apparent, on account that as soon as any sense of a limited self-engrossed view arises, leaving aside the freedom and peace of the selfless present, freedom recedes into the background.

926. The greater the perfection of something, the more freedom it appears to contain.

927. As long as our intention is to continue to love, we are free.

928. What profound freedom there is when we are able to see that behind all things, there is the unabated, unfolding of the universe.

FRICTION

929. Friction occurs between people when egos start rubbing together.

FRIENDSHIP-ACQUAINTANCE

930. The presence of a good friend reminds us of our bond to love and happiness, and of the purpose for our being.

931. It is a normal human response to be outgoing to other human beings, we do not need permission.

932. Sharing something of our deeper self with others forms a deeper bond of friendship.

933. Friendships and associations that fail to live up to our expectations, teach us the lesson of self-reliance, and the need for us to develop our inner resources. The more we develop these resources, the stronger our base will be for relationship and association.

934. It is important that we follow our own truth in acquaintance with others rather than allow associates to influence our way of relating.

935. Most of us want to be accepted, and especially loved in those associations that appear blocked. In these cases we may compromise ourselves in order to widen the grounds of relationship and therefore gain acceptance. However, overly compromising ourselves results in the loss of our own foundation, our own confidence. We become fearful, which then restricts our interaction and communication. We pull back, we become awkward, and may even reject ourselves. Foremost we need to honour our inner truth.

936. Unless there is a heart resonance with another in friendship, we remain on the more objective, ego-separating, thought dominated, quintessentially different paths whenever we meet.

937. In confiding in a good friend, we learn that what life teaches

to one is taught similarly to others. And therefore the experiencer need not be alone in their suffering, or their happiness.

938. Our friends were friends with others before we met them, and will meet with others who will become their friends after we have met them. To try and possess a friend is an attempt to selfishly secure and restrict the free flowing spirit of love that moves in circles between us all.

939. Friendship develops from the recognition and creation of a common meeting ground. The unfolding of friendship often leads to acts of generosity. And finally, the consummation of friendship is seen in wanting to protect the friend.

FRUSTRATION

940. Often our frustrations are subconsciously transferred from our primary unsuccessful desires to secondary peripheral situations. We believe it is not so safe to express our frustration in the area of a primary desire.

941. Whenever we consciously witness the realm of frustration, there is always a reward for our labour, for the boundaries of the ego are being punctured and the resultant insight or discovery will help us move forward.

942. In expressing our frustrations clearly, from an observer's viewpoint, without emotion, we free ourselves.

FULFILMENT

943. It seems not possible to find ultimate completion or fulfilment without all others.

FUNCTION

944. Nothing functions independently. All things function through association.

FUNDAMENTAL

945. Perhaps the most fundamental of things to remember about oneself, is 'I am a soul, my soul is love, I am here to love—now!'

946. The uncorrupted fundamentalist is one who believes in the fundamental, natural, age old laws of life—such as being ecologically responsible, being compassionate to human, animal and plant forms, and fostering universal love and truth.

FUTURE

947. Most of us are constantly preoccupied with wanting to live in a better future, regardless of how good things are. We continually throw our energy into a vacuum of a never arriving time, and by doing so we deny the present, which is the only place our energy can be fully utilised or realised.

948. Being present in the present, will automatically create the reality we desire in the future.

G

GENERALISATIONS

949. If we go about our world seeing others through a cloud of cliches and generalisations, we are already judging, we are already closing the possibility of having any kind of meaningful communion with them.

GENEROUS

950. Unstinted generosity flows radiantly and constantly from the open arms of our soul. When we are in union with our soul, we are open-hearted, and open-handed.

951. Generosity presents its own reward to the benefactor with feelings of happiness in having shared oneself and one's bounty. It seems to open one to the joys of the world.

GENESIS GENES

952. Genetically all life on earth is linked, having a common origin in the earth. And the earth has its origin in the solar system, and the solar system has its origin in the milky way, the milky way has its origin in the universe, and the seed and genesis of the universe has its origin in the divine.

GENTLENESS

953. When we are gentle with ourselves, others, and possessions, we are more mindful; we walk in love's footsteps, we breathe love's air, we listen to love's call, and we rest in love's embrace.

954. The conscious stillness of the gentle soul is where peace, love, wisdom, compassion and humanity are born.

GIFTS

955. Life is full of gifts. Human beings are likewise full of gifts. Humans not only give the gifts of love and kindness but also gifts that are not so attractively packaged, such as the gifts of insensitivity, short-sightedness, irresponsibility, and pointlessness. Insensitivity is the gift to become sensitively responsive; short-sightedness teaches us to have greater perception, insight and vision; irresponsibility gifts gives us trust and determination; and

pointlessness gives us the gifts of meaning, appropriateness and intention.

GIVE-RECEIVE

956. Only the truly potent can give without thinking of their giving. Only an unselfish, open, and receptive being, can receive with an open-hearted love.

957. Unless we are willing to give, it is difficult to gain.

958. If we become more concerned about getting our share, and therefore about taking rather than giving, we are in a state of closing our communion with others.

959. When we give and it is not accepted or appreciated by the receiver, and we withdraw our love and support, our giving proves then to have been conditional. We expected something in return for our giving, and therefore we were not fully in the loving heart, where we can give without thinking of return.

960. Giving without joy is not true giving. It is a pretence centred on one's own self-interest.

961. If it is our custom to ask of others by way of giving, or as a trade-off, rather than seeking directly what we want, we make ourselves poor receivers. This is also the case if we cannot receive without having the need to give in return.

962. We cannot give when self-absorbed. Only by having an outward view are we able to render to others.

963. When we truly have an urge to give to another, then it is naturally done with a sense of respect and love.

964. Any time we take or receive with ego, there is often an impression that we are liable to the person we have taken or received from. We sense that somehow we are in debt, we are captive, not free of obligation or responsibility.

965. Our ability to give and receive (on all levels) is not necessarily sown or harvested in the same situation, or with the same person.

966. When we have the opportunity to give, it is usually favourable to do so, rather than hold back. The human heart thrives when giving.

967. Everyone gives according to their desire and ability; very few inherently believe that they are primarily a taker. And therefore to accuse another of being a taker will not usually mean that they will respond with greater benevolence. Lack of giving usually arises from incomplete knowledge or not fully recognising the need.

968. It is not better to give more when sufficient is enough.

969. Many of us seem less affected in giving up the large rather than the small. Soulfully, we are more connected to the larger scheme of things, which makes giving up the large easier. We are more intimidated by the abuse of small things, because it somehow threatens the human in us, the ego part of us. Giving up the small is a good test of one's true self over one's ego.

970. In asking open-heartedly of the divine, we open our ability to receive to the greatest magnitude. In doing so, the ego's desire to do everything by itself is subordinated. For the controlling ego is not very open to receiving from anyone. If we find it difficult to receive, we are wanting to remain in the control of our own ego.

971. Each of us has a realm in which to give and receive both internally and externally, and it is desirable that we acknowledge and learn to serve both.

GOALS

972. A course of action without an authentic goal is often an exercise in futility. It robs our lives of meaning and purpose. For example, most careers as a statement of life purpose offer meaningless goals to one's existence.

GOLD

973. If all things were made of the currency of gold—the trees, the flowers, the rivers, oceans, mountains, valleys, the sky and

stars, would we be more appreciative of their value? I believe that our answer would be no. What then are we doing in alchemically spinning the lifeblood of nature into currency?

GOSSIP

974. Regardless of what someone has said or even thought behind our back, it is largely not our business. Eventually we realise that we cannot correct everyone's perception. If we still approach gossips with love, they will eventually implode through their own hypocrisy, guilt, self-condemnation and regret. For they will want to return to their own state of love once more, and to do this, at some point they will have to make amends.

GOVERNMENT

975. The possessors of authority in our society must also possess ears that they may truly listen. Hearts that they may have compassion, understanding, and the love of people to carry through with their promises. And eyes that they may behold the consequences of their power, the ability to see injustice, and the vision to lead towards the greater good. If they do not have these things, their authority will be dictatorial, and thus they rule without permission. Their mandate to the people will not be fulfilled, and therefore they cannot demand our compliance.

GRACE

976. When we experience grace we touch the omnipresence beyond self-presence, where one is consciously accompanied by the divine.

977. If we receive what life offers to us with grace, regardless of whether we perceive it as good or bad, we feel the favour and the mercy of the divine. And deeply we know that all will be well. Our actions and speech are refined by this grace, and we are

cushioned from the full effects of the burdens of our own ego mind.

978. The grace of the divine is a supreme healer. It emerges when we finally abandon all fears, false hopes, burdens, and selfish conditions. It is a balsam of compassion, a gentle cloud of peace.

*

GRATITUDE

979. Gratitude for love is the supreme gratitude. It is gratitude for the divine.

980. A life of gratitude contains the gratis of grace and favour, where desires, feelings, and outcomes, are more chosen, seen, and experienced in a positive light, and therefore more able to be satisfied, and we choose to be delivered from all else by infinite providence.

981. When we wholly serve with gratitude, foremost we recognise love. Any kind of duty-bound obligation we may harbour is a secondary, love-tempering phenomenon.

982. The difference between luxury and austerity may more truthfully lie in the amount of our conscious gratitude for whatever we have.

983. When we give thanks for whatever happens in our life, we are placing our trust into the hands of the divine. We realise that our knowledge and understanding are not omniscient.

984. If we have no reason to live, principally we have already severed ourselves from life by forgetting gratitude. Gratitude opens our ability to love, and connects us to the flow of universal energy.

985. Gratitude is the internal state and external act of receiving life with joy. One is gratefully in love with life. Gratitude is the portal to this awareness.

GREED

986. No matter how much greed we face the world with, there will never be enough outside to fill the emptiness inside. Preferably, each of us is responsible for repeatedly bringing to blossom and harvest, an inner crop of love.

987. Greed for the world usually results in a poverty of understanding of one's soul. Greed is not a conscious state; it is a subconscious driven hunger, fuelled by the fear that there will not be enough.

GREETING

988. If someone asks 'How are you?' we have one of two responses—of the ego or the soul. The authentic 'I am' is the soul, and therefore it is an opportunity to re-identify with one's genuine state, so that this becomes the self-determining truth of the moment. It is an opportunity to re-enter the present, and to leave the illusory, constricting, inflated or deflated ego states, which continually and obsessively look for sympathetic support.

GRUDGE

989. To hold a grudge is to actually close down part of our own aliveness.

GUARD

990. Whenever we let down our guard in the presence of someone we respect, or someone who lends us a willing ear, we realise just how close to the surface our hopes and fears are.

GUIDANCE

991. The most effective guidance is inevitably an internal, non-invasive, benevolent, and insightful force.

GUILT

992. If we dwell on the self-condemnation and shame of guilt for times past, we are not taking present moment responsibility.

993. The ego has a tendency to create a pseudo-conscience that is guilt-laden. True conscience does not condemn, but illuminates with truth.

GUILTY KINDRED

994. Every child is born innocent and free. Why then ought the present generation suffer guilt, and because of this guilt, be obliged, shamed, or manipulated to pay for the transgressions of their elders?

H

HABIT

995. The breaking of habits, even occasionally of good habits, allows us a different perspective, and brings new life into our lives.

996. Awareness of our habitual problem begins the process of understanding.

997. Each moment is new, and we are inherently free. We do not need to tread in our habitual footsteps.

998. Self-repetition tends to lead to a state of subconscious automatism, and therefore the repetition of a habit becomes subconsciously directed.

999. During the habitual moment we are consumed, we are inhabited by its power, and other possibilities are curtailed.

HALF-TRUTHS

1000. Half-truths have more tendency to be half lies. They are usually told for the benefit of the one who lies.

HAPPINESS

1001. If we are to live happily, we must live from a greater perspective, embracing our true identity, and all reality, both light and shadow, otherwise we shall be forever subject to the changing moods of ego and the changing manifesto of fate.

1002. The more wholeheartedly unreserved, carefree, and adaptable we are, the more our inner happiness will be unmoved, and the more we shall live in contented harmony.

1003. On the soul level, happiness arises from infinite awareness. On the ego level, happiness occurs because circumstances are deemed to be in one's favour.

1004. If we egoically adjust ourselves to happiness, it can only last for an egoically finite time.

1005. Unless we know who we truly are, we shall not know true happiness.

1006. Happiness is the counterbalance of pain only if the happiness is emotionally based. Happiness based in the divine has no such contrary pole.

1007. 'May all beings be happy' really means may all beings realise their true state, which is the bliss of the divine.

1008. If we expect to find lasting happiness through our ego we are misleading ourselves with ego once again. Happiness is eternally present within our soul. Through the cultivation of our inner presence we begin to join to the edge of lasting happiness.

1009. Our state of inner happiness determines how we perceive our outer situation.

1010. The creation of happiness creates energy. Energy maintains and rejuvenates all systems of the mind and body.

1011. Human circumstances are constantly changing. If we base our happiness on them, we shall experience an emotionally volatile life. Our love and happiness is our own responsibility. It is made more secure when it is aligned in the consistent love of our true nature. We radiate love and happiness for their own sake. An external reason is not required.

1012. A human soul in natural happiness has the bodily characteristics of a youth in bloom, the mental characteristics of an ancient sage, and the simple temperament of a young child in wonder.

1013. Happiness can only be lived now, otherwise it may be a never-ending dream of a never-arrived-at future.

1014. Generally there is great happiness to be found in being outgoing, generous and open-hearted, and we are all aware of this, it feels to be our natural state, although we may not always practise it. And therefore any contrary move to be greedy or mean spirited does not produce the blooms of happiness or fulfilment.

1015. Our great gift from the divine is to share our happiness with others, that we may draw happiness from within them also.

1016. When we feel the fullness of happiness and love, we are living in the fullness of our hearts. When we sense the pains of loneliness, emptiness and fear, we are living in the hollowness of the chattering, confusing, ego mind.

1017. Happiness is an ability to see a fortune of blessings that may not necessarily be apparent. It is a contentedness that arises from seeing the appropriateness of providence.

1018. If we allow ourselves to be receptive to life, to the love that radiates to us from the earth, ocean, sun, moon, stars, and all of nature, we receive the gift of life's happiness.

1019. Real happiness is our natural state of being. It is the measure we have of our ascendancy over life's egoic difficulties. Real happiness cannot be earned; it is already the state of our soul. It is the soul's constant joy and infinite provision. The ability to be open to this love determines one's level of happiness.

HARMONY

1020. All that is in harmony appears to be in accord with its environment. All that is inharmonious appears to be separate and in conflict with its environment. When we surrender our own disharmony, we surrender our broken-off part to re-embrace and merge.

1021. Where there is true harmony, there is the revelation of what ultimate union is all about, and what it shall bring forth.

HARVEST

1022. Because every harvest is different, some greater, some lesser, we cannot count on the individual harvest as being the greatest. However, we can count on all harvests overall being balanced towards the great.

HATRED

1023. The force of hatred is denying of life, and is contrary to supreme love and truth. It is moving backwards against the natural flow of life, which seeks to unite all.

1024. Hatred has no base, no virtue or morality upon which it can rest.

HEALING

1025. The conscious radiance of internal love is a supreme healer to one's inner organs, as well as the peripheral body and beyond.

1026. A disease or a wound, mental or physical, is not primarily healed by external applications or medicines, it is healed by the life force inside.

HEALTH

1027. Supreme health develops from the state of knowing one's divine nature, and with this knowing, the ability to live consciously in love. This state perhaps more than any other creates the highest state of well being.

HEART

1028. Consciously living through one's heart self-actualises love and truth into the present.

1029. When we follow our heart, we are inviting the subconscious feminine to come creatively into the world.

1030. Whatever picture we carry in our heart, is our current incubating creation. But is it our true heart's desire?

1031. When we become devoted to our heart's yearning, then all else that is dear to us becomes clearer and potentially available.

1032. The contained can contain the boundless. Our hearts are boundless, but are themselves contained.

1033. The surrendered heart is perhaps our most natural state. It is a state where there is no need for ego assertion or ego attraction. It is embodied as a deep stillness, filled with peace, gentleness, and a universal containment that knows intimately of love and truth, and speaks them with wisdom.

1034. Soon we shall have to show what is in our heart. Shall we do it this day?

1035. Whenever we choose to be omnipresently centred in our heart rather than ego-centred in our burdensome mind, we become celestial beings in residence on earth, and we celebrate all existence. The freedom of love we seek is not found in ego-centredness.

1036. The pure heart experiences the timeless moment.

1037. Some of the qualities of an open heart are; presence, union, benevolence towards all creatures all beings and all things, constancy, commitment, devotion, truth, reverence, purposefulness, encouragement, sensitivity, inspiration, generosity, mindfulness of passion, tenderness, love, guilelessness, loyalty, faith, openness, worship, intuition, compassion, naturalness, elation, quickening, wisdom, and beauty, all of which together cause wholeheartedness.

1038. The cups of our hearts are constantly filled with heaven's favour.

1039. At the core of the friend, and at the core of the enemy, there is a heart that can be loved equally.

1040. The heart, because it is at the centre, sees only the unity of all things, because it can receive and reconcile all things.

1041. By focusing our attention on the heart when in the company of others or when alone, we are able to move away from the ego dominated thinking of the mind, and more able to relax into our true self.

1042. If we lead our lives from the worshipful heart, we live in tune with creation.

1043. Our heart appears to be where unified subjectivity is centred. From our hearts we co-extensively embrace and are simultaneously embraced. Love is here, truth is here, innocence is here, and freedom is here.

1044. The heart provides love's intimate abode of expression. Our most meaningful challenge is to live this love regardless of anything else that may be happening around us.

1045. If we behold the naked heart of the divine all around us, and realise that we have always been inside, only imagining that we were outside, we shall live with the intent of seeing love and beauty in every setting.

1046. When we open the door of the heart, light pours forth, the creator stands revealed, beckoning for us to enter into the enchanted garden of our soul.

HEARTACHE

1047. Heartache arises from the egoic separating mind. It does not arise from one's heart or soul.

HEARTBROKEN

1048. When we experience a broken heart, we experience the constraints of our ego being softened, broken down, and opened. It has nothing to do with love. In the history of mankind love has never broken a single heart. (See emotions and love.)

HEAVEN

1049. Heaven is the supreme integration of all things. It is seeing the divine uncovered in these things, and therefore knowing this will cause the awareness of an unceasing, infinite bliss.

1050. Whenever we create or experience true happiness, we live in a different world where all things seem possible. The world of happiness is heaven, and therefore heaven must be the paradise of happiness.

1051. If we internally conceive the innocent child of joy in the silent stillness, who takes over from the collected thoughts and habits of the personal self, we are born again, and we emerge into the same place, but now we call it heaven.

HEROISM

1052. A hero/heroine courageously upholds truth and love beyond the boundaries and conventions of selfishness and society.

HIDDEN AGENDA

1053. Surface truths may be revealed, but if there is a deeper hidden agenda, then surface truths are generally closer to lies than to truth.

HOME

1054. Home is the external manifestation of the comforting peace we sense deep inside our heart, which we attempt to create in the world. Unless our homes have heart, we will not feel at home in them.

1055. Until we acknowledge that we are really at home in ourselves, and in our hearts, then we have not fully arrived on earth.

HOMEOSTASIS

1056. A homeostasis of stillness, emptiness, fullness of truth, oneness of love, pureness of innocence, is where our spirit eternally leads us. Yet we continually avoid it with our emotional and physical addictions.

HONESTY

1057. When we labour honestly, we are not inclined to claim more nor less for ourselves than what is rightful.

1058. We are freed by our honesty and imprisoned by our dishonesty.

1059. Being 'honest' can be used as a cover for maintaining our own idea of dignity and self-respect, and to press forward our self-righteousness.

1060. Anyone who is honest innately trusts their inner truth. It is living without a veil. The clarity of one's true self is allowed to shine the light of loyalty to truth.

HONOUR

1061. Honour is the standard upon which our values, integrity, honesty, truth, virtue, fairness, goodness, innocence, reverence, and loyalty are sensitive to, which in turn determines the level of our self-respect.

1062. When we honour another, we realise that their highest, most selfless teacher is within them. We realise that this teacher will instruct and inform them in ways that will delve quicker and deeper into the core of their being than the often self-centred, external perspective of another.

1063. Honour is worth infinitely more than any amount of riches or power gained through deceit.

1064. If we live below the standards of our own honour, we lose power and the integrity needed to keep our will focused upon our life's purpose.

HOPE

1065. Hope is often the beginning of the foundations of faith, and therefore it is instrumental in the power of materialising what one longs for.

1066. There must always be hope, for life without hope is intolerable.

1067. Our hopes cannot be raised and materialised if they are tied down with hopelessness. They cannot soar to where our deepest memory calls—from the heart of the divine.

HOPELESSNESS

1068. Because a situation may seem hopeless at first, does not mean that we ought to close the door to redemption. For we close down to our own possibilities for a solution.

HORIZONS

1069. Where is the horizon of our perspective on life? How far does our domain extend on love, life, purpose, truth, humanity, compassion to all beings, and life beyond earth?

HORMONAL

1070. Hormonal and other biochemical fluctuations and imbalances affect the state of our body/mind/emotions. To a large degree we are ignorant of the causes of these states. Beneath these states however, most of us experience moments of the intuitive centre that makes us strive for balance. These variations in our state that stem beyond the conscious mind, are perhaps another way of experiencing other realms that the conscious mind would not have planned.

HOSPITABLE

1071. The heart/soul is hospitable to all, there are no strangers.

HUMANITY

1072. One's degree of responsibility to oneself, to others, other species, and to the environment, shows also the degree to which one takes seriously the trust and obligations of the spiritually human calling.

1073. Being human means supporting and promoting the materialisation of humanitarian ideals.

1074. The perpetrator of any final act, whether they are praised or condemned, is still only one of the links that binds them to all of humanity.

1075. It is a gross prejudice and an inaccuracy to label an entire race or nation with wrongdoing. It is not the white, yellow or black race that is to be charged, but the dimness of the race of ignorance that has abided amongst all peoples.

1076. A human being is a doorway into infinite kingdoms and orbits of experience, and therefore it is not possible for anyone to give a full and true estimate of the worth of another.

1077. The working foundation of being human appears to be the ability to make increasingly conscious choices.

1078. The beauty and wonder of a human being is made of not only what appears to be perfect about them, but also what appears as being imperfect.

1079. A human being is far, far greater than any one action.

1080. Our current species role appears to be the cultivation of mercy by extracting the deep benevolence of love from our hearts, that suffering may be reduced. However we must ask 'Why is it still necessary for us to continue to base our civilisation morally and spiritually on suffering?'

1081. If the truth of humanitarian humanity is raised to its rightful place, all other things will be taken care of.

HUMOUR

1082. Humour lays bare our partiality, contradictions and inconsistency; it is one of the foremost vehicles for change in the individual and society.

1083. Smiling, humour and having fun are all expressions of love.

1084. Humour is like happiness—it is a decision to perceive oneself and the world through a particular lens. If the lens is set to a wide angle, then many things in life can be considered humourous.

1085. Laughter and humour help to quickly break down barriers between people. If someone is humorous, they show to the world that they are basically content with life at that moment. And a person contented with life is a great balm to those around them.

HURT

1086. If someone approaches with less than love, they are in a place of hurt. They are hurting because they have associated themselves more with the separated and pained ego of the past, than with the true identity of soul in the present.

1087. The deepest hurt can begin to be healed by the slightest gesture of love, a hint of a smile, a pat on the shoulder, a warm glow from the eyes. It does not take a great deal.

1088. No one has ever been hurt by love. We experience hurt when the desires and needs of our own ego are not fulfilled.

1089. When we are emotionally hurt, the ego rushes in to create as well as carry the wounds of unfulfilled expectation and separation from another, whilst at the same time pushing out our remembrance and presence of the divine.

HYGIENE

1090. To make the effort of hygiene is to honour others, as well as oneself, and therefore shows also a certain moral purity.

I

IDEALISM

1091. The ideal is the archetypal design of the divine. The idealist is a visionary who beholds the divine's blueprint and begins to materialise it on earth.

1092. Why is it that so often we live our lives according to the values of others? Each of us was born with our own highest ideals. Only by being truthful to those ideals, can we live an authentic life.

1093. Ideals are the height of our aspirations that lead us onward. Ideals are not in contrast to reality. They are essential in creating new visions and new forms.

IDEAS

1094. Ideas are the conception of form. They give intention, structure, and meaning to our individual existence.

1095. Our ideas are a great gift—unless they are implemented in some way, they are like seeds left unused.

IDENTITY

1096. We all have the same primary identity—the love and truth of our soul. Our secondary identity is the personality ego, which creates a sense of separation and individuality. If we lose touch with our primary identity, we get lost in the separating and contesting tendencies of the personality ego.

IDEOLOGY

1097. When ideology comes before human or social interaction, the ideology is lacking a foundation in humanity. Such ideology is usually based on the narrow, egocentric, power-seeking view of the beholder.

IGNORANCE

1098. Ignorance for the most part is the lack or loss of attention, and the lack of the conscious awareness that comes from a lack of attention.

1099. Of most things we are ignorant, though generally we think our knowledge covers a great deal. Upon deep examination, we find that our personal expertise covers a very slight weave in the fabric of the universe.

1100. We seem to remain unaware and in ignorance until we have the capacity to open to understanding. We can open by love, or by trial.

IGNORE

1101. If we know the truth but ignore it, belittle or embellish it, (which is also ignoring the truth) we become accessories to untruth.

1102. When others ignore us, it is because they do not know us. Often we have not boldly introduced our love well enough.

1103. In the process of ignoring others, we ignore our true self.

1104. Nobody is so large in status that they can ignore another human being. Similarly, nobody is so small that they can ignore another.

1105. When we ignore others, it is true to bear in mind that we are also ignoring the divine in them.

1106. If we ignore another, we are excluding ourselves (but think we are excluding the other) from love, acceptance and union with them.

✳

ILLNESS

1107. When we are acutely ill we usually go through a transition to another kind of self-understanding. Often we are perplexed when others say how well we look during these times. Perhaps the transition is reflected in our face, and we look more true to ourselves. (See Disease, Health, Healing, and Pain.)

✳

ILLOGICAL

1108. Sometimes life appears illogical. Perhaps it is because our logic has not developed the breadth and depth of understanding to embrace that which we currently term illogical.

✳

ILLUSION

1109. Our perceptions are termed 'illusions' by the mystics. However, without them we would be lacking the dynamic drive for truth, love, and freedom. Illusion itself can then be seen to be a kind of veiled truth, and is a necessary part of our journey to the understanding of truth.

1110. An illusion occurs at any time that we have false impressions. When we believe in the impressions, we build erroneous beliefs upon them.

1111. When we are finished with the illusion of ego and time, the eternal will be obvious, and immortality will become conscious.

1112. There is no real illusion in the universe, for the idea of illusion creates separateness of real and unreal. In truth, there is but one manifestation, all is the divine.

IMMATURITY

1113. Immaturity in an adult arises from a lack of self-parenting. On the subconscious level, they are seeking to be parented by others, so they may learn the checks and balances of conscious parenting.

IMMORTALITY

1114. The lack of physical immortality in our present society is, I believe, not so much a lack of knowledge, it is more the loss of things already available, such as the loss of one's true identity, and from this the consequent loss of understanding, love, innocence and truth.

1115. A formula for immortality and agelessness could be when one experiences a co-extensive reality of;

$$\frac{\text{Omnipresence}}{\text{Stillness}} = \text{Eternity.}$$

Which has been taken from the equation

$$\frac{\text{Distance}}{\text{Speed}} = \text{Time.}$$

1116. Immortality and eternity are to be anticipated when one places the personal ego in its rightful place.

IMMUNITY

1117. We cannot make ourselves immune from life. We cannot protect ourselves from what we came here to experience. But we can learn to see what is illusion and what is truth, and live in truth.

IMPATIENCE

1118. When we are impatient, we are not fully in the present moment. The mind is largely somewhere else, and that which is left is demanding to take its leave.

1119. Whenever we act from our own sense of haste and impatience, we have a tendency to quickly decide outcomes, prejudge others and sentence them. As with other emotions, our tendency is to create around us what we are interpreting inside.

IMPORTANCE

1120. What we deem important in our lives is borne out by where we place our priorities, and the amount of energy we assign to them. This measures their true meaning and worth to us, and we in turn will experience the consequences of the amount by which we value their true meaning and worth.

IMPRACTICAL

1121. Sometimes being impractical gives birth to spontaneity, and an experience of great beauty.

IMPRESS

1122. The greater our need to impress others, the greater our insecurity.

IMPRESSIONS

1123. Whatever makes an impression on us, stirs and moves us. The more receptive we become to the impressions of nature, love, beauty, and the infinite, the more we are impressed, inspired, and moved into transcendent spheres.

IMPROVE

1124. If we can improve something, then there is still development and progress possible, and therefore things to learn.

IMPULSE

1125. An impulse can be instinctive (in which case we are driven), or emotionally rash (again driven), or impassioned (which can be either directing or driven), or intuitive (we are directing rather than driven).

INCARNATION

1126. A human being is a messenger of love, an incognito incarnation of the divine, sent from the palaces of heaven.

INDIFFERENCE

1127. When faced with indifference, the only workable course is to love in more sublime ways.

INFECTION

1128. Infections often counter our character and our actions, and they can shake our beliefs. We usually seem tainted by them during the initial stages, but later we feel a certain grace, and we recognise that we have undergone a change in consciousness, we are renewed.

1129. We may choose to be positively infected with laughter, compassion, love, and joy, and use their infectiousness to communicate these qualities to others.

INFINITY

1130. Infinity is the microscopic made vast. It is the boundless made atomic. It is the perspective of molecules and gods.

1131. Infiniteness is the expressive playground of the divine, who watches from inside and from outside creation.

INHIBITION

1132. If we are inhibited, at that point we have lost focus with our true self, and we are being dictated to by the ego.

INNER NATURE

1133. Any time we do not follow the wisdom of our inner nature, we distance ourselves from it. This distancing can be anything as simple as eating when not hungry; being prone to rushing; not caring or resting the body/mind; pushing one's self and one's view into the world; being overly connected to one's emotional state without understanding it; not stopping for beauty; not serving or considering others; not seeing the unity of all things and of all people; and disregarding one's conscience, one's knowing, and one's innate justice.

1134. To be strong in what our inner nature is, we are obliged to love strongly.

INNER PICTURE

1135. The inner picture we have of ourselves is different to the outer picture we project to the world, to the extent by which we live in ego in the outer world.

INNER VOICE

1136. The usual chattering ego voice of daily consciousness in the mind can be a vexation to one's inner balance. It is only one voice, one view, which is often both demanding and confusing. If we allow the wisdom voice of our inner truth to enter, we then have an internal dialogue through which the ego voice takes a more subservient role.

INNOCENCE

1137. The action of innocence is just love spontaneously expressed, without seeking reward.

1138. Continual practice of awareness eventually produces innocence. Therefore we are all in various stages of reclaiming our innocence.

1139. The more innocent we become, the more simple our lives, the less there is to know, speak or remember, the less complex our persona, and the more our face communicates this. An innocent can be taken at face value.

1140. Have we, as innocents, asked our souls to come out to play this day, bringing with them their abundant delights of happiness and love?

1141. To one who has a complex persona or complicated life, an innocent may appear to be either naive, or not wanting to reveal what is perceived by the other, the so-called real self, the ego, warts and all.

1142. Innocence is not an ignorance of offence; it is an awareness and compassion for it. Those who self-righteously place guilt on offence are more in ignorance of it.

1143. It seems to be far better to live 'innocent while experiencing,' rather than 'educated while theorising.'

1144. When we notice the subtlety of structure and form, usually sensed with a degree of wonder, beauty, and contentment, we are more consciously attuned to the spirit of reality, such as that experienced by the innocent child.

1145. Everything throughout creation is in a state of innocence. It is only via the singular, inquiring, exploring consciousness, that things seemingly pass through a temporary state of experience.

1146. Innocence is original nature, and therefore innocence is ignorant of division.

1147. When we surrender ego to our nature of being, we regain our innocence.

1148. It is better to remain in innocence than to assume postures of cleverness and worldliness to impress others.

1149. In order for the innocent child within not to take on burdens, it needs to be constantly reborn so that the child can continue to love freely.

1150. Our innocence sometimes needs to be demonstrated to other human beings, but before the divine it has always been truth.

1151. The innocent child subconsciously assumes that all its needs are taken care of in the moment, and therefore the future is automatically taken care of.

1152. Not only must we know and believe in our innocence, but also in the innocence of others. For in the greater scheme they are one and the same, and therefore before condemning another it is best we apply the same criteria to ourselves.

1153. The state of absolute innocence (egoless divine) has no place where a wound may be made.

1154. Only love can give sustenance to truth. Only perfect truth can sustain original innocence; and innocence is the greatest lover of all. Thereby innocence created the universe.

INQUIRY

1155. The inquirer takes an attentive interest in the customary as well as the extraordinary and mysterious phenomena of life. This often involves challenging and questioning those things which are already accepted, because deep down there is an intuitive knowing of authentic, primordial truth. They have a wondrous curiosity that wants to seek, to explore, penetrate, sift and synthesise from a boundless view. This makes the inquiring life a voyage of recurring revelation.

1156. At times when we inquire of another's welfare or situation, we may be masking a request about our own welfare and situation. The results of the inquiry then become secondary to our agenda.

INSECURITY

1157. Insecurity may arise to temper us, that we may regain our balance during those times when we forget our true self in acts of overconfidence or carelessness.

INSPIRATION

1158. When we are nobly inspired, we are breathing more directly, consciously or subconsciously of the spirit of the divine. And the forces of creativity are nurtured by divine revelation, that we may create anew.

1159. The state of an inspired being, anyone inspired, appears to affect not only the beholder's vibration but also the adjacent vibration of matter.

INSTINCT

1160. Instinct appears to be based in the subconscious ego as an automatic sense of self-survival. However we sometimes confuse instinct with intuition, which appears to be divinely based. Intuition inspires us towards the divine; it does not condemn others. Instinct however, being ego based, takes care of its own body/mind first, which may at times be at the cost of others; others may be condemned by our judgmental instinct.

INTEGRITY

1161. Integrity naturally arises when one aligns heart, mind, and body. When there is concurrence of the love in one's heart with the conscience of one's mind, and the ease and virtue of one's body, then there is a harmony from which integrity issues naturally.

1162. If we truly believe our integrity to be the highest, then naturally we offer our loyalty to the integrity of others.

1163. When we speak and act with integrity, we are drawing together the virtues of our original nature.

INTELLIGENCE

1164. There seem to be broadly two kinds of intelligence. One is imitative intelligence, which is represented by the status quo, and taught in schools and universities, and adhered to by mainstream society. The other is creative intelligence, which is insightfully questioning, contemplative, generally non-separative, and has a world view and beyond.

1165. Creative intelligence is largely independent of regurgitation. Yet that is not to say that a truth repeated is not of creative intelligence. But creative intelligence is certainly more a faculty of present intelligence.

1166. Pure intelligence is the ability to be consciously aware.

INTENSE

1167. The more intense our experience, usually the more passionate and potent will be our lessons and our understanding. It is time for us to become heedful, the lessons have become serious.

INTENTION

1168. Our intent arises out of where we focus our attention. Intention stimulates our will, which in turn drives our commitment towards the aim.

1169. Intention becomes a magic button when we consecrate it to the divine.

INTERCONNECTEDNESS

1170. All human beings are our brothers and sisters, all other things that live are our relations in life, and all things that seem without life are the building blocks of life.

INTERPRETATION

1171. We are constantly interpreting each other and the physical world around us. The clarity of our interpretation seems to be dependent upon our own underlying beliefs, and our dominant perspective.

INTERRUPTIONS

1172. All appearances of creation are aspects of the divine. And therefore if we are interrupted or disturbed, we are being interrupted by the play of the divine. It may be our call to wake up.

1173. The perceived interruptions that occur during the flowing of our day, be they positive or negative, are a direct reflection of our self-generated internal state of learning. Gifts, compliments, and happy spontaneous and serendipitous occurrences are a bouquet. Friction with others, and losses, are 'attention reminders.'

INTIMACY

1174. Intimacy is the desire to be open and allow another to enter our innermost recesses. We are either open to intimacy or closed—either way it is a decision on some level. If we are unsure, we may ask 'What is my inner truth here?'

1175. When there is an active awareness to love deeply from one's inner nature, intimacy arises.

1176. Allowing another intimately into our lives means we give them the gift of equal respect and love that we give to ourselves.

1177. We are in a moving sea of intimacy. Sometimes we are close and sometimes distant. The illusion of distance is created by the ego, but the truth is that we are always in a state of soul communion with one another.

INTIMIDATION

1178. Those of us who use fear and intimidation of others in order to seek their own gain, are in actuality closing down the boundaries of their world from where their bounty comes.

INTUITION

1179. Intuition is a spontaneous insight into essential nature, and is characterised by some of the following:

(a). It comes early, unprompted, and is not filtered through the selfish ego.

(b). It has a sense of right feeling, almost at times a familiarity, a knowing.

(c). It is not usually invasive; it tends to have a quiet voice.

(d). It often fits into a larger pattern, and the more we move into the pattern, the deeper the insight.

(e). If it is not followed, there is a sense that one is going against the flow.

(f). When followed, it feels like one is on a mission, there is a feeling of harmony with life.

1180. Sometimes our intuition will direct us to an intermediary place (though our mind may regard it as a final destination) in order to collect a token necessary for our further development.

1181. A clear belief in one's intuition is desirable if we are to feel the peace and atonement that comes from believing in one's self, and being true to this ideal.

INTUITION, FALSE

1182. We may justify our own stubborn prejudice and refusal to move from a particular view by labelling it intuition. Intuition arises from our inner teacher, the soul, which expresses itself foremost in our heart. And therefore intuition will not deny or attack another, for these are not soul qualities. Unless intuition possesses the unconditional qualities of heart and soul, it is unlikely to be intuition.

J

JEALOUSY

1183. When we intensely focus our emotive needs through another, we suffer jealousy. The other is seen to have the key to fulfilment. It is an abandoning of one's true self, and therefore of one's self-responsibility and of one's self-care.

1184. Jealousy occurs not only because one emotes inadequacy, envy, distrust, and possessiveness, but also because one desires to be the centre of attention.

JOY

1185. Joy cannot be enclosed within the finite ego; it radiantly overflows with exultation. Neither can earth contain it, or sky, or stars. Joy is infinite; it reaches beyond, because it is already there, and here. Joy is *the* most present state of the present. Joy calls to us, for it wants us to live joyfully. And deeply we somehow know that such ineffable joy exists. However, joy points beyond all worldly affairs, for sooner or later, all worldly affairs fail to live up to the desire we have of seeking joyful happiness from within them.

How then, to reach such joy? If joy is within as well as without, it is surely available. If joy is everywhere then it is a prime; it is the essence and fabric of the universe. Yet most of humanity live to a great extent without it. Perhaps we are not truly seeing what is before us, or knowing what is truly within us. Perhaps we are simply not choosing to see or to know an ultimate truth.

1186. The experience of joy is the willed decision to celebrate life. It is the uncovering of the heart's yearning to be grateful for all the wonder and beauty present. The greater our ability to experience and perceive joy, the stronger our trust in life, and the closer we live to our heart.

1187. Joy appears nonexistent to the asleep human. Joy appears hidden and needing to be found by the inquiring human. And joy appears everywhere and in all things to the awakened human.

1188. One of the purest joys occurs when one discovers that one's heart is singing ecstatically for no earthly reason, and that that is its most natural, and profound state.

1189. When one's inner joy is reclaimed it puts all things into perspective.

1190. Joy brings to light the internally sourced rejoicing, for the exalted panorama of divine love.

1191. When we become one with joy, the ego yields, and we

remember and are carried upon the infinite waves of joy rippling through the universe.

JUDGMENT

1192. Judgment without compassion is worthless, arrogant, and vain.

1193. No one can know the full spiritual implications of another's path by judging the levels of their activity or inactivity. Everyone is in a state of learning.

1194. It is morally unjust to pass judgment when we do not know all the facts. If we honestly asked ourselves how often we know the complete facts of a situation, the answer would likely be much lower than the number of times we express our judgments.

1195. The more judgmental we are, the more we are focused in the ego of separatist thinking which draws its conclusions from opinions and prejudice. However, sound judgment is based on the capacity to discern through a conscious sensitivity of perceptions, thoughts and actions, in order to make as clear a decision as possible, of what is just.

1196. Virtually all of our judgments are limited. There always seems to be a greater reality than any individual judgment can contain. And therefore most judgments have a degree of the limited, of the false, because most judgments leave out the infinite. The further removed we are from the infinite, the more limited are our judgments.

1197. The more we pass judgement and see deficiencies in others, the more removed we are from living our own truth, our own perfection, that naturally wants to embrace a soaring benevolence.

1198. To allow one's ego to be judged by another, can free one to continue along one's path without the often heated and defensive debate.

JUSTIFICATION

1199. When we justify ourselves, we are attempting to defend our inner child, we are attempting to shield it from what we perceive to be the forces of external aggression that appear to want to defeat it. But we may also be shoring up, fortifying the barriers, not allowing the liberation that comes with exposure and its consequent forgiveness, healing, and return to wholeness.

1200. Regardless of the justification of our minds, our emotive body will continue to act with fear and guilt when we know we have transgressed.

1201. If we are unduly concerned with self-justification, it shows how little faith we have in ourselves.

1202. We, as ego personalities have a need to justify our actions. But it is not usually justifications that bring people together. Justification tends to keep us separate.

K

KARMA

1203. Karma appears to be the heart and conscience of the universe—the highest laws of love and truth operating together to create an absolute state of synthesis.

1204. Karmic energy fields appear to operate far beyond the boundaries of the individual's body.

1205. Evidently karma operates within and upon the energy field of the individuated self, not the soul. If the soul were subject to karma it would also experience the same kind of suffering as the ego, and consequently the same kind of ignorance.

1206. It is interesting how often we have a small accident, a small self-hurting, immediately after we say or think a cursed thought. And deep down we recognise this law. Yet we tend to forget it when larger and more serious things occur.

1207. The karmic consequences of even the slightest action may have far-reaching consequences. It is necessary for us to stay close to truth.

1208. Karma eventually impels us to an understanding of love.

KILLING

1209. All killings are our collective responsibility. They appear to be a sacrifice towards discovering the truth of our oneness. When we fully realise this, all killing will cease.

KINDNESS

1210. Kindness emanates from the natural benevolence of the inner divine when allowed to act freely, without the intrusion of a credit-seeking ego.

1211. The depth of our explored love determines our degree of kindness.

1212. Kindness, both to the recipient as well as the benefactor, accords a heart-opening experience when conducted with honesty.

KNOW THYSELF

1213. Knowing thyself is knowing well the ego, and knowing well the soul.

KNOWING

1214. To live in knowing is to live with predetermined foresight, to live with the assured knowledge of one's own destiny, and therefore in the purpose and meaning this brings.

KNOWLEDGE

1215. The process of knowledge appears to operate by the sending out of centrifugal beams of information, which are then acknowledged by others or the environment, and returned centripetally to their source, to create an exchange and a synthesis. The purpose of this process of knowledge appears to be to create a fusion of understanding.

1216. Timing is crucial for our receptivity to knowledge. The more receptively primed we are to a particular learning, the more we recognise and understand it, and the greater its impact on our lives.

1217. If we can regard our knowledge as being a child of the divine, we will not need to become a serious minded adult in order to protect it.

1218. We can never force our knowledge on anyone, only suggest it.

1219. Acquired knowledge can lead to greater egotism, and therefore be a veil against truth.

1220. The further we reach into the cosmos, the more our ego/knowledgeable mind will implode in the vastness of universal subjectivity.

1221. Pure knowledge has an intimate understanding of truth, and therefore it is enlightenment. It is a conscious comprehension, a realisation of awareness recognising awareness.

L

LANGUAGE

1222. Language reflects the composition of human consciousness. Mindfulness begets an economy and simplicity of language, which illuminates our inherent wisdom.

LATE

1223. Normally, people do not plan to be late, although we typically accuse them as if their lateness was purposefully devised. On the other hand, perpetual lateness appears to be subconsciously contrived.

1224. The soul is always in the right place at the right time (the eternal present). It is the ego that thinks it is late, on account that the ego cannot live fully in the present moment.

LAW

1225. A charter of true law becomes legitimised in the actions it cultivates; namely peace, love, and truth. When law becomes dogma, and a medium for oppression, it is no longer law but an instrument of disorder, and a mechanism for the anarchy from which it purports to be defending the righteous.

1226. Contemporary law gives little mercy to those who unknowingly break its rules. Without knowing or knowledge of law beyond the natural principles of harmony and conscience, we are innocent victims. Whereas blatantly breaking the law is either a conscious stand for a different perspective of what is beheld to be just, or is a subconsciously originating self-centredness.

1227. Material law tends to be centrifugal and leads to separation of parts. Spiritual law tends to be centripetal and leads to union of parts. Material law cannot exceed spiritual reality, whereas spiritual law embraces physical reality. Finally and inescapably there is only spiritual reality.

1228. Our current system of law is commonly thought to be the upholder of truth. However, upon examination, it appears to favour vested and financial interests, and in making the less fortunate compliant.

In court, adjudication often becomes a financial contest between opposing parties battling over what is permissible, rather than what is truthful. When law operates on the premise that, the larger the financial input the greater the degree of lawyer expertise, we are not dealing with law, we are dealing with inequity and discrimination. Law itself may become expropriated to foster self-seeking, calculated and opportunistic goals.

1229. When officialdom is made the supreme authority for law and government, then law and government will inevitably be patronising, and conditioned by influence, favour, and convention.

1230. If we honestly break regressive laws, then we keep honour and dignity with the law of our conscience, and we stand innocently ennobled with truth.

1231. The love and the light of truth are higher than any love for the formal and conventional laws, or of their meaning.

1232. We may live by laws, but no law is a law unto itself.

*

LEARNING

1233. Learning guides us in a creative, rhythmical, responsive and expansive relationship with oneself into a selfless universe.

1234. Experiential learning occurs when there is a reconnection of apparently unconnected branches, leading to a larger understanding. When we detect the point of union, there is often a sense of rediscovery, and we embrace it once more into our being. Such whole learning contains virtue, wisdom, and transcendence, and it is this that we embrace.

1235. Most so-called learning in our society is a process of information dissemination, which is then stored in the recipient's memory, and regurgitated when required. This is mind programming, it is not learning. It seems that there is little in the way of self-creative exploration or self-understanding involved.

1236. Logic, inspiration, imagination, intuition, and contemplation, are essentially complementary aspects of the art of learning.

1237. The art of learning is an art only if it is artfully pursued.

1238. If we were really honest with ourselves, we would realise that our outer experience is indicative of an inner need. The circumstances provide an opportunity for us from which to learn something.

1239. When we can allow another to learn a lesson for themselves without needing to show them the way as we see it, then we have moved away from the ego's need to evangelise. Finally, we have reached a place of contentment in ourselves, as well as begun to love the reflection of soul in the individuality of others.

1240. The inspirations as well as the strains we experience, are an indication of the dynamics occurring, and the opportunities present, from which to learn and grow.

1241. The lessons of the physical world all have spiritual content. The more adverse conditions become in the physical realm, the more these conditions are pushing us to probe our spiritual depths, and radiate spiritual law and understanding.

LEFT OUT

1242. Whenever we see ourselves as being on the outside—locked out by others, then our primary quest is to embrace more highly, embrace more supremely.

LESSONS

1243. If we believe that we live in a divine and compassionate universe, then all the lessons of our lives are appropriate to our current stage of development.

1244. When we boldly move through our challenging life experiences, we move quickly through our lessons.

1245. If we redeem the understanding from just one of life's myriad lessons presented to us each day, we will live increasingly in the assured embrace of our soul.

LIBERTY

1246. Whenever we feel a sense of liberty we are opening to a more bountiful, wholehearted world, where truth is increasing and more readily present.

LIFE

1247. Life results from the breath of spirit, which creates the vital spark that illuminates the essence of our being.

1248. There do not appear to be any singular or isolated incidents as being sole causes in life.

1249. If we want to live fully and freely, it is beneficial we learn not to deny our life force, or another's life force, by any thought, word or action.

1250. Somehow we must grasp hold of the seemingly impossible but logical truth of creation; that nothing in life works against us—all things (eventually) advance us.

1251. We become more at home in our body and with life, when we know that we are loved and cared for by the fundamental as well as the subtle forces of creation. From then on we begin to put aside the burden of attempting to make things happen to our advantage, to get on top of things, or to worry about the things that seem beyond our control.

1252. Life appears to be the most fragile as well as the most tenacious force in the universe. It propagates its precious essence with zest and extravagance and therefore it must be infinitely willed, and resolute in its purpose.

1253. We have only two responses to all that life offers: 1. As an individuated ego. Or 2. As the divine. Both have their place.

1254. When we begin to see that life is a play, a drama of immense proportion, we realise that we do not have to be so consumed, lost, serious about it, or overly concerned what others think.

1255. Everything in life teaches—without exception.

1256. Life is a moment-by-moment experience; we continually live on the cutting edge of change. The challenge of each moment requires an ongoing commitment of our will to love.

1257. To really live we have to be alive!

1258. What are we saying to the world, what are we offering to the universe, by the manner in which we are living?

1259. If we tackle others and life itself head-on, rather than being receptive and open-hearted, we will inevitably find that frustration and anger are our companions.

1260. The more content we put into life (awareness) the more we live life.

1261. We have all been created from the sweetness of heaven and the salt of the earth. And therefore life requires us to taste of both.

1262. Do we have the conviction that this great design of life is purposeful and has intent? To acknowledge this is to give meaning to this very moment, and to place ourselves as servants of life who live with assurance.

1263. We chose to come to this world to be intimate with life here. If we do not choose to be intimate with others, with nature, or with our bodies, then we are denying the lifeblood, the vitality, the wine and the intoxication of life.

1264. When we live fully in the moment without holding conditioned thoughts or emotions, we live in the presence of love, and we experience exuberant co-extensivity with everyone and all things. We deeply know and trust in life, what is occurring, and what we are creating. On account of this we live in passionate devotion to and joyous expectation of life, and we are intuitively alive to its spontaneous, synchronous, and serendipitous occurrences. We feel peace and contentment, and because of this we live in a state of spirited gratitude, knowing that fulfilment in love is our present as well as our decree to the future. Therefore we love boldly, we relish love, we are eager to love, and we see love bubbling everywhere.

1265. The transcendental forces of life come into being through the fertilisation of matter by the attracting forces of love, and the potency of light (truth). Wherever there is love and light in the universe, life will be close.

LIGHT

1266. The light in a human face has travelled from the very beginnings of the universe, through the creation of our galaxy and our sun, to shine light-heartedly upon this radiantly aware visage.

1267. Truth is the energy of light. Light kindles our spirit to lift up to revelation, awareness, and joy.

1268. Light travels at 300,000 kilometres per second, therefore the pure moment of the present is one 300,000 ths of one second/ kilometre. However, according to Einstein, time stops at this speed. The more we live in the light of the present, without the shadow of our ego, the more light-filled and timeless we would become, as perhaps indicated by the light emanations of saints. Paradoxically, in this immense stillness and peace of the present, we would also be travelling at the speed of light.

The radius of our light-filled presence would continually expand at this speed. An observer would record the radius of our light body expanding to 18 million kilometres in one minute, and in one hour to over 1000 million kilometres, a distance that embraces the orbit of Jupiter. The distance to Pluto, the outermost planet of our solar system, would be embraced in five to seven hours.

However, according to Einstein, light has no mass, or to say it another way, its mass is infinite. Therefore, to the consciousness that reaches the speed of light—its subjective mass would become instantaneously infinite, while its length, or ego singularity, would disappear altogether; time would stand still, and everything in the universe would be present and perceived from stillness. Thus the universe is both eternal and infinite, yet in the moment it is present and able to be embraced. To give an illustration of this: when we are meditatively present on a beach, we may also find ourselves present on a universal shore, where each star becomes a grain of sand, whilst on the terrestrial beach, each grain of sand becomes a star.

LIMITATIONS

1269. If we are not ready to listen to the lessons of our life, or to the well-meaning advice of others, we have not learned the full import of our present limitations; or will be ready to move beyond them.

1270. In recognising our conscious limitations (ego), we can invite our super conscious (higher self) to participate in our lives by surrendering to its boundless wisdom and love.

LISTENING

1271. Just how willing are we to listen to another without our self-interest arising; or only listening to those who espouse our self-interest? When we truly listen and when we are fully listened to, there is emptiness of mind, and attention, followed by consideration, recognition, and union. This union is love.

LIVELIHOOD

1272. Whenever we do not invoke the delight, majesty, and blessings, of the vital spirit of life in our livelihood, then we are merely subsisting.

LONELY

1273. If we are lonely, we have not developed our relationship with the divine.

LOOKING

1274. When we look with a hard single-pointed focus, the ego tends to be brought to conscious attention. However, if we look with a softer focus, taking in more of the peripheral view, the ego tends not to arise and we stay centred. This gives us an indication of our biological-spiritual-psychological context, that the ego tends to see only one thing at a time, whereas the soul takes an overview.

1275. The more earthbound our vision, the more we look to our own bodies, the room around us, or to the limit of the horizon and no higher, and consequently our individuated ego is inclined to arise, for the earth is the ground of our ego. However, the more we look beyond the horizon and into the sky, the more the sky becomes the ground of our being, where we are lifted into our soul faculties, and we become aware of ourselves as beings of the stars.

1276. Surface eye contact with another during usual daily consciousness triggers the ego to arise; this is objective looking. Deep eye contact allows each to enter the soul; this is subjective looking.

LOOKING WITHIN

1277. We have been made with the curiosity to look inside—into a book, a box, a world, a sky, a mind, a soul; eager to discover the remarkable treasures within. It is how we begin to integrate ourselves with the universe.

LOSS

1278. At those times when we transcend the personality self, we lose all sense of loss.

1279. If we lose something such as money or possessions, it can indicate that we are in debt to life. Attempting to reclaim it by false means will place us further in debt.

LOSS OF CENTRE

1280. At any time we lose our centre, or our balanced way of being (which primarily occurs in our ego relationship with the egos of others), we are moving into the uncertain and unsettling no-man's land of ego, which has no firm foundation in which to be. The ego can entice us (with an accompanying memory loss of one's true identity) and hoist us out of our centre with vanity, false pride, and arrogance. Or devalue and lower us from our centre (again by not knowing, or forgetting one's true identity) with condemnation, rejection, and low self-worth. We help regain our centre by such things as radiating our love; living in the present; breathing consciously; meditating; being and acting mindfully in stillness, slowness and gentleness; serving others; cultivating happiness, wonder and joy for no reason; and remembering one's true identity.

LOST

1281. When we unconsciously lose ourselves, it is because we have betrayed ourselves, we have turned our back on the divine within.

1282. If we have the impression that we are lost, it is usually because we sense a loss of intellectual control of our life. Yet when this happens, we are given the opportunity to regain the serenity and wisdom of our heart.

1283. It seems we cannot be found, nor can we be instrumental in helping others find, unless we have first become familiar with being lost.

1284. Losing oneself in order to fit in with others, is the abandonment of one's own uniqueness and the loss of one's faith and will.

1285. The universe is one, therefore nothing can ever be lost. Things only appear to be lost because of the illusion of time. In the present moment, everything is present in the universe.

LOVE

1286. For generations love has been burdened with false concepts. Many of them are exposed in the following contemplations. They are intended to help free the spirit of love from our accumulated centuries of oppression.

1287. Love is fundamentally who and what we are; it is the uncorruptable fabric and substance of our true state of being. And secondarily it is having the awareness of this state of being. Paradoxically, the secondary state usually appears first.

1288. When we realise that our essential nature is love, and that the universe is a manifestation of love, we are at home in ourselves and in the universe, and we live in the awakened moment of love, to love.

1289. The presence of love in the world is the presence of the divine. This love presence is the continually evolving process coursing through mankind, drawing us towards the divine. It is the blossoming of the divine's presence throughout the world. It is the transcendent force that sanctifies all mind and matter to celestial holiness.

1290. Love is the most adored expression of all the divine's impressions.

1291. The more love we radiate, the more receptive and responsive we become to others and to life.

1292. We become sensitive to our soul when we allow it the freedom to be evident. A mind full of thought does not allow it this freedom. A mind in stillness allows the presence of our soul to shine the expression of our original unity of being—Love. Without thought, without the intervention or inhibition of our ego mind, we observe rather than think, we love for no reason other than to love for its own sake, while all separateness is unified in virginal awareness. And at once, peace, gratitude, and the contentment of love become an enveloping balm.

1293. Perceiving that another does not love us, need not take away our ability to still love them. True love is not mutual back rubbing, it is independent of selfish requirements.

1294. When we are in love we break through the confines of our selfish ego and we see a similar animating principle operating in another. Love becomes our invitation to leave duality and re-enter unity. The more soul passion we feel, the more we lose ourselves (our ego) in the ecstasy of union.

1295. It appears to be of little use to try and persuade another to love us. The stronger we become in our own potency of being, our own self-determining purpose, integrity, and devotion to life, the more that others will feel drawn to us to love.

1296. Regardless of all circumstances, it is preferable that we love, for it is also our very own joy, to love.

1297. When we love, we are secure in ourselves and in our world. When we selfishly hold back our love, our world becomes insecure and appears threatening. The awareness and expression of love is the one place where we may find internal peace and happiness. With every lesson we are presented, life points steadfastly to love, that we may love.

1298. Love heals us, transforms us to a higher understanding, a higher level, to give meaning and purpose to our own lives and to all life.

1299. All of the hurt, all of the killing, all the desperation, suicide, anger, depression, hatred and so on, is something else wanting to come through. It cannot be for more of the same, for it would be lacking in the desperation that all these things carry. It must be for something noble; for something on the opposite shore—perhaps it is for love, for love to be given birth.

1300. If another does not allow us the receptivity for our active expression of love, and we are curbed and rejected, then we are likely being given the opportunity to work through the rejection of our own needy ego love, to uncover our stronger, more radiant heart love.

1301. Do we really give love? How able are we to bestow and allow love? Do we as an ego just usurp love? And how capable are we to receive love without wanting to possess it and turn it into a demonstration. For the ego cannot love, it simply desires, and mistakenly calls this desire love.

1302. The discipline of love is to love without possession. If we truly love someone, we do not possess them, and there is no need to set free that which we do not possess.

1303. Whatever occurs in our lives can be distilled into a message of whether we are loving or not loving. If we get carried away with the form of the message rather than the message itself, we will miss its simple and truthful intent.

1304. When we are truly ourselves, we are internally still and at peace. From here, we naturally express love. The degree of difficulty we have in expressing love is to the degree that we are not being true to ourselves.

1305. The deepest love is essentially a state of benevolent, peaceful, all embracing universal radiance, directly flowing from one's inner being. Whereas most social expressions of what is considered to be love are the expression of emotional need, and the selfish yearning for the possession, but impossible fulfilment of such needs. Love is the essential nature of our inner being. It is up to each of us to move away from false love in order to be in the real.

1306. When our thoughts, words and actions are no longer dependent on egoic recognition, then we are beginning to truly love.

1307. Love is the greatest wisdom. Love is the energetic state where unconditional intelligence joins with unconditional heart to reflect unconditional soul.

1308. True love essentially awakens us to a remembrance of the divine.

1309. Love sees through, above and beyond the illusion of one's ego and thus of the drama of life.

1310. We exalt love when we focus upon giving love rather than in getting. In this way one's inner channel to the source of love becomes unimpeded, rather than blocked by our attempts to influence, win over and acquire love from others. When love's inner channel is open, love flows effortlessly, and happiness becomes the natural present and the future consequence.

1311. The more we practise the outflowing of love, the more radiant and magnetic we become. Our love is transmuted into an unmixed, clearer, more innocent and truthful state.

1312. When we fall in love, we are falling into the abyss of emotional neediness and possession. If we rise in love, we are rising into the heavenly realms of unconditional giving of our love.

1313. It is 'innocence' that is written on the doorway of true love, not 'temptation.'

1314. If we approach others with a love of life, then how can we possibly be regarded as strangers to their life's experiences?

1315. We can only love in the present. If we are fearful of loss or commitment to relationship in the future, we are being unavailable to love now.

1316. All situations in life appear to be teaching us love as well as giving us the opportunity to love.

1317. It is our nature to love, and if we have forgotten, it is the most important thing to remember. It is the most important quality to offer, the most important solution to problems, the most effective way to transform and transcend.

1318. If we have difficulty loving another, it is due to the constraints of our ego. Our lesson is to love for the sake of loving.

1319. Love's open nature spontaneously serves, with happiness, upliftment and union.

1320. When we live in the pure present, it is easy to love, the moment facilitates it, and there is no forcing required.

1321. In an atmosphere of ego-based love, the expression of love is not only conditioned by the giver, it is also immediately assumed and possessed by the receiver, which creates an ongoing need and an unfulfilled desire in both people.

1322. The ability to love confers the utmost in efficiency, in terms of getting things done with cooperation, emotions management, living harmoniously in the present and seeing ever greater possibilities and combinations. It is the management tool par excellence.

1323. It seems we cannot have great love without great faith, great trust and great knowing.

1324. True love is not blind, it is the most conscious of all states. It is the ego that is blind, which creates the states of illusion, possessiveness, and self-neediness that masquerades as love.

1325. To those we love, there is always a willingness to forgive.

1326. It is difficult to be a receiver of possessive love, for it contains the fears of rejection or being imposed upon. Yet when love is expressed purely, it can be shared purely, with innermost freedom, joy and lightness.

1327. Our essence is love. Whenever we have difficulty in life, it is in order that we may learn to express our love more, and in deeper ways, so that we become more acquainted with our essence.

1328. A balance of one's needs and the needs of others, is a sign of a conscious, aware love.

1329. When we love life, we feel life returning love to us.

1330. If love is foremost seen to be an obligation, it no longer has freedom of expression. Love becomes an onerous work, it is no longer a joy. Neither is it love; the form is lacking the content; the function is empty; the wine cup is missing the wine.

1331. When our needy emoting ego finishes its futile game of attempting to prevent the soul from experiencing its freedom to love unconditionally, we shall begin to truly love.

1332. Love renders the ability to embrace evermore, into the realms of the infinite.

1333. The more we move towards loving the soul of another, the less we sense being addicted to love and the less we wish to emotionally possess them.

1334. Love appears to be the all-pervading essence of awakened reality, and therefore the background essence of unawakened reality. This reality contains a transcendental purity that reaches beyond even our slightest desire to possess it. Perhaps, like our own ungraspable soul, love is the distillation of the character or very soul of god. Thus for love to arise, and for our soul to be given life, love must contain a transcendental purity.

1335. Without divine love, all knowledge and wisdom are empty.

1336. Essentially love is constantly alluded to; rarely is it directly touched. It is generally experienced as that which creates openness, attentiveness, caring, happiness, kindness, generosity, appreciation, acceptance, forgiveness, compassion, courage, devotion, friendship, romance, understanding, peace, tranquillity, excitement, enthusiasm, playfulness, humour, laughter, smiling, expansiveness, wonder, creativity, spontaneity, commitment, passion, confidence, honour, patience, boldness, positivity, adventure, trust, health, wisdom, joy and so on. The more we enter the present in awareness and transcendence of these states, the more we touch the unconditional truth and innocence of the infinite state of union beyond them, that is love.

1337. Love is the essence of our being, the underlying ground of our existence, and thus it is always present, but whether it is apparent, is another story.

1338. If we could make our love completely innocent and unconditional, nothing would seem impossible. The possibilities of the universe would all lie open.

1339. When we do something with love, we do it with consciousness.

1340. Openness, attentiveness and caring are the fundamental inductive qualities of love upon which all other emphatic states of love are formed.

1341. Genuine love operates within a steady state of acceptance and equilibrium. If love is regarded as a steady state, this allows us the freedom to be fully communicative, not holding back for fear of having to protect the fragile state of love.

1342. The potential to love ever more greatly is always higher than the beholders of love, and therefore to aspire in love is a continuing process.

1343. How often have we missed an opportunity to draw from the depths of love within ourselves because we were not bold enough?

1344. All are capable of great love and beauty. To restrict seeing these qualities in only a few, is to make oneself blind to the infinite possibilities of these expressions in everyone.

1345. Love qualitatively, is a state of being. All giving, receiving and uniting are embraced in this state of being.

1346. The soul is already love. It is the separated, rejected, wounded ego that wants to be loved.

1347. It is the ego that claims ownership of another ego under the guise of love. When there is soul love, love is expressed with honour, unconditional giving, and joy.

1348. The more conscious we become of love, of what love is, the greater our ability to love.

1349. Our true essence is love. Human life seems to be about actualising our essence through mind, speech, feeling, and action.

1350. The (misguided) yearning energy for love relationship is perceived as being that which produces impatient desire, craving and covetousness in the individual, which then gives rise to wanting to capture, bewitch or dominate the person who is currently the most tempting. This is not love.

1351. It is often the case that one's own situation and state of being are automatically cared for in the outpouring of love for others.

1352. If we want to live with love in our lives, we must be prepared to look for the love in others, no matter how deeply buried it may appear to be.

1353. Authentic love demands no return, it returns naturally.

1354. Being reticent with the expression of love is quite contradictory. It is attempting to hold back that which is naturally expansive.

1355. Love is always present. It is up to us to awaken to it.

1356. When we love purely, we are in tune with the eternal. And therefore 'Thy will be done,' is being done. We are aligned with the principles of eternity, and thus one with eternal love.

1357. True love is truth in love.

1358. If we are being a true lover, actively giving our love, we will not experience the unfulfilled expectations and pains of wanting to be loved.

1359. What we love we become, and therefore it is incumbent upon us to love the deepest and the highest we can conceive.

1360. Love by its very nature is inclusive, not exclusive. We may love an individual greatly, but if by that act we exclude others, we deny our love's full expression.

1361. Because we came here in love, we came here for the greater reason to serve others and the divine, not the selfish ego.

1362. To give blessings of love to those we are in difficulty with, opens us to yet more love.

1363. Clear, unqualified love is at the core of all beings. If we related to each other from the core, all relationships would be in a state of absolute.

1364. Love is not a reward. If another does not provide us with what we want and then we withdraw our love, then our concept of love as well as the quality of love we are offering are both conditional and therefore contrary to the true value and meaning of love.

1365. To the lover, the whole universe becomes a heart. And the lover becomes a servant, working in its service.

1366. Love is the courage to extend one's consideration beyond oneself.

1367. We are loved! This is a great realisation. And since we have love, a greater realisation is that we too may love, no matter how great or small we stand upon this earth.

1368. If we love and worship the divine first and foremost, then all things are embraced.

1369. When we truly love; the face softens and shines, the body becomes relaxed yet filled with vitality, the mind stills and peace enters, the heart grows and fills with joy, the spirit reaches out to all, and the soul basks in the radiance of the wholeness and communion of body, mind, heart, and spirit.

1370. To be able to love, we have to be living in the present; otherwise our avoidance of the present is conspicuously reflected in our avoiding to love.

1371. Who is the 'I' that loves? The question is an enigma on all levels except the universal. Then we recognise that the only true lover is the divine soul. However the ego attempts to claim ownership of this love for itself. But really there can be no ownership of the power of giving love, it is simply the presence of the divine.

1372. If we really examine our attempts at love, much of it will be seen to be selfish ploys to gain love.

1373. When there is true openness between people, then the attracting forces of love pour out between them and around them, radiating outwards and inwards.

1374. Fundamentally, it is preferable we love rather than think. The energy of thinking tends to enter into obsessive circles of routine, fear, and worry. Yet when we love its energy is radiant. Moreover when we focus on love we allow the space for our intuition to naturally answer those questions that we usually think about.

1375. We create love when we selflessly give our care, understanding, compassion and upliftment to another.

1376. True love, paradoxically, is impersonal, for it soars beyond the objective personality of self and others where there is no need or seeking of gain, and in this way it is similar to divine love.

1377. We cannot love another more than we love ourselves, for in our loving of the other we are embellished by love.

1378. When we live our lives integrated with love, so that love is not a separate thing, then we are treading our true pathway.

1379. The place that love asks and perseveres for, is to come before all other thoughts and actions, so that love leads our way.

1380. What we are really looking for is love's constant joy. Everything else is an attempt to find this.

1381. Love cannot be used for anything else but love, otherwise it is not love.

1382. We have come to earth to express our love, not to go hunting for it from others. We are here to love, rather than to seek to be loved.

1383. Inanimate things can be loved through our awareness and appreciation. When we love them in this way, our enjoyment, knowledge and gratitude for them are enhanced. And we become more receptive to the deep and subtle sentience that pervades all things.

1384. Apparently love is the most sublime power in the universe. If we align our love with our belief (conscious, objective), and with our faith (conscious, subjective) we make whole the energy to manifest our desire.

1385. Love works at constantly sifting the ego to an expansive place of resolution.

1386. Actively serving with love naturally creates inner happiness for the one who loves.

1387. When we know ourselves, we know that we *are* love.

1388. Our pure essence and identity is love (the soul). Knowing this, we have the capacity to love boldly and constantly. When we boldly love, love becomes our self-actualising present, and our self-propelling destiny.

1389. In the state of love we are most open, most conscious. Our reality is expanded, we understand and know more of creation.

1390. When we see with love, when we act with love, we are seeing truth, we are living truth.

1391. Love is never a half-measure, either in the giving or receiving, else it is not love.

1392. We are love divine, but we have largely forgotten this, and we vainly look for it in human love all around us, finding at best, only a reflection.

1393. We must sooner or later choose love, for eventually we will discover that there is no abiding truth in any other choice.

1394. Love, by its very nature, demands the highest commitment; the total commitment of body, mind, heart, and spirit. Otherwise it soon makes apparent any state that is less than this.

1395. When we consciously walk the path of love, we address

things less and less with doctrine, and more and more in presence.

1396. We may believe that we know a lover, a situation, a condition, a problem, an opportunity and so on, but love always knows more, and sometimes the expected does not eventuate. Then love will mould us in a new way, present us with a new opening, and a new path.

1397. When we open ourselves to others, we are also more able to feel the love in them.

1398. It may in some instances be more loving not to be outgoing to another, but to let them progress with their own learning.

1399. Although we live in a trade-dominant world, love remains free of all estimation or forecast. The adding and subtracting rules of commerce have no meaning or value where love is concerned.

1400. There are many problems in the world, but only one real solution—to love. For when love is not present, everything becomes a problem. The power of love opens the doorway to solutions.

1401. It appears that all things have a reason, but that also everything is subjective. Yet beyond reason whilst embracing it, beyond the subjective whilst embracing it, is love.

1402. When we open our hearts and allow our love and understanding to fly to another, a wave of healing flows out infinitely beyond the two involved.

1403. We are all successive links in the immense, incalculable chain of love. Love is inexhaustible in all directions, all dimensions, and throughout eternity.

1404. To be less than loving is to acknowledge lesser states as being more powerful than love.

1405. The saying of 'I love you,' is really a statement of being and intent, in that I have decided to give my caring and my service, and to be in this love with you. And therefore as a statement it doesn't mean a great deal unless intent and being actually accompanies it. It also shows that these are more important, more honest, than the possibly egoic need for the saying of 'I love you'.

1406. From the edges of the heart, love flows, like the waves of an eternal ocean.

1407. Authentic love will overcome all, overwhelm all obstacles, and prevail longer than all opponents, to triumph and rise in glory and majesty. For such love has purity of power, innocent authority, and pristine dominion.

1408. To really allow someone to look into our eyes, and for us to look deeply into theirs, opens a door to each other's innermost secrets. And the deepest secret is the same. We find that we are both innocent creations of love.

1409. Throughout the history of mankind has anyone ever been able to possess another being through love? Love is always available but it seems beyond our grasping of it.

1410. If we are coming from the place of love, then this same love will protect us from hurt.

1411. When we love, we naturally trust and want to serve.

1412. To love now within the ecstatic present moment of eternity, this is sublime, this is truth.

1413. Love that is undemanding gives the gifts of utmost radiance, bliss, joy, peace, health and magnetism to the lover.

1414. The universe seems to be fashioned for us to focus on the self-enlarging and unifying act of loving. And therefore if we focus on being loved, we may experience the constricting pains of separation and loneliness.

1415. When saying 'I love you,' it usually issues from need, pity, recognition or service.

Need:

I need you.

I say it to break down barriers.

I want your acceptance.

I have to say it because it's the done thing to say.

I say it to show how loving I am.

I say it with another in order to have a mutual back rub.

I say it to create our own exclusive bubble around ourselves.

Pity:
I am sorry for you.
Recognition:
I admire you.
I recognise the love of your soul.
Service:
I want to serve you with my love.

1416. We may believe in our self-love, but we cannot presume the love of another.

1417. To be bold with one's love usually requires a certain vitality and health. If one's energy is sure, even, and harmonious, there can be a greater ability to love.

1418. All things that do not appear to lead to love could be said to be the yearning for, and learning from, love's ways. So that our desiring, possessing, and greed for others and material goods, on a deeper level, are a yearning for love.

1419. The ego is not the true lover. When we can love without largely being egoically aware of it, then our loving springs from our soul's presence, steadily, bountifully, and truthfully.

1420. Love of the divine is the same as love of one's true self, as well as love of one's beloved.

1421. To those who approach the world with an open love and understanding, we may bare our souls. But to people who approach the world without this, it is generally best we remain silent, our actions will speak for us.

1422. Our degree of compassionate love is the degree of our understanding.

1423. Once we have grasped the truth that we are eternally loved and able to love eternally, then our fears of being without love or support begin to fade.

1424. Love embraces infinity and eternity, simultaneously.

1425. When all our methods and techniques fail to help others in their understanding, then our most valuable support is simply love.

1426. Love requires a clear and free space from which to function. In attachment it cannot have a full expression.

1427. Unless we are centred, breathing consciously, feeling with an ease-filled mind and body, it is more difficult for us to love.

1428. The state of being of love is the blossoming radiance of beauty from the open heart.

1429. When we consciously say 'I love you,' we are actually saying the divine is loving.

1430. Perhaps if we gave our all to love, in body, mind, heart and spirit, we would fulfil our innermost longings. We would be unstoppable.

1431. If we give love its freedom, it bestows a blessing of grace upon us, and we receive an even greater ability to love and be loved.

1432. When we are truly ourselves, the essence of love emanates and perfumes our lives.

1433. Whenever love is not encumbered by selfishness, it is divine. Worship of the divine is the gateway to infinite love. All things are then seen to be a manifestation of the divine.

1434. Love is a state of being, a conscious awareness of cellular, intimate fusion, a rapture of happiness, exploding and forever extending.

1435. The radiation of truth and love by us into our environment causes us to become like the sun and the moon, both mindfully creative and receptive.

1436. The stirrings of love arise spontaneously in all at some point. It is not necessarily passed on from generation to generation, and therefore it must live in the unconscious realm of our being. It is present already in the body's ability to experience pleasure, comfort, renewal and service. It is present, though undeveloped, in the ego mind as the seeking of the highest good for oneself, and the extra pleasure gained in wanting to share this highest good with others. And it is present in the desire to create an environment that is comfortable, harmonious, and reflective of beauty and pleasure. Eventually we learn from our self-giving to reach out and express love to others. And ultimately we move beyond the ignorance of emotional ego masquerades to an awareness of the love state of our soul.

1437. Awareness is the conscious foundation of love. In order to activate love in the world, we are required to use our will to build love.

1438. The deeper we become enmeshed in the egoic mind, the more difficult it is to spontaneously break through conventional and restrictive barriers to love.

1439. Love is a celebration. The celebration of love occurs when we love beyond our self-requirements.

1440. When we are *in* love, then love is all around.

1441. If there needs to be a reason to love, it is not love.

1442. There cannot be more love than what already exists—it needs only to be expressed.

1443. If there were only one atom of love in all creation it would surely be enough, for its infinite expression would radiate throughout the universe.

1444. Love cannot be constrained by anything at all, else it is not love. All of our methods, techniques, requirements, philosophies and psychologies that say love can only be reached by a particular way, or that only certain things or people deserve love, are failing in the understanding that love is infinite, universal, and is the all-embracing totality of creation. All of our unrest springs from not admitting this truth—the universe is love and we too are thus love. If we deny that we are love, we are denying the truth of creation, and we deny our very own life.

1445. Pure love moves us beyond the gravity of the selfish ego and into the inspired atmosphere of a boundless sacred sky.

1446. If we love first, we have the clearest, deepest, and most confident foundation for what we want to create. Yet many of us think that we have to create something first, before love will come.

1447. One of the most penetrating discoveries we can make in our lives is to love boldly. Loving boldly in gratitude for what is, and what has been, and in trust for what may be. When we are bold with love we break through our self-limiting judgments of others and ourselves. We feel energised, our mind and body are aligned with the deeper reason for our being, and suddenly we are empowered in the most powerful way possible, that of one who is being a courageous lover.

1448. If we see, if we really listen, if we feel, we know that love always prevails, always transcends, suggests the highest, and guides us perpetually.

1449. Where there is true love, there is no competition amongst lovers.

1450. Each of us is a manifestation of love, largely unknown. We are surrounded by a creation of love, largely unseen. We are love existing in love and we do not know it. Yet we exist in love now. We have existed in love for eternity. Our love is infinite and we do not know. But sometimes we gain a glimpse, a veil falls briefly, and the sanctum of love overwhelms us.

1451. The primary state that love creates in us, that removes the barriers for, and pierces the armour to do, is to create openness, that we may have union with that which is within and that which is without.

1452. Our immature understanding of love is like 1+1=2 + the myriad separate forms, and -1-1=-2−the myriad separate forms, ad infinitum, repeating these cyclical variations. But true love is the eternal never-ending 1+1=1, +1=1, +1=1, ad infinitum.

1453. Humanity is an expression of divine love. In turn our highest expression is that of divine (unconditional) love. Love creates the openness to unite humanity and to reunite with the divine.

1454. Love leads us into the formulary of creation, where all sense and vitality are conceived and birthed into the void—further and further, increasing creation into the uncreated.

1455. Inexorably, love will open us to infinite, eternal beauty. We will not experience this from one viewpoint, but as infinite eternal beauty itself.

1456. In the end nothing matters so much, except how much we love.

LOVE REALM

1457. As soon as we leave the love realm of the present moment and enter into any negative state, we are also leaving the joy and at-one-ment of the present for the uncertainty of the states of regret, fear, and longing of past and future.

LOVE, DIFFICULT

1458. To love thy neighbour or thy enemy is very difficult, if we attempt to use or force the separating quality of the ego mind to create love. It is preferable we just open our hearts. And the sign of an open heart is the urge to love.

LOVE, PERVERSE

1459. Many intimate relationships in our society are based on perverse love. This love may have one or more of the following characteristics:

(a). Taking for granted the person who is lovingly available.

(b). Chasing the person who is indifferent and unavailable.

(c). Wanting independence from a lover, whilst at the same time wanting the highest commitment.

(d). Not thinking that one is worthy enough to be loved, when truly all are worthy.

(e). Thinking that the love being expressed by another is too good to be true. And therefore thinking that I had better withdraw before I get hurt and rejected, especially when they discover what I'm really like.

(f). Being attracted to a lover that we think we can dominate.

(g). Being attracted to a lover that we think will dominate us.

(h). Being attracted to and wanting to possess the person who most fills our emotional neediness, and thinking that this need is love.

(i). Thinking that one is not able to love fully again because of past hurt. And therefore only being able to offer a reduced version of oneself to any future lover.

(j). Creating games and diversions to make a lover more doubtful about our love in order to create emotional neediness in them, so we can be more in control.

(k). If rejected by a lover, to become frantic about reclaiming the lost love, even though we know deep in our heart that this is not true love.

(l). Confusing temptation, lust and sexual intimacy with love, and thinking that once consummated this means we are now in a committed relationship, regardless of how well we relate on other levels with each other.

(m). Thinking that displays of dependence, possessiveness, and jealousy are proof of love.

(n). Thinking that love is mutual back rubbing, scoring point for point. A subconscious/conscious tally is kept of rewards. And if the tally is not kept in some kind of balance, then the one not receiving tends to feign withdrawal, which is usually an emotional play for control.

(o). Thinking that we love a person because they have the right looks, credentials, status, career, and so on.

(p). Thinking that if we agree on everything we must be in love.

(q). Continually putting a lover down, in order to take control of them and the relationship.

(r). Suddenly becoming more interested if someone else shows interest in our lover.

(s). Having left a relationship, still wanting to control and not let go of one's ex-lover, especially if they show signs of being interested in someone else.

(t). Thinking that our wanting and needing to be loved is an indication of our availability and ability to love.

In reality, perverse love has nothing to do with true love. It is the cry of the wounded, emotionally needy ego, wanting recognition, and wanting to be loved.

LOVE, SELF

1460. If we attempt to love ourselves from the ego perspective, we will experience a consistently changing, erratic self-image. Self-love is properly founded in the steady radiance of the irenic soul. The soul lives in the eternal present, therefore a soul-centred love is always a present-moment affirmation of love, it is not dependent on the past uncertain history of our ego.

1461. Balanced self-control and self-love are wholly synonymous.

1462. We may love ourselves, but on occasion, especially when downcast, we may see the love in another more perfectly reflecting this all-embracing love. It is a reminder of our true state.

1463. Virtue and integrity are governed by one's self-love, which in exaltation outpours in love for others.

1464. Self-love is not self-neediness. It is the conscious call of one's soul into a state of human 'being'. This invitation is performed with love, devotion, beauty, and play, as if one is with a true lover.

LOVE, UNCONDITIONAL

1465. The glory of the unconditional, manifests whenever love is freed of all encumbrance, false theory and belief.

1466. Loving unconditionally is already an agreement between souls. It is the divine in love with the divine. If we see others and ourselves principally as separate personalities, then no matter how great the love between us, this love will be conditional, and we will still be learning about the pain involved in conditional love.

1467. In order to be in a state of unconditional love, all traces of ego have to be removed from one's impressions, then one's expression will follow accordingly.

1468. Unconditional love is not recklessly thinking that we have to accept all the actions and beliefs of another, it is more a recognition of the underlying ground of soul love that unites us all.

1469. The ego is not absolute and therefore cannot love unconditionally. To attempt to love unconditionally through the ego is futile, because the ego is a conditioned expression.

1470. To love unconditionally, to be able to receive negation with grace, can only genuinely occur when we know who we are. When we realise our divinity, then it occurs naturally.

1471. Unconditional love is not love in the conventional human sense. It is a state of being finely tuned to the compassionate view of life. It is not a forcing or giving of love, it is a rising into the divine. There are no personalities involved, no elements, only the one.

1472. To be unconditionally loving seems to be the destiny of human beings, that we may once more be innocent.

LOVER-BELOVED

1473. The Beloved exists whenever and wherever the divine becomes apparent.

1474. All true loves, are the revelations of the beloved.

1475. Our heart's yearning is the yearning to be with the beloved. Whomever our heart is wholly with, is our beloved.

1476. Until there is a conscious communion with the divine, we will probably not be awake enough to meet the divine beloved. If we attempt to do so without divine communion, our ego will likely project on to the other's ego the attributes of a god or goddess; however, such ego-projected divinity cannot last. It seems that life is constantly teaching us 'As above, so below'. When we experience 'One above,' we shall likely experience 'One below'.

1477. Because the beloved worships this form that I am, she (her spirit) resides within this form. Therefore I may worship her by worshipping her in me, as the manifestation of this form that I am. Surely, the more I love this form, the more attractive I make this form to my beloved, as the home for her to reside in.

1478. The experience of a totally open, doubt-free heart between lovers is the supreme experience of the meeting of lover and beloved.

1479. In the beginning relationship to the beloved, we know already. There is no need for wondering, forcing, hoping, or manipulating.

1480. Unless we know that our love for the beloved is forever; unless we feel that we will create a universe and fill it with our love creations—our children, a family of divine lovers; then we will be operating on the level of finite attraction, subconscious projection, and emotional neediness, where love is stunted and unable to blossom universally.

1481. Between a lover and a beloved it is the divine in each that causes attraction, and the wandering, egoic mind that causes separation.

1482. If we are living fully conscious in the present, and therefore in our true state of being, then meeting and recognising the beloved will occur at first sight.

1483. A belief in immortality and eternity is necessary for the lover and beloved; otherwise they may be separated by the conventions of society, based on such things as age difference, looks, image, and social standing.

1484. Is it really too much sentiment to ask of the mechanistic, reasoning mind, to regard the earth and the sun as lovers, and by the power of 'As below, so above,' to believe that there is romance in the heavens.

1485. The lover and the beloved bring heaven's joy to earth. They incarnate heaven on earth.

1486. Our beloved is not placed on our path, they are the path itself, just as we are their path. There is nothing on our pathway that they are not touching. If we can simply become more aware of them in all that we do, we shall live embraced.

1487. Before the beloved arrives, we are required to be the lover. Before mother earth arrived, father sun was alone. This action of the lover brings about the beloved.

1488. We see the divine in the beloved, in the radiance of their soul. They embody the beauty and sanctity of the divine that makes us want to worship at the altar of their body.

1489. Everyone is looking for love, but how many of us are love? We have found love when we become love. Perhaps when we become love, the beloved will enter.

1490. When we meet a true lover, we experience the most profound knowing of another, for we are able to look into their soul, and they are able to look into ours. This is commonly called 'Love at first sight,' but really it is 'Love at first soul sight.'

1491. It appears to follow that the truer we are to our true selves, the more the beloved is attracted to us.

1492. When we trust in the spirit of love, we are more confidently potent in our own being and direction. Our most powerful purpose is revealed upon this path—the purpose to love. This path is also the most powerful for the beloved to walk. And thus the spirit of love arranges the purposeful rendezvous.

1493. The yearning for the beloved is also the yearning to be in more intimate union with our soul.

1494. Because the lover exists, is proof that there must be a beloved. The more purely and actively we love, the stronger our magnetic pull towards the beloved.

1495. If we are looking for the beloved in an ego form, even if we find them, we will not gain or create what we are looking for . . . which is the ultimate state of unconditional love. How can this come from an ego form? When the ego is embraced, beloved's can then embrace. A beloved is then seen to be the being with whom the state of oneness is experienced.

1496. All are beloved. It is the beliefs, expectations and conditioning that determines the depth of our intimacy with another. For all souls at their highest are in union.

1497. Ultimately we shall discover that the true lover and beloved embrace in a state of being, not of finding.

1498. Lovers operate from unified subjectivity; they are co-extensively one and beyond. When they meet they recognise their oneness. Calling one's lover from the place of separation (one's ego) will call forth the phenomenon of separation, since one is separated. Being in oneness, the play of the universe reclaims its unity, love shines and attracts itself. Lover and beloved are one.

LOYALTY

1499. There are basically two kinds of loyalty. One is loyalty to our ego, the other is loyalty to one's soul. If we place ego loyalty above soul loyalty, we shall be moving contrary to our true inclination and path in life.

LUCK

1500. Luck is a symbolic covering of gratitude from the inner divine. If we persevere but cannot build our providence on a particular path, then the divine does not support this path for us, and therefore our good lies elsewhere.

LYING

1501. When we lie, we know that we are breaking our own vow to truth, the supreme truth that our conscience naturally sustains.

1502. If we know or sense that another is lying to us, and we in turn embellish our account to strengthen our case against them, who then is the greater liar? On truthful examination, the greater lie may be found in our superior, condescending, self-justifying exaggerations, which we have probably chosen more consciously than the person we accuse of lying.

M

MAGIC

1503. The world becomes a magical place when we realise that love contains the most magic.

MALEVOLENCE

1504. Blindness (or ignorance) of the selfish ego is at the root of all malevolence.

MANIFESTATION

1505. The forces of truth and love are behind any manifestation of integrity. If we see our idea, hope, thought or desire in truth, and raise it with love, it will surely have more possibility of success.

1506. An assured, relaxed, receptive, and timely knowing, helps create the harmony and attunement necessary for the manifestation of our desires. The struggles involved in wilfully disciplining and attempting to force ourselves can often be detrimental to our cause.

1507. Manifestation that somehow reflects our soul's intent rather than our egoic, material desires, will inspire us to manifest excellence.

MANIPULATION

1508. In the end we cannot manipulate another into a position that suits us. But we can love, and that love will align us both to the highest of possibilities.

1509. Most manipulation is not consciously intended and therefore appears to be generated from subconscious wounding, or ignorance of the other's needs.

MARRIAGE

1510. Marriage is foremost a pledge to honour the love between unveiled souls. This pledge is higher than all legal and social expectations or commitments.

1511. If we desire a marriage made in heaven, then we may be required to surrender all our perspectives and expectations to the divine.

MATERIALISM

1512. All the material things of the world—our bodies, food, clothing and housing, can be traced back to the beginning of this earth, and even beyond, into the universe, beyond again to the beginnings of the universe, and on into the creative mind of the divine.

MATURITY

1513. Apparently the more we are able to live in the brilliant fullness of the present, without the darkening process of the conditioned mind, the more ageless and innocent we become, and the more this is reflected in the development, maturity, and understanding of our ego.

Young children live largely in the moment until they reach adolescence when they begin to spend more time in the conditioned mind. At this stage the understanding and maturity of the ego dramatically slows, for it has fewer moments of 'being present' reflected to it from which to develop. Thus many egos basically remain in a state of immature adolescence throughout their lives, developing only methods and habits of pseudo cleverness and avoidance.

1514. Maturity occurs from moments of presence, it does not necessarily result from experience, or the passing of years. It is being at peace with oneself, whilst having an acceptance and awareness, as well as commitment to the earth and to life.

MAY THE FORCE

1515. No one can avoid the inevitable clash of love with unlove, and truth with untruth. Life requires that we make a stand.

MEANING

1516. With all things, there is the outer experience as well as the inner meaning.

1517. Helping others helps put meaning into one's life. We seem to have been created for service and mutual dependency, in order to give meaning.

MEANING WELL

1518. If we mean well to others, we must be careful. Are we truly giving, or are we seeking our own gratification?

MEDIA

1519. When the foundations of our media become unbiased, then they will be able to render an unbiased perspective and an unbiased presentation. Generally however, the current view of reality is based on a dual perspective, which suggests we still have to work with the conditional in order to reach towards the unconditional.

MEDITATION

1520. The act of meditation allows oneself to be consciously loved by the divine. For this to happen we need to make ourselves sensitively receptive. Such receptivity follows from relinquishing the chattering ego mind to one's nature of being.

1521. To meditate or pray with the intention of selfishly ennobling one's position without seeing it within the background of universal atonement, is to deny the larger picture. We are all mysteriously connected to life and to each other. Our very existence is proof. (See Prayer.)

MEETING

1522. Upon meeting others, it is more truthful to begin with an embracing attitude, regardless of circumstances, for it mirrors the deepest reality of our oneness.

1523. What is it that determines our introduction to another. Is it the person, or is it our prejudging, our placing of them into a category?

1524. Unless we are at ease and comfortable with ourselves, how can we expect others to be comfortable in our presence? The key to meeting others lies in becoming more familiar with who one really is.

1525. When meeting another, we have the opportunity to enlarge each other through the creation of a bond. This bond is most deeply felt if it is formed with heart on the personal level. The forming of this bond is the connecting link that joins us to the wider circle of humanity, and eventually to all beings.

1526. Our first contact with others is an opportunity to impress ourselves upon ourselves, that they will then have a truthful first impression of us. And so in meeting with them again in the future, we can be at ease and be ourselves.

1527. Upon meeting others for the first time, it is desirable to be fresh and alive to the experience. To allow ourselves to be conditioned by previous negative experiences, is to narrow the present possibilities and to dull the spontaneity of the moment.

MEMORY

1528. The ability to recall and have memory, both human and planetary, gives our lives continuity, and gives the earth and humanity cohesion.

1529. The great purpose of memory is for remembering who we are, and why we are here on earth at this moment.

1530. Memory requires the passing of time in order to become an impressionable phenomenon. It is the individuated ego that is impressed with these passing images. For it is only the ego that can live in the frame of time, the soul lives in the eternal present. The more we can make memory (and all history) a faculty of present mindfulness, the more we live in the soul's eternal present.

MENTAL BLOCK

1531. A mental block is rather like a cul de sac—we are required to turn around and open our perception to a wider view.

METAPHOR

1532. All of life can be viewed as a metaphor of the soul. And all that occurs can be seen as a direct or indirect revelation of it. With this awareness we may live more fully in grace.

METAPHYSICS

1533. The arcane and metaphysical sciences such as astrology, divination, chiromancy, alchemy and so on, exist for the guidance and tempering of the personal ego, and not for the inner divine.

These sciences are metaphysical only in that they help lead the ego to its home.

✳

MIND

1534. Mind is present in anything that has consciousness or awareness.

1535. The mind is similar to a focusing lens—whatever we focus upon, internally or externally, becomes our picture of reality. It is therefore the source of our bondage as well as our freedom.

1536. When we do something mindfully, we do it without ego, and it is done precisely to what is required.

1537. The more mindful we are of the implications of our actions upon others, the more we can make both our pathways easier.

1538. 'Having to' and 'wanting to,' are for the most part subjective states. Our external circumstances may sometimes appear to be limited, but we always have a choice about our state of mind within those circumstances.

1539. When we live with a unified mind, we generally live with an attitude of 'and . . . and'. When we live with a disunited mind, we generally live with an attitude of 'either . . . or'.

1540. The ego mind tends to have a mind full of mindlessness. The soul is mindful of emptiness.

1541. If our minds are full of discursive thoughts, opinions, and judgments, we deny the inner divine a voice.

1542. The so-called everyday conscious mind is mostly subconscious ego mind. The entering of the heart however opens the door to conscious, conscious mind.

1543. Just as we cannot sow seeds on barren ground, neither can we sow new thoughts within closed minds.

1544. A mind that is filled with constant checking, fears, hates, anxieties, depressions, guilts, hurts, inhibitions, self consciousness, and so on, is unable to respond freely and confidently in the moment. The state of emptiness, of empty mind, without the egoic constraints of a full mind, is able to live freely in the moment, to respond spontaneously and confidently, with humour, wisdom and love.

1545. Children are creative with their minds. Most adults are reactive with their minds. We can only be self-empowered in the creative mind.

1546. Small-mindedness is the world's greatest problem. Small-mindedness is the result of lack of understanding and knowledge. It is desirable that we forever broaden our knowledge and understanding of each other that we may become large-minded, having great tolerance, and freely allowing the natural diversity of life to flourish.

1547. It seems that unless there is an observing awareness of the everyday conscious mind, then we become immersed within its egoic confines. Once we observe it, we begin to live from a more conscious, ego-less state.

1548. When the mind is already set, it is very difficult for us to see and hear something new.

1549. In order to remain open-minded, the familiar must in some sense be transcended.

1550. To be mindful about what we speak to others is often a good way of finding out what we need to hear ourselves.

1551. Any past viewpoint repeated without present mindfulness becomes the master of the speaker.

1552. Selfish thought characterises the ego mind, which tends to operate through judgment, opinion, ignorance and rashness.

The soulful mind is characterised by seeing the wave, and its connection to the whole—it tends to operate through silence, meditation, intuition, contemplation, attention, mindfulness, loving kindness and selflessness.

1553. When something is not quite right, it is often because our mind is set on too small a parameter. When we expand our mind's vision, we are usually able to arrive at a greater understanding, or a solution.

1554. In the creative mind there are an infinite number of levels, which imaginatively could be entered as a skyscraper, with each floor representing a different level of consciousness that we can access. It could include a floor of the inventive mind, a floor of music composition, a floor of beauty, a floor of transcendence, a floor of art, writing, timelessness, the universe, microcosms, other dimensions, angels, comedy, fears, gardens, telepathy, healing and health, confidence, will, performance, love, mindfulness, truth, kindness, devotion, worship, happiness, history, the future and so on.

1555. The empty mind is more able to bring close the soul's presence.

1556. If we are to continue with this obsessive self-interested chatter in the ego mind, let us at least make it descriptive and affirmative of the present moment. And for our aspirations, let us give them faith and reality by proclaiming them in the present tense also.

1557. A mind that is given a new set of instructions requires that we follow through with an active will, in order to programme the act with the intention.

1558. Levels of Mind:

* Unstructured thought—arises spontaneously from the subconscious mind.

* Structured thought—one actively thinks and reasons in an attempt to find facts and seek resolution, by using one's daily conscious mind.

* Intuitive thought—one experiences the mindfulness and wisdom of a super conscious mind (the heart/soul, collective unconscious, or planetary mind and beyond) where one listens actively or hears inactively.

* Channelled thought—one apparently listens to other minds without any input from one's structured-thought mind.

* Creative thought or visualisation—one actively enlarges one's

senses, or one is suddenly inspired by an experience of a greater reality.

* Subconscious thought—the mind/body control and exchange for centrifugal and centripetal data, including memory and instinct.

* Dream thought—the seemingly unstructured, symbolic thoughts and images of the subconscious and unconscious mind.

* Unconscious potential thought—arises from the collective unconscious.

Collectively these levels of mind constitute a sense of the individual. Beyond these levels we are sometimes able to experience the beholder, the one who witnesses all without the intolerance or bias that may exist on some of the other levels, and we realise that we are more than mind. The beholder is felt to be our transcendent reality.

1559. If one is largely living in the unstructured-thought mind, one will be living from the fears and vacillating emotions of the subconscious ego.

1560. Mindfulness is much more than a quality of mind. It is aware-fullness of one's infinite nature.

1561. The composed mind, without ripples of thought, exists timelessly, with great gentleness, and without spatial boundaries it radiates and is one with forever. Nothing is lacking, all is complete. And a passive oblivion envelops the small self and its many cares, revealing the serenity of the universal.

MISINTERPRET

1562. Most misunderstandings between people are unintentional, and created out of ignorance of the other person's perspective. Yet we often blame the other person as though they had intentionally created a conflict.

MISSION

1563. Each of us (behind our earthly appearance) are highly intelligent, compassionately aware, spiritual beings, on a mission of love and truth, from the centre of the universe, through the centre of our being. This is our deepest truth.

1564. We are all on a divine mission. When we place our attention on the heart of this mission, our reality becomes aligned with our mission. In this attention, the love that bade us to come here becomes apparent and outshines the material realism that seeks to resist, invalidate, and void all memory of our divinity.

MISTAKES

1565. Humanity would not have progressed without the revelations of mistakes. A mistake is merely a 'missed take' on one path for the 'take' of another. It is a deviation, a missed step, an oversight, a slip-up that allows us to see other possibilities and to return us to ourselves with a more rounded view.

1566. What may at first appear to be a mistake or an accident, can in fact be a great discovery. It is one of the methods our subconscious uses to teach us.

1567. It is not easy to admit to mistakes, but the ability to do so confers the freedom of being human. When we openly admit our mistakes, we begin to release ourselves of shame, and disarm those who accuse us.

1568. Mistakes are for the purpose of learning and education, they are not made for the purpose of instilling guilt or blame.

1569. Our mistakes are the initiating steps to the area where we find understanding. They provide the necessary contradicting signposts to our headlong journey. In hindsight, 99% of the value of a mistake is in the understanding gained.

MISUNDERSTAND

1570. Being misunderstood puts us back into our own hands, that we may not only see the ego's loneliness in being misunderstood, but also connect with the deeper understanding of our unity with all, regardless of what happens in the external reality.

MODERATION

1571. In many situations, moderation is the point of balance and justice between the extremes of avoidance and excess.

MOMENT

1572. The eternal moment is imperturbably composed. There are no questions, no answers, only omnipresence.

1573. What a disservice we do to ourselves when we allow worn out beliefs and old psychologies to ruin the freedom, vitality and oneness of the moment.

1574. In order to be able to live more in the freedom of the moment, it seems essential to heal our habitual, repetitive thoughts and motions.

1575. From the universal point of view this moment is totally fulfilled, totally divine.

1576. When we are in the moment, we are also in full presence.

1577. From out of the mass of sleepwalking existence that most of us occupy, those who truly and utterly experience one moment are sublimely blessed. This moment becomes a joyous keystone to their life.

MONEY

1578. Money and/or riches (not necessarily financial) appear to be the resulting energy of spending one's time valuably.

1579. Because of the very nature of money (and possessions) being passed amongst us all, there can be no attitude of any long-standing that says 'This money is mine.' It is owned by all of us temporarily (in the singular) and permanently (in the plural).

1580. Money has risen to the peak of influence in most societies. It governs our lives so that everything we do has an underlying monetary value on our time. Our humanity, ecology, relationships, health, creativity, passion, and spirituality have been seriously eroded by the cost of what we see is worthwhile.

1581. When money is given or received with enmity it tends to become dead money. It has no vitality, no real promising ability for the exchange of good energy in the future.

1582. Fairness in money dealings is more important than the exchange of money itself. If someone is in integrity and proffering their best exchange, which may even involve a sacrifice on their behalf, such honour and honesty pronounce their heart's involvement in the exchange, and it is to this level of exchange that our own inner-fortune and harmony best responds.

1583. Money appears to be the promise of value. We largely foretell the return of its value by the attitude and manner in which we give it back into circulation.

1584. The mind and body are so valuable that no amount of money, not even all of the money in the world is enough to compensate for the distress caused to them by money worries.

MORALITY

1585. The judgment that arises out of moral comparison is largely valueless and opinionated when compared with the divine.

1586. We cannot ask immorally of another what we ourselves would not do. If we do ask, our own principles of morality are questionable.

MORE

1587. Frequently, more seems to lead to a desire for more, until we realise that the more may be harmful to us. For example when we eat more, we often desire to eat even more. Similarly for drink, drugs, money, power and so on. The more inevitably leads to a loss of one's inner centred state and its replacement with a more unconscious state.

MOTIVATION

1588. Motivation wells up from an inner passion that inspires and inflames us into action, to move us to our goal. If emotions such as apathy, anxiety, boredom, confusion, guilt, shyness, depression, loneliness, rejection, self pity, sadness, and worry predominate in our lives, we have forgotten that happiness is our true nature, we have forgotten the commitment to our own dream, we have forgotten gratitude and we have forgotten to love.

1589. Our level of motivation seems largely dependent upon how clear our emotional body is. Though we can be motivated by emotions such as anger, fear, hate, self-righteousness, impatience, indignation and frustration, we tend to burn out quickly from such emotional motivation.

MURDER

1590. All murder is an unconscious act, perpetrated in ignorance. True consciousness promotes life, truth and love.

1591. When a life is extinguished, the waste of our accumulated oppression lies blatantly before us.

1592. Though most of us have not murdered another's body, how many of us are innocent of the crime of murdering another's thoughts, character, or sensibility?

MUSIC

1593. Music affects our emotions and feelings, as well as stimulates our mind and body. It may unite and bring us together, or individually lead us into the boundless. Essentially though, music creates melody and rhythm to harmonise with life and nature. Without the harmonic proportions that create melody and rhythm, music would not exist.

MYSTERY

1594. Mystery is the divine's game of hide-and-go-seek played throughout the universe. It is a sign that the divine is in hiding.

1595. The inner worlds of the universal unconscious and subconscious are far larger than the world of daily consciousness. If this were not so, we would live in a completely known world, nothing would be a mystery.

1596. Everywhere mystery reveals itself . . . a falling leaf from the fingers of a tree: a lost hair reverently placed; a broken twig on our path; a passing face in the cloud; a beam of light slipping underneath a door; a still voice in an empty room. They are curious signs of things hidden, the skylarking flight of the divine.

1597. The cloaks, riddles, and enigmas of mystery, are all required. For they cast a charm and fire our imagination to forever lead us into the great unknown.

1598. We are a mystery to ourselves, no matter how much we probe and reveal; we cannot grasp this bottomless mystery. Our own face is a veil that hides the secret of our sacrosanct, everlasting, universal legend.

1599. Mystery is the invitation for us to explore the revelations of freedom, clandestinely concealed inside the infinite passageways of the unrolling universal unconscious, which enticingly escorts our voyage to the primordial womb of creation.

1600. The divine is love. Love is the sweetest mystery. The

divine therefore purposefully works in mysterious ways, for love will open us and bring us to the mystery of universal fusion.

✳

MYTH

1601. If we look at our lives historically as myth, rather than fact, we can distance our perception enough to see the growing thread of our journey—our very calling along a particular path.

N

✳

NAIVETE

1602. All beings throughout time have lived in a state of profound naivete. No one really knows all.

✳

NAME

1603. Essentially a name is a selected vibration that draws the spirit in a particular direction, that it may be perceived and personalised.

1604. If we associate our own name more with our inner being rather than with ego, whenever we call or hear our name we shall bring a deeper consciousness into being.

✳

NATURE

1605. Nature, and the presence of original self-nature, are the same. The more unconnected we are to outer nature, the more removed we have become from our own noble nature.

1606. Every one of us has been a reaper of nature, which in part shows the interdependency of all life. However, our lesson seems to be to balance our true needs with nature's ability to provide, along with our own ability to return and restore. For this to occur, we need to raise the status of nature from being our bonded slave to that of an exalted priestess. (See Earth, Universe.)

NEEDINESS

1607. Neediness is often an anxious diversion from the immense state of our true being. If we eat when we are not hungry; do for the sake of doing; desire love and sex to fill one's emptiness; want the company of others to assuage loneliness; take drugs to avoid oneself—we are creating a distraction from the present, and from what we fear may be the dark void of our inner being, which essentially is our deepest abode of peace and fulfilment. The fundamental call underneath such longings is for us to enter a state of being, not of seeking or of doing.

1608. Most need is created by the compulsiveness of unremitting ego inadequacy. This inadequacy can create many emotive responses, from anger to depression, to fear, worry and so on, which create a tempting but fearful desire for that which is perceived as being missing. However, the missing part is not something from outside; we are missing the state of 'being' from inside, as seen in the conscious 'being' states of love, joy and happiness. These states do not create need.

1609. The opposite of emotional neediness is love and compassion. Our ability to give love and compassion heals our need at the same time.

NEGATIVE CULT

1610. In our society it appears fashionable to be cynical, angry and negative, and unfashionable to be happy or to speak of love and joy. When fashion dictates to us the soul faculties of love and joy, then there is an element of mass mind control occurring.

NEGATIVITY

1611. The amount of negativity in our lives is often an indication of the amount of ego-minded struggle and resistance to flow, change, and transcendence.

1612. Our negative perceptions can be a key to an unfolding of our reality if we allow ourselves to experience what the full implications of the perception might be, and from where it arose.

1613. How much of our lives are negatively self-preset? The level of personal freedom we perceive usually indicates whether we are living in a self-preset negative mode, or experiencing the fullness of happiness and freedom in the present moment.

1614. When we sense a negative judgment forming within ourselves, it is forming because our own conceptions of life, others, or ourselves, is too narrow.

1615. Whenever we experience a negative situation, it is an opportunity to look at the shadows of our subconscious with the light of consciousness.

1616. If we hang on to a negative, or find it difficult to let go, then it is necessary to inquire why in the first place we picked it up, and why we continue to pick it up. It seems that we continue to pick it up out of unconscious habit, and the payoff for its continuation appears to arise from the greed of the ego. The ego wants to keep gnawing on old bones, and keep us in a negative area of the past, away from the freedom of our true presence in the present.

1617. Is there really any point in carrying the burden of a negative view of another?

1618. Generally, if we are not experiencing love, we are not fully in the present. If we are experiencing a negative thought or emotion, it will be found to be based on past judgmentalness or a conditioned thought.

1619. To conclude that something is negative because of our own past conditioning, or because of what others conclude, may in some instances narrow the range of possible actions to being outside of the area of our redemption.

1620. If we choose by our own beliefs and perceptions to see the negative in others, we are dishonouring the ongoing force of love inherent in life that seeks unity. For until we have conversed with the deepest aspect of another's being, we do not know them. When we do converse with their deepest aspect, we find that there is only love.

1621. The pervasive quality of the negative can easily spread unconsciously to other parts of one's life, if not consciously checked.

1622. If we cultivate a more mindful sense of unity with others, and with life, then we help destroy the ego's ability to sow and reap the negative.

1623. Our attitude of negative expectation of others, radiates to them, and helps keep our perspective of them in a negative place.

1624. If we cannot understand and clear ourselves of the recent negative responses we have had towards others, or ourselves, how then can we expect to clear the subconscious negatives from our deep past? It seems necessary to focus first on the present and the recent.

1625. One way to be free of negative thoughts is not to hold them. We do this by not claiming them.

1626. When we exist with a negative expectancy, we exist with the ego burdens of anxiety, fear, self-pity, worry, hatred and delusion. We exist without the freedom to be true to the love-nature of our soul, from where we live, not just exist.

1627. Negative speech and actions are usually heard and felt loudly by their initiator, if they are not absorbed and reacted to by their target. Most people react to the negative, which helps deflect the intensity of the initiator's consciousness on the issue, and therefore keeps the negative in a state of unconsciousness in the mind of the initiator. However, the initiator will often require of un-reactive or creative people, some kind of soothing interaction as a balm to their own self-inflicted ego anguish.

1628. To perceive something negative about someone and to disdainfully comment on it, magnetises and enlarges some of the same quality in ourselves.

1629. If we take aboard the negative fallout from another, we are taking aboard another's impressions and forgetting our own true reality.

1630. Most negative relationship states are caused by ignorance, not vindictiveness. However vindictiveness itself is a deepening of ignorance.

1631. If we look at those things in our life that seem to have a negative expression, those things that seem beyond our control, they are the very things that we are learning to have greater dominion over through our interactive experience. One way in which we can have more conscious input is to prepare as though we do have dominion, and live this way.

1632. Almost always, our negativity arises out of our focus on not being loved. We forget we are a lover—we came here to love. When we remember to love, we recover love's peace, and we meet love's joy.

1633. Any time we speak, think, or do the negative, we are helping to decrease the love, truth, and life force within ourselves and our world. Because we are still here, and the earth and the universe still exist, is proof of the abundant blessings of love and truth.

1634. It is very difficult to say something negative on a universal level. It is the divisive, separating mind that requires an object for a negative attack, from where most negativity is directed, at the personal level. When we experience the unified mind, negativity is annulled.

1635. The further removed we become from having an open, loving, understanding, purposeful and compassionate view of others and of life, the more the internal forces of negativity, anger, depression, worry and so on increase. The wisdom that life is attempting to impart, is that the way to love, peace, and fulfilment is for us to open and to open more and more.

NEGOTIATION

1636. Negotiation from a purely egocentric point of view is based on selfish demand, and is inevitably confrontational. However, negotiation is really an opportunity for those involved to learn a deeper reality, by being of service to each other. When we want to serve another, we understand them from their perspective, we fully listen, and we express our truth lovingly. This allows an agreement to be based on appreciation, consideration and awareness, which in turn helps create conciliation, harmony and peace.

Negotiations and agreements that have no peace indicate that there has been an excess of selfish involvement.

NO

1637. If we were to regard 'no' as not being a denial of our existence, but as indicating 'yes' in another or opposite direction, then 'no' would lose its sting of rejection.

NOBLE COMPANION

1638. The noble companion (one's soul) is always fully present, and thus being fully present, lives in the fullness of love, truth, and innocence. From such consciousness the noble companion must possess infinite awareness and infinite understanding. And therefore the noble companion is the unfailing friend to the ego and its experiences.

NO THOUGHT

1639. When we have no thought, we can experience the peace and contentment of the infinite's love realm, in the timeless present.

1640. The state of 'no thought' is an ego-less state. It is the ego which constantly chatters in the mind, attempting to fill the soul's love presence.

NOURISHMENT

1641. Just as food feeds us, so too do many other things, including contact with others, watching the sun rise and set, being in nature, being inspired, making love, being creative and productive, acts of love and generosity, finding understanding and meaning, and acts of prayer and meditation.

NURTURING

1642. In practical terms, our ability to nurture is indicative of the depth of our love. Nurturing is the physical embodiment of love.

O

OBJECT-SUBJECT

1643. Habitually, we consider our ego-self as subject and soul/god as object. However, if we reverse this and regard our soul/god as subject and the ego as object, we immediately feel at home on earth. We feel embraced; immediately there is love, peace and knowing.

1644. The seeming objective world relates more to the ego. The true subjective world relates to the soul.

OBLIGATION

1645. Unless we are willing to fulfil our obligations, we will likely make them a burden to ourselves. A burdensome obligation becomes a breach of one's self-promise.

OBSERVATION

1646. When we observe, we discover, we notice the new, and we more fully appreciate the known. When we observe, we embrace that aspect of life into our being, and we take heed of it. Therefore the more we observe, the more consciously attentive we become to the moment, the more we discover, and the more we live life.

1647. Amongst the greatest of things is to merely look, listen and feel; to take the time from our self-imposed anxiety-causing race through life.

1648. If we observe something purely for what it is, the mind naturally stills. Out of the stillness, the essence of what we are observing communicates with our own essence, and there grows a quiet appreciation and a gentle respect that reaches out beyond the time and space of the moment. From this we are left with the realisation and confirmation of the oneness of creation.

OBSERVER

1649. At those times when we are aware of our perceptions of knowing, thinking, and feeling, we become aware that there is an observer within us who watches the proceedings. When we begin to live more consciously aware of the observer (our soul) the mind is directed more to wisdom, and the speaking of it, and the heart to a devotional gnosis.

OBSESSION

1650. Most obsessions result from a lack of balance between body, mind and spirit. During the period of obsession, one is literally possessed by the spirit of the accumulated thoughts and emotions of the thing obsessed over. The exorcising of one's obsession begins with broadening one's view, both mentally and actively.

1651. If we are overly obsessed with how things ought to be, we are covering over the much larger portion of our lives where there is peace and love.

1652. An obsession with getting the externals right usually arises because of a deep internal unhappiness, the belief being that making the externals right will bring happiness. But external things are subject to change, so it becomes a difficult path.

1653. If we let go of those things that distract, obsess and diminish us, those things that especially occupy our minds to their detriment, we clear the pathway to receive what was on the other side of our obsession.

OBSTINACY

1654. An obstinate temperament finds it difficult to open to new possibilities or to change beyond the narrow confines of a rigid set of boundaries. Such a person wants to dictate their beliefs and values on to the world, and to close off to all other possible factors. But ultimately no person can be at such odds with the world and win.

OBSTRUCTION

1655. The obstacles in our life are there to create—prevention, interruption, a detour, or make apparent a new opportunity. Obstructions can be seen as either a limitation or as an opening to broaden and deepen our concepts.

OCCUPATION

1656. I believe that the reason why so many people find it difficult to keep to a course, an education, or a career path is because very few are satisfying to the true self. Trying to discover a satisfying occupation within the paradigms of present society requires great determination.

OLD

1657. Perhaps the most enlightened understanding of the word 'old' is that which keeps faith to its original essence and intention, and is therefore uncorrupted, harmonious, accepted, and perennially current, whilst embracing and yet transcending all change. And therefore it becomes an archetype for excellence.

OMISSION

1658. The truth hidden from others by one's omission is heard just as loudly as a lie by one's conscience.

OMNIPRESENCE

1659. Omnipresence begins to show with the blossoming open of the heart. The further we go inside, the more we experience the emerging wisdom of omniscience, and ultimately the radiating sovereignty of omnipotence.

1660. Wherever we may be, the forces of love and truth are there also . . . . inside us and about us . . . . no matter what may appear to the contrary.

ONCE

1661. If we live in the moment, we do everything only once, and it is done forever. If we do not live in the moment, it appears we can do the same thing many times.

ONENESS

1662. When we are one with our spiritual ideal, we are also one with the greater spiritual dominion that extends beyond the earth, and beyond space and time. However, when we are one with the mundane world, there is only limited extension or union possible.

1663. All states are temporary and changeable, except the state of oneness, which includes the fullness of love, truth, and innocence.

1664. If everything is within us, and we are in everything, we are not only healing ourselves but also the universe, simultaneously.

1665. When we are truly one, there is no separation and all yearnings disappear. The level of anxiety we hold in relation to our unfulfilled yearnings reveals also the level of our closeness to the state of being one.

1666. The more we practise the arts of oneness throughout the day, for example by—meditation, cultivation of mindful awareness, conscious breathing, honouring nature, enlightened sexuality, doing creative acts, acts of kindness and generosity, seeking inspiration, creating beauty, choosing feelings, forgiveness, gratitude, loving, sharing, prayer, practices of devotion, being empathic, practising compassion, serving others, promoting laughter, singing and dancing for joy, eating slowly and mindfully, purifying one's body, living in the moment, cultivating a childlike wonder and curiosity, being happy for no reason, cultivating poise, accepting all, working for the divine, remembering the divine in everything and everyone—the less we will experience the pain of separation and duality.

1667. All is one mind, one body, one heart, one spirit, and one soul. All is the divine one. All is continual existence of one being.

There is only one voice (all voices), only one listener (all ears), only one vision (all eyes), only one who acts (all actions), only one thinker (all thoughts) and only one who feels (all feelings).

1668. How does the two (ego and soul; ego and others; ego and creation) become one . . . . there is no two.

1669. Finally there is only oneness, the butterfly and cocoon of creation are always in union, always in a constant state of transcendent transformation, flowing from one into the other. There is never any separation.

OPENNESS

1670. The secret of the universe is that it is open, and that it is we who are opening to it. The universe is composed of the divine, the divine is love, and the paramount action that love creates in human beings is that of opening.

1671. The greater our openness to what life presents to us (and it is present because of our conscious, subconscious, and unconscious invitation, in order for us to learn and experience), the more we live life, and the less we withdraw into states of stasis, characterised by prejudice, narrow-mindedness, and intolerance.

1672. What are we afraid of when being unable to be open? Why do we draw back in fear and imagine threats from others, particularly those that act or dress differently to us, which then adds to our judgmentalness of them? Consequently we find ourselves only able to be fully open to certain kinds of people, such as good-looking women or men who dress appropriately. Surely, variations from the norm give us all greater freedom of expression. Principally we are learning that our judgmentalness imprisons us, while our openness, attentiveness and caring, frees us.

1673. When another takes steps to open and reveal themselves to us, this is not the time to start pointing out inadequacies that we perceive in them.

1674. The open mind is constantly creative and free flowing, not limited by fears or judgments. The open body is relaxed yet vital. The open heart is constantly in love and loving, with the wisdom and understanding of beauty. The open soul is in love with the nature and expression of eternity.

1675. Open senses, such as wide, wide open eyes (like children have) creates an open and expanded feeling of wonder, joy, love, excitement and innocence. How wide-eyed are we? How open-eared? How open-hearted?

1676. Openness is a sign of a communing soul.

OPINION

1677. When two indignant opinions vie equally for the truth, the one who yields to the other first is the one whom truth loves most. Truth cannot be upheld by the blind opinion that leaves out love for others.

1678. Mostly we have differences in opinion, and because opinion is not utmost truth, we inevitably fight over untruth.

1679. Opinions are meant to be catalysts for deeper thought, they are not meant to become dogma or be used to convert others.

1680. Giving an opinion is valid only when it is recognised as an opinion.

1681. When we give an opinion and pass it off as fact, we are shoring our ego, and barricading it from the forces of truth and insight.

OPPORTUNITY

1682. The moment of opportunity passes very quickly if we are not truly present. But the one who loves life will be adventurous enough to create a new opportunity.

1683. The key to the doorway of opportunity is called boldness. The next step is one of affirming action.

OPPOSITION

1684. The closer we are to living harmoniously with the law of truth that naturally pervades the universe, the quicker it seems to act whenever we oppose it. In reality this is because we become conscious earlier to the forces of opposition.

1685. When we are opposed, we are being tempered and balanced.

OPPRESSOR

1686. The oppressor contains within themselves the seeds of their own downfall. That is, the lack of a foundation based on wisdom, and a conscience to direct it.

1687. From the spiritual viewpoint, that which is oppressed must by nature return to its oppressor, physically, mentally or spiritually.

OPTIMISM

1688. The truly optimistic appear to be more in alignment with a higher truth, which sees beyond the illusions of egoic earth life. Sometimes this manifests with the optimist being optimistic for no apparent earthly reason. Whereas, those who live in cynicism as a way of being are more aligned with their negating ego.

ORACLE

1689. When we consult an oracle, our own state of being is the primary force in the revelatory process.

ORDER

1690. Order occurs somewhere in the midpoint of the beholder's mind—either side of this, there is a tendency to see chaos. The circumscribed mind cannot fathom the order that exists in what is apparently perceived as chaos. In chaos there may in fact be a more complex, higher degree of organisation, symmetry or sequence than what is normally perceived as being a conducted arrangement of order.

Order is therefore relative to the perspective of the beholder's view. The larger the perspective, the more that order tends to be beheld. For example, when we view the night sky, we see and feel an impressive order, though the stars are apparently (from an earth dweller's perspective) held in a chaotic pattern. Intuitively we are aware from the soul's point of view of the larger cosmic order.

ORDINARY

1691. There is no such thing as 'ordinary.' If we say or presume that something, someone, or a circumstance is ordinary, then we have missed something special.

1692. When we enter the seemingly ordinary knowing that beneath the surface dwells the extraordinary, our fascination produces delight.

ORGANISATION

1693. Organisation is a process of linking organic parts to become a whole system. From this, freedom arises. And freedom engenders the vision of unity. From unity, benevolence is born. And benevolence appears to be the cohesiveness that holds the universe together.

ORIGIN

1694. Everything has a source prior to its manifestation in a conception of mind. The seed of a plant or a tree contains the pattern of its creation to set in motion the evolution of form. When we perceive the beauty of the forms around us, we are also seeing the patterns conceived in the creator's mind.

OUTGOING

1695. In order to be outgoing to people, foremost we need the inner psychological space and freedom from which to move. Love creates the space, freedom, and the opening to be outgoing. (See love.)

OVERCHARGED

1696. If ever we are overcharged, our biggest challenge is our own sense of outrage at seemingly being disadvantaged by life itself. But the transcendent attitude is that all things are in a continuing perpetual balance in the universe. All action, reaction, and non-action are part of this balance.

OVERCOME

1697. When we overcome a situation, it is preferable that we do so by self-ascending, by seeing a higher truth, than by using our power to subdue.

OVERREACTION

1698. Whenever someone overreacts negatively, it is because their own subconscious fears, guilts and angers have recently been stimulated, and are now beginning to rise to the surface of their consciousness.

OVERWHELM

1699. We tend to reach a state of overwhelm when our perspective attempts to cover all the bases at once that occupy the middle ground. If we look from the larger, universal ground, we regain a true perspective, then we can return to the small ground where we operate best doing one thing at a time.

OWNERSHIP

1700. Only the ego thinks it owns the land, possessions, and others.

1701. In the realm of pure existence, where there can be no perception of ownership, there also cannot be theft. Theft of possessions, or of life cannot occur, since there is no division or separation. All of the so-called misdeeds on earth, when really looked into, are actually forms of theft. However from the perception of pure existence it can only be pseudo theft.

P

PAIN

1702. Pain is apparently the force of separation of body/mind from soul, which offers an opportunity to learn what the ego is and what the soul is, thus allowing us to reconnect with our source in a deeper way.

1703. Most emotional pain seems to be a combination of fear, loneliness, hurt, anxiety, and a deep sense of rejection resulting from our personal relationships. Emotions of helplessness alternate with self-destructiveness. They appear to be a subconscious effect resulting from a past limited ego perception. They urge us to look at what beliefs we have chosen, and to make changes that will align us with our inner peace.

1704. Pain softens the ego and allows us to re-enter the gentle heart.

1705. Joy lifts pain, both surface pain and deep-seated subconscious pain. The more we live in the consciousness of joy, the more we lift and clear pain. Interiorly we already live in joy, we need only realise it.

1706. If we are running from pain, we are actually running in pain's footsteps.

1707. The less ego we carry, the less pain we experience.

1708. When there is great love, even the course of pain runs sweeter.

1709. Pain appears to be the ego's pledge to the soul, that it will return the experiencer with greater understanding.

1710. Our pain is not a punishment from god. It is a call to pursue our wholeness.

1711. Just as we experience and create pain on our path towards maturity, so also may there be pain in proportion to our return to innocence from our state of maturity.

1712. Pain is primarily experienced in the mind, but the voice of pain is asking us to move into our heart.

PARADISE

1713. To live with love foremost, with wonder and praise for every aspect of creation, with joyful gratitude for all things, would be to exist in a sublime paradise. Though many would probably call it extremely naive, and ask 'What about the pain and suffering in the world?'

Yet, each of us can only live in the space of the moment, subconsciously—consciously trusting in the design and purpose of the divine, which for most of us is unknown. And who amongst us really knows the modus operandi of life on earth? Thus with each moment that we surrender our dabbling to the divine, we regain the peace of our own divinity and we reap a moment in paradise.

Inevitably at some moment, with the increasing of consciousness, with the realisation of our divine nature, all ignorance, all inhumanity, all savagery and despoliation will fail to satisfy our unconscious, small-minded motivation, and paradise will become evident to us all.

1714. If we consciously go about seeing the divine in others, we already live in paradise.

1715. Innocence and paradise are mutually inclusive. An overly full mind surely invalidates innocence.

1716. Paradise is living the life of our own supreme conscious choice wherever we may be.

1717. Whenever we lose consciousness of our divinity, we leave the garden of paradise.

PARADOX

1718. Paradox provides the necessary force of contradiction to our circumscribed expectations, or our inability to live fully in the moment. Paradox dances between the attraction and repulsion of opposites, whilst indirectly leading us to the yielding of our ego through the merging of these opposites, by trusting in the divine.

1719. Looking from the microscopic human view, the universe appears to be a mystery and a paradox. If we attempt to live our lives by a formula, whilst leaving out mystery and paradox, we will find ourselves living from a background of anxiety and fear, hoping that the unexpected will not arrive. However in a world of constant change, the unexpected may arrive suddenly and surprisingly.

1720. When we let go of our headstrong hold on life, the previous irreconcilable paradox transforms into the joy of synchronicity, where all things have value and can be considered. Our drop returns to the ocean, co-extensivity becomes conscious, and the drama of life is seen from the view of the playwright and not the self-obsessed actor.

PARDON

1721. Pardon is primarily the taking of self-responsibility rather than receiving an acquittal from others. It is the move towards freedom from self-guilt through self-forgiveness. It arises from the illumination through trial of a more truthful path. It follows with the surrendering of something that does not work, and a yielding of resistance towards accepting that one is here for a greater purpose.

PARENTS

1722. The role of the parent is not to dominate or subjugate. Parents are to guide, inspire, draw in and draw out, the souls of their children.

PASSING

1723. All things in the universe are apparently in a state of continual refinement. And therefore all things that we claim to know now, such as the elements, life, other beings and the earth, are in a state of passing.

1724. Those things we are egoically attached to, when viewed against the eternal universal background, are seen to be a passing phenomenon.

PASSION

1725. Passion transports us out of the confines of the ego and into the inspired and heavenly spaces. That which we love, that which inflames and absorbs us, is our passion. It is our sacred gift, and our use of it is our service to the divine.

1726. It is the duty of each of us to seek and follow our own passion, our own unique path, and our own unique style.

1727. Passion is a dynamic movement of creative energy, which can be experienced internally with oneself, another, or the divine. It is initiated by allowing an expectant emptiness for inspiration to flow from the fullness of the supreme.

1728. To help us attain the state we desire, we can choose to associate and be in harmony with the historical sphere as well as the present sphere of our passion.

1729. Pursuing our passion not only gives our lives meaning; its rapture also heals us at the same time.

1730. There appear to be two kinds of passion in love relationships—that of ego passion and soul passion. Ego passion is the fire of the indigent wounded ego, seeking its home and completion in another. Soul passion is the ecstatic love call of the divine, and is open to voluntary choice. Ego passion is a dim reflection of soul passion; it is a limited experience of the entanglement of egos, and tends to be driven and therefore lacking in choice and divine grace. Soul passion is direct, all embracing and enlightening; it is seeing the divine unveiled in another without needing oneself to be worshipped—rather it worships the divine from the most accessible and beautiful perspective of a human form.

1731. Passion is present when we live self-empowered. This self-empowerment in turn arises from one's self-love. When we live boldly and brightly, trusting in the infinite resourcefulness of our self-love, we live empowered and impassioned.

PASSIVE-AGGRESSIVE

1732. Our current reality requires a duality of expression in order to create a potential learning dynamic in our daily lives. A passive-aggressive dynamic can be observed throughout all relationships in humanity and nature, which are in the process of learning.

1733. If we have an aggressive stance or attitude we tend to attract reciprocating energies from others, such as more aggression, or fear based passivity. Alternatively, a passive attitude may attract an opposing energy of aggression, or even more hopeless passivity.

Life seems to be guiding us towards a midpoint. This midpoint between extremes becomes an interior key to unlocking one's inner peace and equilibrium. Love that is beyond being ego objective, or in other words ego detached, seems to be both the midpoint as well as the key.

1734. When we observe that the dynamics of daily life are largely created between the extremes of aggression and passivity, we can watch the proceedings with a greater degree of equanimity, without losing oneself upon an emotional seesaw.

1735. The closer we get to making our use of language unadorned with either aggressive or passive egoic, conditioned beliefs, the more we move towards truth, and towards the crux of our essential nature.

1736. We can witness the passive-aggressive response in the introvert and extrovert personality, and in the emotional life of the ego. We see that emotions such as anger, hatred, self-righteousness, impatience, resentment, indignation, contempt and judgmentalness arise from the aggressive extremity. Whereas the passive extreme can be witnessed in emotions such as anxiety, apathy, boredom, confusion, depression, embarrassment, fear, grief, guilt, hurt, loneliness, regret, rejection, shyness, sadness and worry. Some emotions such as jealousy and annoyance for example, may be experienced at either extreme. However, it is evident that life is teaching us to move towards the path of balance. This path is characterised with a love of life that is detached from such extremes of ego variation.

*

PATHWAY

1737. If we know that we are treading our true pathway, then all the things we truly yearn for are actually part of our path.

1738. Any path that does not lead to an embrace and to union will in due time lead to barrenness.

1739. The pathway is not meant to be a secret, it lies before each and everyone always. However, it requires of us to recognise the realm of our soul and the creative pathway before it.

1740. If we follow our true path, but are accused by society of being out of step, then it is society that must enlarge its boundaries.

1741. As soon as we have true understanding for the particular path or detour we are making, we have then the reason that propels us with the required energy to persist.

1742. Unless our path has a feeling of joy, we are forcing ourselves, and force against force will produce consequences we do not desire.

1743. When we are on our valid path, we can be firm and bold without getting angry. We can be assertive without being pushy. We can have a healthy self-esteem without being egotistical.

1744. On the true path, there is a feeling of something happening, of progress, even though externally at times there may be little or no apparent confirmation.

1745. When we are on our natural path, we flow with life and our egocentric struggles lose their importance.

1746. We may not agree with what another says or does, or even with what shows up on our own path. However, for those things beyond our current ability to influence, an internal acceptance allows us the personal freedom to continue to walk our pathway with integrity.

1747. It is our own individual responsibility and honour that we keep our life's pathway as clear and clean as possible, leaving behind us as little physical, mental, emotional, or financial mess as possible.

1748. The path we forge through life is our offering to the divine.

1749. If there is truth and true freedom for an adherent upon a particular religious or spiritual path, they will be free to explore other paths.

1750. When we step suddenly onto our real path, there is an

immediate sense of upliftment and joy, our level of vitality and well being is profoundly raised.

1751. At any time we are tempted to separate from our true path, we generally experience great unease, lack confidence, and question our own honour.

1752. If we are no longer destined to walk a particular path, it will break up rapidly and completely. If elements of a path persist, there are still things for us to learn upon it. And sometimes, a seemingly backward step is eventually seen to have been a step forward.

1753. From the metaphysical point of view, we are all eternal beings, and therefore every path becomes self-evident, self-correcting, and self-determining . . . eventually. There are just different qualities and experiences to be integrated. The experiences of now will inevitably lead to the eventual.

1754. The more we live our true path, the more we are embellished, and the more meaning and purpose life contains.

1755. Every individual life is unique, with its own unique path, its own unique mission and quest.

1756. The path we walk through life will have many mountains, valleys, plains, passes, gardens, crevasses, beaches, and rivers to cross. If we lose ourselves on the journey by intimately associating our sense of selfhood in the landscape, forgetting our true nature, our attention will be subverted by the instability of our own emotional outlook. The landscape has then become more important than the explorer. It is important for us to witness and accept the ever changing flux and reflux of one's path, whilst still being attentive to one's inner nature.

1757. The test of a true-path experience is in whether we feel wholly empowered, more open, more loving, more truth-filled, more grateful, and more committed to the unfolding of the universal state.

PATIENCE

1758. Patience requires the attention of awareness.

1759. When we keep faith with our own will and destiny, patience arises more easily. When we know where we are going and live in this confidence, we can take more delight in the side-roads that life provides us.

1760. Patience is more an optimistic, trusting state of mind decided upon, than the result of learning from negative experience.

1761. When we are steadily patient, we are not in a place of waiting. We are in a place of loving.

PATRIOTISM

1762. The true patriot is a lover of people, not of artificial boundaries.

PEACE

1763. We cannot depend on outside variables for our peace, it needs to come from the stillness within.

1764. When we make peace with ourselves, the inner stillness, the gentle calm and contentment that is ever present beneath the layers of ego minded struggle and anxiety, comes to light from out of the intimate chambers of our blithely rapturous heart.

1765. Those who live their lives mindful of conciliation are the true peacemakers.

1766. How can we find genuine peace unless we become one with our soul, in body and mind? Until we feel in harmony with our body as our soul does, and in our mind with every unconditioned thought as creative cause?

1767. Unless we yield to and understand what the real nature of love is—that it is a state of being without ego conditions, we shall not find the freedom and serenity of authentic peace.

1768. Our level of peace seems dependent upon our level of intimacy with the divine, along with an honourable acceptance of life.

PERCEPTION

1769. True perception is the basis of our transcendence. True perception has its foundation in pure receptivity. Pure receptivity is selfless, open-hearted, and open-minded, where all senses are innocently open. Perceiving this way gives rise to love, truth and innocence in thought, speech, and action. Whenever we do not perceive this way, we tend to perceive selfishly, which in turn creates constricted thought, speech, and action.

1770. Each of us exists from our own perceptions box. Through the act of enlarging our perceptions by embracing others and by embracing a universal view of life, we can then begin to move out of the box.

1771. Our perception that the nature of life is chaotic, suggests that we are still too closely attached to our own ego as being who we think we really are.

1772. It is how we perceive others, ourselves, things and places, that give us all the seemingly good things in life and all the seemingly negative things. Perception is an internal quality. We can either be held captive by our perceptions, or we can comprehend them.

1773. When we devotedly perceive the world, there is no ego mind. The perception of true reality occurs before the ego mind starts to interpret. The longer we delay interpretation, the richer our perception.

1774. It is not so much the outside events of life that can make us happy or sad, but our inside perceptions of them.

1775. Pure perception is something we intuitively understand. We understand what is perceived in relation to the whole. We tend to see its beauty, its simplicity, and we honour it. We feel a sense of having known this; it feels like a process of remembering. Fresh perceptions that do not contain these guides ought to be questioned for their truthfulness.

1776. How we perceive another is only one facet of the totality of perception, which may or may not say something about them. Others who enter their life can perceive them quite differently.

1777. It is perception that separates us, and perception that unites us.

1778. Through an honest perception of our environment, of the elements, and of the senses endowed us, we realise that practically all is a comfort, a bringer of peace, happiness and beauty.

PERFECT PLACE

1779. Why are we so often at odds with the place we find ourselves in? When essentially this is the most perfect place for us to be now in the entire universe, for universal energy has placed us here.

PERFECTION

1780. Perfection seems to operate from both ends of our path. It appears as an absolute supreme already in existence that may be realised in a moment, or it is seen as an ideal to evolve towards. The soul views perfection from the absolute. The ego tends to view perfection as the possible fulfilment of a long, difficult, and impossible journey.

1781. We often measure others against the standards of perfection, and naturally the outer egoic form that we see of others as judged by our ego, fails to live up to those standards. If we take their outer egoic form as our criterion for viewing them, we are ignoring their infinite, sublime and blameless soul.

1782. Placing more importance on the perfection of our actions in the world, than our love and pleasure obtained from doing them, is synonymous with believing that one's obsessive ego has arrived at godhead.

1783. No ego is perfect. Everyone is learning. Perfectionist moralism creates an impossible guilt-creating standard to live by.

1784. The belief in stern perfection can distort the wonder of our exploring experience. Perfection without beauty, joy, and simplicity, becomes a rigidly mental labour of perverse rule making.

PERFORM

1785. When we perform, do we do so for our own ego or for the divine? If we perform for our ego, we will experience much to be emotionally insecure about.

1786. Whenever we sense the pressure from others to perform, it is then our inner duty to be ourselves.

PERSEVERANCE

1787. Perseverance to a noble cause confers the ability to persist with patience (love). It grants the surmounting of difficulties from a higher perspective (love). And it furnishes a compelling devotion (love) to complete one's purpose.

1788. Without love, perseverance will be fundamentally lacking in such things as stability, vision, integrity, and worthwhileness.

PERSONAE

1789. We all appear to live with a variety of personae. To some we are wise, to others we are a clown, to some we are domineering, others submissive, a lover, an enemy, a friend, a student, a teacher, a father, a mother, a child, and so on. Some relationships flow while others appear blocked. When we interact with another, a persona is largely formed by those elements in the subconscious that require to be brought to consciousness through a process of reciprocal projection and reflection. Different personae raise different elements from the subconscious. When one persona meets another persona fully, there is a flow. If not fully met there is awkwardness, an obstruction. However, once we begin to see that our personae are not our true state, we can begin to radiate the truth of ourselves regardless of the changing states of personae.

PERSONALISING

1790. Personalising and imbuing the seemingly separate parts of creation with the presence of the divine brings presence of mind and ritual to the practice of daily living. All objects, all beings, and all activities become sacred. The god of pens, the god of paper, the god of writing, the god of crossing out mistakes, become just as present as the god of sunlight, the god of rain, and the god of bread and wine.

PERSPECTIVE

1791. Thinking negatively places us in a narrow perspective, and we tend to become ignorant of other things.

Thinking positively expands our perspective, and we think large, we think universally, and we begin to embrace all.

1792. If we have a view of someone (this is more applicable to a negative view, but can also apply to positive views) we may not be able to interact fully with that person. Instead we will tend to see, hear and act only within the guidelines we have set. Having any kind of a view of another human being is short sighted.

1793. The ability to see above and below the surface confers a more rounded view.

1794. Individual perspective is like viewing from one spoke of a wheel. Often we want to convert others to seeing from our exclusive point of view. However, when we see from the hub of the wheel, we see all points of view inclusively, without being attached to any of them, and we are one—we have let go of our egocentric struggle.

1795. Many of us appear to have self-limiting views. We do this by looking but not really seeing, and hearing without fully listening, understanding or questioning.

1796. If our perspective is narrowly based on our own needs, we are missing the part available to us in the larger picture, which takes in the needs of others, and beyond.

1797. When we look from the egocentric point of view, it is often narrow, selfish, and confronted by obstacles. When we look from the universal/humanitarian view, it is usually with love, compassion, and unity. A large view helps to foster benevolence.

1798. Most of us see each other as two-dimensional beings, of body and mind, leaving out the dimensions of heart and soul. But it is through the dimensions of heart and soul we truly get to know each other.

1799. Whenever we speak of more than one, as in gender, religion, race, household, community, generation or nation, we are expressing a limited viewpoint, having not experienced the full range of possible encounters, it will be prone to bias.

1800. We all seem to possess an innate sense of belonging to a greater whole than is apparent to our individual perspective.

1801. If ever we find ourselves wholly condemning a particular place or country, we are claiming a small-minded view for ourselves. Similarly, if we praise a particular place or country, it is fitting that we do not view it as exclusive, but rather as the outgrowth and blossom of the entire planet.

1802. When we look from the view of love and truth, all other views are pulled together under their sky.

1803. Perspective appears to be unique to each individual member of each and every species.

1804. When we see with the eye of the divine, our perspective is no longer self-centred.

1805. An open mind sees a boundless view, a closed mind sees boundaries. A limited point of view will in the end defeat us.

1806. There will always be a superior view, comprehension, and capability, above our current impressions.

1807. Yes we can learn from people who have a narrower viewpoint than our own; they remind us of states we have moved beyond, but let us not forget their importance, on account that we become conceited and disdainful.

1808. When we see others only one way, we deny them as well as ourselves a boundless view.

1809. Our perspective is a self-adjusting, microscopic-telescopic view of life. We may choose to be a micro-experiencer, a macro-experiencer, or an experiencer of the numerous states between them. I have found that a conscious micro or macro view can nullify an overly fixed view on constricting states.

1810. When we have a view of someone, we often exaggerate that view so that we can catalogue and rank that person in our mind. And the result is that we have unreal perspectives on others, roughly divided into good, bad or indifferent.

1811. Perspective is a window into a particular world. This perspective seems always to be encompassed in the perspective of a larger window of another's perspective, ad infinitum.

1812. The overcoming of struggle and the triumph of success require a similar treatment, that is, an attitude of embrace. If we embrace, we are automatically coming from a larger perspective.

1813. It seems that currently we can only see a perspective of something, we cannot see anything fully as it is. There is always more to experience, not only with our senses, but also beyond them—a higher heaven, a deeper ocean. In the immensity of the universe and of its dimensions, there will exist mountains that are beyond having a summit; skies that stretch not just between horizons but between galaxies; starry gateways that shine brighter than all the assembled stars of earth; valleys that are more lush than Eden multiplied a thousand fold; rivers and oceans that stretch vertically; stones that laugh and cry; flowers that leap and dance, and birds that fly in clouds of flame. These things will be seen from the molecular to the macrocosmic. When the blinkers of our educated reality are put aside, we shall really see, we will grow in stature; our vision will become boundlessly creative. We will no longer be spectators of the universe; we will be artistically at home within it.

1814. The picture we carry around of ourselves is constantly adjusting according to the changing state of our ego. It is this adjusting picture that we see others and the world through. It is not surprising then, that there are so many incorrectly attuned pictures of ourselves, others, and the world.

1815. No matter how saint-like we may live our lives, others may view us differently. One of the greatest examples—Jesus, was both loved and hated.

1816. The whole view is greater than any part view, and it is the infinitely expanding whole view that perpetually inspires us.

PETTINESS

1817. Pettiness is a sign of something deeper, perhaps a deep-rooted anger. A person in peace and happiness is not concerned with petty issues.

PILGRIM

1818. We are all pilgrims who have journeyed from the centre of creation to worship upon the shrine of earth, to seek, delight, and reveal the clarity of love in this temple.

PLANET HUMAN

1819. The overview of planetary human consciousness encompasses all other limited points of view. The divisiveness of mankind's religions, politics, social issues, sexual issues, racial issues and ecological issues are understood by the planetary human who creates embrace and spiritual integrity. This view is more in keeping with the unconditional view of the soul.

1820. The planetary human stands tall upon the earth, and looks with wonder, appreciation, and acceptance into the cosmos.

PLAYFULNESS

1821. Adult play is not just meant to be passively watching a movie or the television, going to a restaurant occasionally, drinking with friends, participating in formalised games, or having sex. It is more naturally the activity of innocence.

When we play unconditionally, we lose much of our serious self-controlling image, and with it the defensive, judgmental and censuring barriers that largely form adult inhibition and suppression in our socialised existence. These barriers are abandoned for the spontaneous and informal intimacy of play; we do not fear being wrong, or undergo performance anxiety, serious competitiveness, or guilt.

The body/mind is liberated from daily work routines and habits, and allowed to re-enter an unfettered domain of fun, freedom, fantasy and aliveness. In the rapture of pastime, we are transported beyond the confines of time and into the active life of the present.

Play tends to be more social than solitary. Often the best play outside of the creative process involves two or more people, in which we mutually accept and support our playmates in the happiness of play.

We are renewed by playfulness, our expression is opened, our spirit skylarks into the open spaces once again. We are energised with an increase in joy and wellbeing, which is reflected in our relationships to make all things graced with ease, simplicity, and greater possibility. And we see and remember that nature herself is playing also.

Yes, the entire world is a stage, and we can choose to make it a structured tragic drama, or an engaging gambol through a playground.

PLEASURE

1822. We are wired for a preference to pleasure. Our circuitry encompasses vast sensitivities that can carry us to heaven, and return us with a fountain of ego-annihilating joy.

1823. Pleasure is the sublime preference to feel one's ecstasy and one's joy.

PLEDGE

1824. The ancient concept of the 'pledge' was a sacred contract and obligation held until completion, or forever. This protected both parties on their life's journey, and produced commitment of the highest degree. Perhaps today we have need to reaffirm the pledge, that we may again find commitment to our goals, relationships and ideals.

POSITIVITY

1825. When we live with positive anticipation, we live in greater freedom, we carry fewer burdens, we live closer to our original nature of spontaneity, innocence, and childlike wonder and curiosity.

1826. Whenever we speak, think, or do something positive, we are helping to increase the love, truth and life force within our world and ourselves. The supremacy of love, truth, and life is evident on account that the earth and the universe still exist, they have not been destroyed by the forces of negativity.

1827. If we cultivate a more mindful sense of unity with others and with life, then we help increase our ability to sow and reap the positive.

1828. To create a positive perspective for ourselves, we need to claim positive thoughts and then consciously live by them.

1829. Without a positive, life-enhancing attitude, our lives become filled with burdens.

1830. To notice something positive about someone and to comment on it, magically rubs something of the same quality on us.

1831. When we discover that life, that the divine loves us, it produces in us a positive, majestic expectancy of life's offerings.

1832. It is more a person's inner tendencies that decree their state of aliveness and enthusiasm. If they have chosen positive, life-affirming principles to live by, they will choose to step above any negative situation in which they find themselves.

1833. An attitude of positive expectation of another radiates to them, and they are able to confidently use this energy. This in turn helps keep our perspective of them in a positive place.

1834. When we experience a positive judgment forming within ourselves, it is forming because our own conception of life, others, or ourselves is expanding.

1835. On the universal level, we can only speak of the positive, for the infinite is beheld to be so much greater than the pettiness of a negative judgment spoken about it.

POSSESSIONS

1836. The more of our ego we imbue into our possessions, the more attached we become to them.

1837. We can collect material goods, knowledge, desires, and even emotions, but unless we are careful not to become possessed by them, they will enslave us.

POSSIBILITIES

1838. The world is full of possibilities. Every change effected by each individual or life form can potentially affect the whole.

1839. In seeing the positive, there is always a leap above the mundane, which produces lightness, happiness, and a more boundless view of possibilities. In seeing the negative, there is a narrowing, falling, and a closing of possibilities.

1840. The possibilities of the universe are at hand. The activation of universal consciousness begins to call them forth.

1841. Whatever we can conceive in our imagination allows us to think beyond present possibilities. We are then drawing infinite possibilities into our lives.

1842. The perpetual, boundless, all-embracing possibilities of truth and love are revealed from merely watching the sunrise, or a million suns in a deep night sky.

POTENTIAL

1843. Each moment contains the universe, and therefore contains the potential of the universe.

1844. We are constantly being asked by life to accept a greater part of the unused, unrecognised fullness of our essential self and give it consciousness. If we do not accept these gifts, we deny our full and true expression.

POWER

1845. Personal power is not just the energy of creating force or meeting opposition, it is the embrace, the integration and continuance towards one's destined truth. This embrace and continuance is love. Love is the most potently generous fuel for power.

1846. Power can be both centripetal and centrifugal. Apparently, centrifugal power is more creative in the outside world, whereas centripetal power is regarded as being more receptive to the inner world. Historically however, the most benign power has been that of a radiant centripetal power.

1847. Unless we act from a place of inner potency and power, we will probably act from a place of fear, need, and worthlessness. And if we fall into powerlessness because of the seemingly negative external situations in our life, we are believing that the outer symptoms are more powerful than the inner potency of our soul.

1848. Most of us spend our lives slowly losing power, gradually being defeated by our perception of external symptoms and situations, until we become enervated, ineffective and powerless. Without power we go fearfully, we lack confidence. In order to walk tall in our power, we need to become mindful of our true worth and state of being.

1849. When we live from our love, we live from the very source and essence of our infinite power.

POWERLESSNESS

1850. If we live helpless and powerless, we will be lacking the necessary energy of will, sovereignty, faith, vision, determination, and focus, that comes from knowing that one is a universal being of the exalted, most powerful states of love and truth.

PRAISE

1851. Praise gives honour and re-establishes one's conscious love. It is the act of heightening one's awareness of what may have become colourless or lost in the routine of the everyday, so that one reclaims gratitude for the love of infinite providence.

1852. Gratitude seems to be intimately linked to praise. Those greatest examples of lives lived in gratitude, such as Christ and the Buddha, are also the greatest praised.

PRAYER

1853. Prayer is the act of invoking the divine, in order to commune with the source of love.

1854. 'Thy will be done,' directed to the soul, would seem to be the greatest sentence of prayer.

1855. The most natural form of prayer appears to be practised in a meditative, contemplative spirit, where the ego personality is largely quelled.

1856. Prayer cannot be for the edification of our plight to an omniscient god, but rather, seems to be to strengthen our faith towards our purpose.

1857. We read in the bible: 'Ask and ye shall receive.' But who is doing the asking? If we ask as an ego personality we are cut off, we are asking as beggars, pleading to a distant mother-father god. From such a position we may never assume the fullness of the origin of our universal source. If we are to truthfully ask, we can only ask by decreeing from the fullness of the nobility of our souls presence.

1858. When we pray, it is preferable that we first place our ego in its rightful home. Then we pray from our divine self to our divine, where 'I will' and 'Thy will' become as one.

1859. A sign of our communion during prayer is that we re-enter the world charged with love and wanting to share this love.

1860. If the divine is within and all-knowing, then the divine knows our needs already. Our prayer then is to recognise and give thanks for the perfection of creation. Such communion with the divine will bring forth our faith as well as embellish our energy.

1861. Prayer does not necessarily need to be separate from eating, from sleeping, from making love, from work, or from any aspect of life.

1862. That which we genuinely pray for others is by the power of omnipresent reflection given to us also.

1863. How can we expect our prayers to be answered if we do not place the divine foremost?

1864. If we supplicate the divine to bring us our heart's desire, we may be inadvertently inviting an intermediate process of chaos out of which the circumstances of our desire will come to fruition.

1865. When we finish praying, it is apt we do not finish with a goodbye to the divine, but a welcome.

1866. Most prayer appears to arise from the ego-self, for the soul has no need of supplemental prayer, it is itself a living prayer already. This also explains why many of us have a sense of contradiction and discomfort during prayer, as we are attempting to force what we intuitively know is a spiritual ideal, through the body of ego that we are trying to avoid.

1867. Dare we seek to be in the divine's presence in our prayers? Or do we talk about ourselves all the time and not bother to listen?

1868. The human body is a living prayer. The more consciously we place the body into postures of sacredness, the more conscious our prayer, and the more this posture affects our attitude and state of being. The posture itself is the prayer. Words are not always necessary.

1869. Whenever we pray for the upliftment of one person, we are praying for all, for in the life of the universe we are all connected. Just as we cannot pray for one wave and leave out the ocean, or pray for one flower, without the valley filled with flowers.

1870. When we pray from the ego, the prayer is usually directed towards the ego-self. When we pray from the soul, it is directed towards the love of all, and this we find to be the most charged prayer of all. For prayer to be effective, it needs to be charged.

1871. If as quantum physics says that all time is present, then all hopes, desires, loves and manifestations are in existence now. Prayer then becomes a means of uniting dimensions.

1872. When our prayerful requests are long and complicated, we are praying with a certain anxiety in wanting to cover all bases, and therefore our faith is not entire. A simple prayer lovingly focuses our faith.

1873. If we pray from below the object of our prayer, we may lack the potency and confidence that more readily arises from praying above and embracing our objective.

1874. In our prayers if we supplicate for our ability to love, all other things are embraced.

PREACHING

1875. The desire to convert another to one's own point of view is a sign of one who is acting out of insecurity, the hope being that others' acceptance of one's view will confirm it. Fundamentally though, one has not come to a loving acceptance of one's inner being, from which a state of grace arises that precludes the need to convert.

1876. It is very compelling for us to preach to others what we ourselves need to learn.

1877. When another interprets our actions, assume they know, and then make decided statements, they are likely attempting to preach to us.

1878. If we practise what we preach, then there is probably no need to preach. When preaching, there is a tendency to overemphasise in order to convert the other. This practice of exaggeration seems to arise more from the preachers' lack of faith in themselves, lack of faith in their doctrine, and lack of faith in those they preach to. In short, it appears to be more a battle of faith within the preacher to consolidate their own doctrine.

PREFERENCE

1879. That which we give preference to, decrees the pattern of our individual and collective evolution.

PREJUDICE

1880. Prejudice is a selfish, preconceived action of the ego, defining itself as being small-minded.

1881. If we approach something with prejudice, it will not reveal itself purely to us, nor will we be able to appreciate it fully. But if we approach open and pure, it too will likely reveal itself.

PREOCCUPATION

1882. It is preferable that our preoccupations do not interfere with our sense of humanity.

1883. If our preoccupation denies us present-moment awareness, it is leading us into the realm of the unconscious.

PRESENCE

1884. Presence induces the state of being, and similarly being induces presence. They are synonymous.

PRESENT

1885. In the present we receive and create with each in-breath and each out-breath. Our calling is to become mindfully aware, allowing the receptive and creative forces of creation to occur naturally.

1886. When we are surrendered (not holding mental or emotional constraints) we are present.

1887. The full present belongs only to the awareness of the one who loves life. It does not belong to the ego and its many constricted or overly inflated energy formations that live always in the past or future.

1888. As soon as we think a conditioned thought or emote a conditioned emotion, we tend to move into the ego and away from the present.

1889. In order to live completely and freely in the present, we need to absolutely drop hold of our unnecessary baggage from the past.

1890. If we lived fully alive in the present, there would not be the need to spend so much of our time reflecting on the past.

1891. When we are not fully aware of the present, our past predisposes us to the seeming security of old judgments and beliefs.

1892. Each time we meet someone is a new present. We can either choose the truth of this present, which is to be in the state of love, or we can allow the ego-constricted thoughts of the past or future to interfere.

1893. The images we carry from the past, both positive and negative, can become an automatic response to things in the present. It is beneficial that we endeavour to perceive the present as fresh by perceiving ourselves as virginal beings.

1894. When we are present, we flow with the flow of life. When we are not present, we tend to resist this flow, to resist change, and in turn it is we who become fixed.

PRESUMPTION

1895. In presuming, we believe we have the right to make the prime move according to our own needs.

1896. Most presumptions do not apply to the situation. Most presumption is the egocentric mind's unresolved judging chatter.

1897. To presume beyond the familiar, is to prejudge a situation, and therefore likely to be one sided and without full knowledge.

1898. It can be both arrogant and foolhardy to presume of anyone. But sometimes it is better to live with the idea that there are helping hands and hearts everywhere.

PRETENCE

1899. Pretence is conditional upon there being a lack of truth between one another, which is a result of little or no love. Honesty is conditional upon there being a love of truth.

1900. To pretend that one knows something in order to save face means that we have created a new face, which has no knowledge of its subject matter.

1901. We cannot pretend and truly love at the same time.

1902. When we know so little, why do we pretend we know so much? Pretending to know so much means that we will be at odds with truth.

1903. To pretend to work for the success of something, while at the same time wishing for its defeat, creates self-defeat regardless of the outcome.

1904. Pretentiousness of some sort is a phase most of us pass through in order to reach towards the real.

PRIDE

1905. If our pride is based on ego-fantasy or ego-achievement, we will experience a changing, tempestuous sense of our self-worth. Unfeigned pride is more deeply based in the nobility, honour, and dignity of our soul.

PRINCIPLE

1906. A principle implies that one's actions are guided by the very highest understanding of love and truth. However, in presenting a point, when we say 'It is the principle of the matter,' it is often not a principle at all, but more likely to be our own stubborn refusal to move away from old dogma.

PRIVACY

1907. Privacy is founded on the belief that particular material things and activities are exclusive and belong to the individual. However, it will be increasingly difficult to protect the freedom of certain aspects of privacy in the face of ever-expanding information gathering and exchange. We need to define for ourselves what is most private. Clearly, the more we wish to conceal, the more our need for privacy. This calls for us to look at our raison d'etre, to specify our reasons for concealing, and whether these grounds are our best option.

In the end we discover that the only thing that does belong to us is our own internal experience, which is always private, no matter how well we can convey it.

1908. Only the ego thinks about privacy. The soul has no need of it. The ego wants to separate and enclose itself in its own private, self-oriented world view.

PROBLEMS

1909. We generally consider problems only from the problem perspective. Our resistance then reinforces them, and they loom larger in our consciousness. However, we grow in understanding and inner-awareness of our power by the re-routing possibilities provided by creatively viewing our problems. Such as reflecting on what may be the positive aspects, the opportunities, the learning, the payoffs for having them, what supports them, and what are the different ways we may approach them. We need to ask 'What do we truly want?'

1910. Most of our problems seem to have their cause in ego-assertion.

1911. When viewing a problem we have with another, if we take the emotive personality out of the problem, and instead place the problem against their soul, the problem loses its ego sting and we can begin to love again. (This can also be done with one's self and one's personal problems.)

1912. Rather than keep a problem where it may have started, in the past, without any possibility of a present physical solution travelling back in time, we bring the problem into the present as a new situation, we then have the potency of the present to bear a solution upon it.

1913. Everyone has the same fundamental problems in life, it is only how we face those problems that we differ.

1914. If we look at our problems as not being what is wrong with our lives but actually as assistants to help increase our awareness and discernment, we can step back a little, be more comfortable, less anxious, and more able to create beneficial changes. Furthermore, when we realise that our experience is largely perceived by how we think, then our evolution of consciousness becomes focused on an internal detachment from holding on to those perceptions that help generate extremes of experience.

1915. The biggest problem any individual seems to have is with constantly identifying the egoic bag of impressions as oneself, as one's primary focus of attention and being, when this is plainly not true.

1916. Personal problems and world problems, when viewed against the infinite universal background, take on their full and correct meaning, as well as assume their proper perspective.

1917. Any time we are submerged in the chaos of our problems, to remember the divine brings immediate grace.

PROCRASTINATION

1918. Procrastination is the avoidance of the fullness of the present moment. It is the exclusion of our true state of being—this is at the heart of procrastination. The most important factors are to reclaim our inner-peace and to begin.

1919. We can only act now. Our habitual avoidance of now, creates ongoing procrastination. We avoid now because we imagine it will bring unhappiness. However when we are fully present, without carrying emotional baggage, our experience of now is usually pleasant and fulfilling.

1920. The procrastination of pleasure is just as unhealthy, if not more, than the procrastination of business. To persistently delay the use of one's present energy denies the full expression of our immediate aliveness. Moreover, the carrying of this unused energy becomes a burden to us.

PRODUCE

1921. When we create and produce, if we draw on the virtues of the earth, our product will have the utmost value and harmony with life.

PROFESSIONALISM

1922. If we exchange our humanity for the posturing of professionalism, we are trading our inherent love for the vanity and selfishness of our socially conditioned ego.

PROGRESS

1923. In the modern world, 'progress' and 'development' are often euphemisms for selfishness and destruction.

1924. We must be very careful about what we say to others of our own progress. For in stating it, we give notice to the universe that we have gained to such a degree. In broadcasting it, we set ourselves up for a trial by experience on the very nature of our assumption.

1925. All progress can be determined and measured by its development and contribution to the humanitarian ideal.

PROJECTIONS

1926. We often subconsciously use others as a screen for our projections, or the ground for our shadows. These shadows and projections are an indication of the constraints of our own makeup. Our level of reactivity to others is an obvious sign of these constraints. On becoming aware of this, we can begin to reclaim the shadow, reclaim the projection, and reclaim our wholeness.

PROMISE

1927. A promise is a pledge to the future, which in the present, raises hope, trust, and capability.

1928. Only someone who is wholly living in the present can give a valid promise. If a promise is broken, very likely the one who promised was not living in the present moment when the promise was made, and therefore did not have the authority, or the necessary energy to carry it through.

1929. If we make a promise to another and we break it, we are also breaking faith with our own conscience and losing our self-integrity.

1930. What promise did we make to ourselves, to others, to the world, the universe, and to the creator, before coming here?

PROPHECY

1931. Love is the will of the divine. A true prophet speaks of this will. A prophecy that does not contain a revelation of love is not of divine will.

1932. We are individually more powerful than any contrary prophecy.

PROSPERITY

1933. All abundance, all prosperity, has its source in the divine.

1934. Every moment well spent in abundant, mindful happiness and wellbeing, automatically opens one's door to fertility and fortune.

1935. We can create something very valuable, but if we do so in isolation, we make it more difficult for others to render to us for our labours. For prosperity to flow, it seems preferable to have a radiant channel into the community. The more channels we open, the more possibilities become available.

1936. In union with the divine we can experience without separation 'To him that hath shall be given.'

1937. When we mindfully breathe the spirit of divine consciousness, we bear our original bond to the majestic realm of the soul, where power continually overflows into fertility, and we are freely able to render honour, quality, service, success and celebration.

PROVIDENCE

1938. That we are here on this spinning blue world, suspended in space by unseen forces. That there is land for us to live on, which science tells us is composed on its finest level of nothing but light. That there is air for us to breathe, and sunlight, food and water, is all a great and most miraculous creation. But this arrangement is also so obvious a setup, as to be heartily amusing.

PSYCHOLOGY

1939. The prevalence of pop psychology thinking, which its adherents often blindly espouse without fully investigating the thought structure behind it, is creating a new, perhaps more insidious, more subconscious, automatic cliched thinking than the cliches of the previous generation it purports to be insightfully replacing. Such blanket beliefs must not be allowed to cover an individual's ability to be self-discerning.

PUNCTUALITY

1940. Being punctual not only shows respect for others, but also gives one the freedom of reaping the full benefit of one's timely obligations.

PURPOSE

1941. Our primary purpose and reason for being is to love. If we forget this, our ego will tend to occupy our attention with erroneous and selfish purposes, and self-limiting fears and doubts.

1942. The difference between what one truthfully wants to do and what one thinks is the accepted, conventional thing to do, is that the former is found to serve one's soul and therefore the earth, while the latter serves the ego and leads to separation and frequently, depredation of the earth.

1943. We give our lives meaning through the purpose with which we imbue ourselves, and the ensuing faith and commitment of our will.

1944. Life purpose is a progressive and evolving design, which for most of us is lived piecemeal. If we look at those areas of our lives that are not being fulfilled, we may ask 'What is the purpose here?'

1945. Having a true purpose in life drives us onward. Have we addressed our purpose?

1946. True purpose operates against a background and a foreground of love, with the objective of making love ever more active and consciously apparent in one's life.

PUSHING

1947. If we are pushing to find a way, we are often avoiding 'being.'

Q

QUALITIES

1948. When we admire and pay homage to the qualities of another, we are helping to consciously raise those qualities in both of us. By this act we help transmute our own resistance and incompleteness.

1949. To be able to see the greatness of love and wisdom in another being, means we are beginning to become aware of these things, and consequently will yearn to express them ourselves.

QUESTION-ANSWER

1950. Predominantly, there are two types of questions we ask of others. One is a genuine inquiry, and the other is an attempt to belittle the one questioned.

1951. The more reactively a questioner springs to the defence of their question, the more self-interested their questioning of another is. Similarly, the more reactively an answerer springs to the defence of their answer, the more factitious, insecure and self-defensive.

1952. When being questioned, no matter how searching or critical the question, we can remember that our place in the world is already a reality.

1953. The answer to any question, or at least the first step to its discovery, seems to be somewhere within the sphere of the questioner; it is always close at hand. Answers are all around, not hidden. Hidden perhaps only by our habitual patterns of not looking, not listening, and not knowing that all around us is a unified field of life.

1954. If we ask a spiritually based question of another, it will be found to arise from our ego mind, and be addressed to their ego mind. We will not find the infinite in a finite question or finite expression of ego, and therefore the search from these perspectives will be ongoing. Neither can we ask an ego based question and direct it to the 'being nature' of another, for instantly we would recognise our own 'being nature.' Between 'being natures' there are no questions or answers.

1955. A constricting negative statement or question requires and deserves an expansive answer. The answer then becomes a statement of reality or intent, whereas the question was a statement of limitation.

1956. It appears that *all* questions arise from the ego personality. However, true answers will sooner or later draw us to the sacred.

1957. The question and its answer are not separate from each other, they naturally attract, they are halves of the wholeness of understanding.

1958. All questions and answers come from within us (singular) and within us (humanity). But inherently it is only the separation of consciousness that creates questions and answers. On the universal level all is one, and therefore there are no questions or answers.

R

RADIANCE

1959. The more a person expresses their inner radiant energy, the more they are interested in others, and the less self-absorbed.

1960. When we are internally radiant, we create more of the reality we desire, rather than being fearfully withdrawn and creating a reality we do not want. This is the difference between having the confidence in one's free will, and the resignation of fatalism.

RAISON D'ETRE

1961. Is there any greater raison d'etre for a human being than to love?

RANDOM

1962. Acts of randomness *appear* as unplanned acts of chance, probably because randomness occurs over deviating and larger time spans than are apparent within the perspective holder's time range.

1963. In the pure moment all randomness is in synchrony.

RARE

1964. The timing of something rare that enters into our lives has a greater sublime symbology.

REACTION

1965. The more impulsive and headstrong our reactions, the more subconscious they have become. They are an indication of old attitudes and beliefs we still carry.

1966. How much time do we spend on reactions rather than intentions?

1967. Our knee-jerk responses to particular situations, where we react without prior thought (not taking into account instinctive bodily survival reactions) seem to operate from our ego survival urges, which strike a righteous claim for fear of losing oneself, in order to keep hold of one's individuality.

1968. In reacting negatively to someone, we tend to suffer not so much from what they say or do, but more from our own state of avoidance of love, our heightened sense of ego, and the self judgmentalness that arises from this.

1969. Whenever we emotionally react, we are losing

consciousness, and likely to be gaining ignorant, or needy, or arrogant attitudes.

1970. When we react we are becoming unaware; we are falling into the abyss of our past unresolved wounds. If we hold on to the edge of the present by wilfully choosing to love, we make this moment conscious. We transform the abyss, we rise above it, and we create a light in the darkness of the subconscious.

REALITY

1971. Reality appears to be a constantly changing fabricated phenomenon. Therefore our reality and that which we think is real is in a state of change.

1972. The so-called 'realists' in our society are those who consider current reality as being almost set in concrete. This view is an illusory one (as agreed upon even by our science). A more truthful definition of a realist would be, one who sees reality as an ever-changing ocean of created possibilities, filled with ongoing waves of visions and ideals.

1973. Whenever we realise (understand), or realise (accomplish), we give those things consent to come forth, awakened and quickened into our reality.

1974. For many of us, reality is that which we comprehend. And such comprehension is largely based in the ego patterning of the mind since childhood, not the unbounded vista of heart or soul. Such a reality habitually extends only to the boundaries of the ego, and societal ego mind.

1975. With the enlarging of awareness, many past realities became obsolete. Similarly today, much of our present reality is being changed, or will be discarded.

1976. Reality is objectified (whilst also leading us into the boundlessness of the subjective) in the act of making truth more conscious.

1977. Our consciousness is drawn into whatever we value and

appreciate, and these things become more real for us.

1978. Visions, ideals, and imaginings are the forerunners to changing present reality.

✳

REALM

1979. The soul's realm is infinitely greater than the ego's realm, but often in our daily life the ego demands that its realm be made paramount.

✳

REASON

1980. The process of clear, consecutive, evolving human thought and understanding becomes what we call, reason.

1981. If we use reasoning to extract and justify a prejudicial decree, it is not pure reason. Pure reason intelligently embraces ethics, so that as far as possible, it is free of preconceived opinion and emotional bias.

1982. There is a greater reason beyond all human reason. It will remain an unfathomable mystery until humanity moves beyond the reason to have reasons.

✳

RECEPTIVITY

1983. Our ability to be receptive, which includes openness, sensitivity, empathy, patience, compassion, unselfishness, and attention, opens our hearts to love and opens our minds to wisdom.

1984. So often we push to gain more, but the very act of pushing can move the 'more' further away. Very few of us know the art in being a receiver of life's grace.

1985. If we are mindfully conscious, and our energy is outgoing to others, there is nearly always an immediate response in favour of the receptivity of others towards us, and a seeking of common ground.

RECOGNITION

1986. Whenever we meet another for the first time, yet we recognise them, then we are drawing upon our soul's memory, where they are already assimilated. It is a reunion with that part of our reality. It is easy for us to honour and appreciate them. Really, the more we love, the more we recognise.

1987. When someone recognises and flows with who they truly are, the outpouring of their joy kindles to life the joy and excitement in others.

RECONCILIATION

1988. Reconciliation occurs when there is a yielding of one's selfishness to the greater reuniting aspect of love. The conscious use of a detached and loving will, helps create a reconciliation of opposing forces.

1989. Ideally, before any kind of relationship can recommence after a dispute, there needs to be a reconciliation, a place of meeting, otherwise the dispute is swallowed, and becomes a long standing knot of ill-feeling and hypocrisy. It seems that forgiveness on its own is not enough. Reconciliation must follow.

1990. If we are not open to reconciliation with others, how can we live with ourselves, or with others?

1991. Whenever we heal a misunderstanding, or make friendship with a former enemy, the world seems to rejoice, for we have thrown off our shackles, and given love its freedom.

RECURRENCE

1992. If we have a recurring thought, word, action, or way of being, we also have a shadowy subconscious investment in those states.

REDEMPTION

1993. Love redeems us more than anything else. Love restores, liberates and delivers us with innocent atonement.

1994. It seems a basic human quality that we give each other a chance for redemption. In any civilised society even the most hardened criminals are given a chance. If we as individuals cannot give a chance to our lovers, friends, acquaintances or even strangers, it shows that we are closed to faith, and to the possibility of our own future contentment.

REFLECTIONS

1995. When one is centred, one is aware of the grace, true providence, and love and beauty of creation. All is witnessed with a subjective awareness. When one is not centred, it is as if one is viewing creation from an oblique angle, from where myriads of mirrors reflect ad infinitum. One gets lost in these lesser reflections, for there is no centre, no reference for who one is.

1996. The human body, mind, spirit and soul are all mirrored outside the surface of the body. Likewise, all that is outside of the human body is mirrored inside it. If this were not so, the earth would be totally alien to us, instead of feeling benign and existing as a place of beauty.

1997. Each area of our life is in some way, reflective of all other areas.

1998. It is a little simplistic to believe in the popular psychology that all that we perceive in another is within ourselves. Surely the emphasis ought to be placed on the word 'active.' Yes, all possibilities are within each of us, from the saint to the sinner, but which of these reflections are active?

1999. The reflections we see in our world, are just that. However, it takes direct seeing to see beyond. It takes direct knowing to know.

REFRESHMENT

2000. Just as we treat our body with the refreshment of bathing, the mind is refreshed and ennobled with a treatment of intent, and the soul with a treatment of stillness, quiet, and listening.

REGRET

2001. The value of regret is in the soul's gift of highlighting a more considered path, rather than remaining chastened with guilt and remorse. Honest lament is transformed in the actions of requital.

REJECTION

2002. It is the fundamental nature of souls to seek union with others. Whenever we are rejected, we sense the very basis of this calling has been denied.

2003. When another rejects us, our sense of selfhood is threatened, and we become aggrieved, in order to try and reclaim the apparent loss of our position. But what has been lost? It is not our own view so much, as the other's. Upon closer examination we realise that we cannot keep our position enshrined in anyone else's estimation of our merit. In fact the more wayward another's view, the less they know of us, and the more they are reacting from their own repressions.

2004. To be rejected is to be given back into the keeping of oneself.

2005. On the soul level we accept each other entirely, and therefore the most damaging of human activities is to be rejected and attacked by another human (soul). We interpret this as being unrecognised for our true self. During these times, it is important to remember who we truly are and if necessary speak of this, rather than get caught in attacking and rejecting another.

2006. Only an ego can reject another's ego. Our essence is permanently within every heart.

RELATIONSHIP

2007. When two come together to perpetuate their relationship, the supreme purpose of this coming together is for soul union. If egoic causes and conditions such as image, wealth, age, social standing, career, family ties, race, religion, nationality and so on, are regarded as more important than soul union, then we are hiding the truth under veils of illusion, whilst ignorantly thinking these veils are permanent reality.

2008. All so-called love relationships are in a state of passing if the lovers are not giving their love in truth. However, all relationships contain lessons to be learned, and therefore there is no such thing as a completely failed relationship.

2009. Most relationships appear to begin on the attraction level, physically and/or mentally, rather than embracing the deeper connection on a heart and soul level. Attraction is also the most likely level of subconscious projection of one's anima/animus onto another.

2010. There are many levels of relationship. Because a relationship may work on one level, for example sexually, does not mean that it is qualified to work on all others.

2011. Each of us seems to have received a wound of denied love in childhood, with a consequent inability to be pacified. When we mature and seek a loving relationship, many of us alternately chase a partner who is unavailable (childhood denied love), and deny someone who is available (inability to be pacified). We get fired up emotionally in those who don't want us, and are apathetic to those who do. Furthermore, if the one we are pursuing does suddenly show interest, often, after a short while we lose intrigue and attentiveness. The push-me-pull-you dance of relationship is something we all probably recognise.

This behaviour appears to be a reflection of our childhood

wound. Once again we are in the helplessness of that time, and are unable to satisfy our needs. In terms of self love, the subconsciously operating psychology seems to be that if we were not considered worthy of being loved unconditionally as innocent and open children, then how can it be possible for someone to love us as adults now?

2012. During the early stages of a lover's relationship when romance is strong, both lovers are pouring their love forth to the other, and to life itself. Often, after a while one of the lovers begins to doubt, and they look at what they are gaining out of the relationship. If they sense they are not getting back what they have put into the relationship, they begin to withdraw their love and demand more love from the other. At this point, their focus changes to a more selfish position, and it is this selfishness that makes romance wither. Yet genuine romantic love is always an empowered, unconditional giving, of a noble, beautiful, gentle love.

2013. In an intimate relationship that is unbalanced, there is usually conflict between the holder of 'emotional neediness' and the holder of 'emotional power.' The one who has the power imposes their will, whereas the other person's desire to please leads to a loss of self-identity. However, the one holding power is as much dependent on the other, for if their base of power, their partner, should leave or become assertive, they often collapse. Likewise, the emotionally needy one is dependent on seeking approval and placing conditions on their requirements of love.

At the start of this kind of relationship, the one who appears emotionally strong usually takes the power position, and the one who seems emotionally fragile, takes the emotionally needy position. However these roles can reverse during the course of the relationship.

This kind of relationship, though common in our society, has little to do with love. It arises from a wounded, temperamental, egoic inadequacy. Understanding these patterns will allow us to see the overall picture of relationship, including the primary relationship we have with ourselves, so that one day we may live in love.

2014. The principal cause of pain and trauma in relationship appears to be an emotional inequality between partners, which often results in blaming each other. This usually stems from a difference between what is implicitly expected and what is explicitly expressed. This difference is centred on the requirements for intimacy, in close combination with the levels of power and dominance. For example, one partner may be assertively dominant and passively intimate, while the other is assertively intimate and passively dominant. With such differences it is difficult to achieve emotional equality. However it is the implicit expectations that drive these behaviours, and it is these that need to be revealed and resolved.

2015. If we do not become aware of our ego's game and the ego games of others in relationship, then we will live as unconsciously reacting pawns.

2016. When we are emotionally needy for relationship, we are saying that we are available for unconsciousness, helplessness, upset, judgmentalness, reactiveness, aggression, manipulation, suspicion, withholding, and the loss of one's centre. Unfortunately it is the availability for a battle of wounded, emotionally needy egos. This is in contrast with being available with one's feelings where there is no wound or neediness. (see emotions contemplation No. 675)

2017. With true love in an intimate relationship, the lovers usually have a sense of wanting to slow the mating process, to allow a much deeper courtship to be savoured and delighted in, in order that a firm foundation for union be established.

2018. If we withdraw from another because of a perceived attitude that the relationship is difficult, we are withdrawing from the outer reality. The inner reality, regardless of our emotions, is ultimately one of connection with the other, and all others. The awakening to our inner reality is the responsibility of each of us.

2019. In adult relationships, the habit of attempting to correct and control another creates the false idea that the gaining of the upper hand will lead to self-freedom. Freedom arises more from the willingness to love rather than the desire to control. We did not come here to focus on correcting and controlling others.

2020. No matter how difficult our relationship with another may be, when we focus on those aspects that we love in them, then we are seeing the truth. If we choose not to see any love aspect in the other, we are denying the truth.

2021. When emotional conflict arises between a couple, it is easy for both to establish opposing camps that vainly attempt to win over the other. The other will usually respond in their own way, regardless of what we say. We cannot make them communicate in exactly the same way as we do.

Even with the best intentions and the wisest, most carefully chosen words, a high level of reactivity and a sense of blame or fault-finding ensues, to which one of the partners, sooner or later, warily accepts guilt. However, to keep peace and harmony, essentially each has to find their centre. The most accessible method is through conscious breathing. If each of the partners retreats to breathe for a while and find their centre, a sense of detachment from the emotional situation will result. Being centred is a great gift to one another. Once both are centred, love naturally merges the previous opposing sides. When this occurs, nothing really needs to be said. What is required is to trust the centring process. For who are we to preach to our partner? Their own soul is guide enough. And if we can trust implicitly now; witness life as it is without the contraction of our judgments, all that is left is gratitude.

2022. The societal expectation of relationship is that 'forever' is the underlying text, even in casual relationships. Our deepest yearning seems to be for a 'forever relationship,' whilst at the same time many of us keep ourselves occupied with a myriad of relationship experiences. It seems we need an intermediate term to describe this state, such as having a 'relationship experience,' a 'bonding adventure' and so on, without the unsaid but evident expectation of forever.

2023. When our primary relationships are in turmoil, we often experience transference of their turmoil to other relationships. Similarly, when our primary relationships are harmonious, we also experience transference of that harmony to other relationships.

2024. For the most part, our resistance in personal relationships is caused by a state of egoic unconsciousness, which results in opposition, confrontation, and standstill, in that we have not learnt to transcend our resisting experience. If instead we can recall our inner love, which naturally circulates from the heart, we shall more consciously move with others.

2025. In intimate love relationships, saying 'I love you,' often implies a sense of ownership and commitment, as well as suggesting, 'I want you to love me.' This is fuelled by the impression that the object of this love has instilled in the beholder a wanting and a needing. However, this wanting and needing is really a state of ego self-attraction. And therefore is contrary to the true meaning of the 'I love you' statement, which is that I have consciously chosen to give my love, my care, and my affection to another, primarily without looking for return, for to love is a joy in itself.

2026. The over-compliance of views in beginning, close, or unequal relationships, are gambling the broader range of the vitality of independent views for the seeming comfort of the narrow adjusted view. Such a view often leads to less truth, less passionate magnetism, and less love in the relationship.

2027. There usually needs to be an ongoing, conscious redefining of what the grounds of relationship are. For it is often subconsciously redefined by the input or lack of input of both parties.

2028. Being emotionally needy creates an energy of opposition to our lover which will eventually repel them. However, unselfishly giving love creates an energy of attraction that will make us more magnetic.

2029. The flow of energy in relationship and between relationships often follows a self-possessing or self-rejecting pattern.

A relationship may be formed where a self-possessed person holds the power position, whereas the other generally holds a self-rejecting or needy position. At some point the self-possessed person ends the relationship. After a time of grief and reflection, the needy person pulls in their energy and they apparently become more centred. They then appear to be self-possessed and often attract a self-rejecting person themselves. Meanwhile the former self-possessed person loosens up, becomes more sensitive, open and vulnerable, and forms their next relationship from the position of a self-rejecting person looking to one who is self-possessed.

This circling flow of energy can perpetuate until we begin to become more conscious. In neither position of being self-possessing or self-rejecting do we get what we truly want, which is to be nurtured either autonomously or protectively, for in both we lose our inner state of balance in attempting to get these needs met.

2030. It may be that in our obsessive yearning for a lover, we have not yet learned of the effulgent fullness of our own love.

2031. Seeking a lover is ultimately not a pursuit but an unveiling. The state of love is an evolution of awareness. The more consciously aware we become, the greater our ability to love. The more we love, the more we can be loved. This evolution of awareness may occur in the course of one relationship or in many.

2032. There appear to be two kinds of intimate lovers, the awakened lover, and the lover asleep.

The awakened lover loves because they recognise the soul of their lover. They love deliberately, intending to raise them to a perpetual state of joy. They steadfastly reflect on how this is to be done, all the while acting for, and taking into account the highest good of their lover.

The lover asleep operates from a place of dependence and obsession—primarily they crave a return for any effort. They continually fear their love will not be returned. And when love is not returned, or not returned in the manner expected, the lover asleep loses themselves in the societally accepted maze of lover's emotions, such as anger, anxiety, depression, fear, hurt, jealousy, loneliness, sadness, rejection, and hate. Ultimately the lover asleep is not a lover at all, but a selfish addict to their own estranged and wounded ego.

2033. The purpose of relationship appears to be to produce the dynamics for the unfolding relationship of the planetary human and beyond.

2034. It is not possible for an ego to merge in love union with another ego. If one or both partners in a relationship keep hold of ego as their means of true self-identity, they will be unable to merge soulfully in love.

2035. The emotionally possessing energy that most call love, which particularly occurs in relationship, needs to be seen as being entirely different from the truth of the non-possessing state of love, otherwise we will continually hurt and fool ourselves when this pseudo love operates, or when it departs. If we are honest we will realise that what holds most intimate relationships together is not love but ego based emotional control.

2036. Relationships on earth appear to be relative, but in universal terms are absolute.

2037. It appears that the primary foundation for an intimate relationship rests upon three pillars. They are: Passion, which includes sexual passion; Intimacy, which includes romance and friendship; And commitment, which includes the commitment to be fully communicative. All three pillars reach towards a single point above where the soul of love dwells unconditionally. To embrace unconditional love is the purpose for which the pillars of relationship are built.

2038. In surrendering our egoic needs in relationship we are surrendering to love's larger capacity and bounty. We open to the desideratum of love, where bidding and request flourish in place of demand.

2039. Deep in our core we yearn for the eternal lover. Unless we bring this yearning to our conscious attention, we will likely form relationships that will lack ultimate commitment, and therefore be limited and fleeting, even though they may last for the length of a life on earth.

2040. If we believe in heaven;

If we believe that true marriages are made in heaven by souls who are fully conscious, who do not take into account, looks, age, status, money and so on;

If we believe that timelessness is greater than time;

If we believe in 'As above so below,' that the sublime earth is a reflection of heaven;

If we believe that we are souls on earth;

If we believe that the soul primarily expresses itself through the heart;

If we believe that the heart is where love dwells; then we are open to the greatest possibilities of intimate love relationships with others.

RELATIVITY

2041. Everything in creation exists in association. To analyse an aspect of it without taking into account its relation to supreme love and truth is to deny the sublime relativity of all things.

2042. Einstein's famous equation E = MC2 interpreted metaphysically may read;

E (energy) = S or spirit

M (mass) = M or mind

C2 (constant light velocity) = T2 or truth, which is timeless.

The equation is now: S = MT2. All energy is spirit, and is interchangeable and flows into and from mass, which is the bringing together of the concepts of mind to create manifestation. It appears that the greater the innocence of mind (which is unconditional), the more powerfully attractive to love—love being the supreme force of union in creating form. Light is a constant and most powerful symbol and essence of truth. Supreme truth is universally timeless and thus without doubt. Therefore the relativity of creation may be expressed as, spirit = mind (form based on unconditional love) and raised in the universal timelessness of truth without doubt.

RELAXATION

2043. Whenever we relax into ourselves, the body/mind instrument becomes more playable. We are more able to express the deeper notes—the notes of love. We are more focused, more guided; our lives are conducted by the music of a greater symphony which surges beyond selfish concern.

RELIGION

2044. When our belief, worship, and ritual are founded upon love, and used for the exaltation of love, then we are practising the religion of the divine.

2045. Religion should not require anything harmful to the body, mind or spirit. And it must advance the eternal arts, mystery and understanding of the soul.

RENEWAL

2046. Daily and nightly we are renewed. Daily we are renewed from our experiences of heaven, and in heaven we are renewed by our experiences of earth. With each breath we are restored, with each heartbeat we are revived, with each sense we are enlivened, with every stillness, inspiration and understanding we are renewed.

RESENTMENT

2047. Resentment occurs from a perception of inequality, or that something we expected did not eventuate, and therefore we believe that we were not understood or valued enough by others.

Resentment often precedes wanting to get even through revenge. If we focus on resentment, we will likely seek revenge. Instead, it is preferable for us to re-focus on our deeper aspirations, whilst taking into account the meaning of our failed expectation.

RESISTANCE

2048. Unexamined and unexpressed resistance, for example to aspects of work, relationships, family and so on, will inhibit our own joy and vitality. Unexamined resistance creates stubbornness, indignation, defiance and self-righteous confrontation.

2049. Often, the more we resist the more we become fettered, and we remain shackled to our own antagonism. When we let go of the ballast of our point of view, we gain altitude from where we may see a panorama of liberty.

2050. The ego's resistance to truth is also synonymous with resisting love from others and from life.

2051. The greater our resistance to an idea, usually the less we understand it. Understanding is necessary for the acceptance of an idea. It may then be realised that only an idea, which has a sense of wholeness with an accompanying soundness of morality, can be fully understood.

2052. Most resistance is reactively emotional rather than intelligent. If we deny another or ourselves because of our emotional reactivity, we are not making a decision, we are being dictated to by a conditioning belief.

RESOLUTION

2053. The power of resolution is in transformation, for when a resolution is reached, one's previous beliefs, intentions, or way of being are transformed.

2054. Merely knowing that there is enough love and sympathy to resolve past resentful issues with another, can be enough to resolve it all. For it resolves the biggest wounds of all—the rejection and separation that both have felt.

RESPECT

2055. We may respect convention, or we may respect the soul. It seems difficult to serve both.

2056. To one whom we respect; we cannot help but speak our truth; it comes tumbling out.

RESPONSIBILITY

2057. Responsibility arises from our ability to respond, not just from surface egoic levels, but with honour from our conscience.

2058. When effort becomes strain, overwhelm, and struggle, we are not taking full responsibility for our direction or for ourselves in life. When our energy is consciously directed, responsibility becomes more effortless.

2059. Whenever we take self-responsibility we continually come into being, we naturally embrace greater energy, courage, and determination.

2060. If we do not take hold of our immediate responsibilities, how can we expect to take care of the earth or our fellow human beings?

2061. We are not responsible for what another says or does (excepting perhaps our children). We are not the guardians of fellow adults, and therefore it is necessary to release ourselves from carrying such a burden.

2062. I believe this era to be one of taking greater personal responsibility, rather than one that is bound by old scriptures, old formats, and old dogma.

2063. We cannot run away from the inherent duty and responsibility that wells up from inside, for we take it with us wherever we go. Similarly, the course of action and events that are attracted to our inner-duty and responsibility will also follow us wherever we go.

RESTRICTION

2064. Our most significant restriction is our self-imposed inability, holding back, and unavailability to love. This closes more opportunities than all others.

2065. As adults we need to ask ourselves: 'Who has the right to restrict another adult's life experience?' And, outside of the issues of health, safety, and consideration: 'From where does the authority come?' If it issues from wanting to control, then surely we are denying them their right to freedom and self-expression.

RETREAT

2066. It is to the benefit of all that we respect one another's fundamental necessity for retreat and privacy. From out of the rest of solitude, without ego arising because of the presence of others, we may partake in society in a renewed way.

REVEAL

2067. When we reveal ourselves, we may become vulnerable, but we are also allowing ourselves the possibility of greater union with others, for that which we are, is no longer hidden.

REVELATION

2068. There is enough revelation in each moment to satisfy the deepest of universal insights, if only we were to inquire what is deeply happening?

REVENGE

2069. Revenge is based upon the ancient disorder of unforgiveness, which created the divisive adage 'An eye for an eye.' Revenge is no longer the cardinal, self-righteous response for a human being who has deeply realised the oneness of humanity.

✳

RIGHT

2070. When we prove ourselves right, is it the kind of rightness that leads to an enlarging consciousness of our being and the being of others? And is this right consistent with the love of truth?

✳

RIGHTFUL

2071. To know what is right for us, a right goal, right work, a right desire and so on, we have to know who we are, so that we may choose a path and a goal that is aligned with this.

✳

RIGHT PLACE

2072. The right place appears before us when we experience being in the heart of all things. It is our being present in the present, yet it also becomes a calling when we are not present.

✳

RIGHTS

2073. If rights are made exclusive, are the rights and the exclusivity in accordance with the highest principles?

2074. It does not seem possible for an individual to make a selfish claim on divine rights.

✳

RISK

2075. We are already successful if we take a risk on releasing our inner potential. Even though we may stumble along the way, these experiences widen our perception and increase our understanding.

RITUAL

2076. Ritual helps not only to ground heavenly energy, but also to ground scattered earthly energy. If we approach ritual with fresh energy, we remain conscious and are able to feel the potency of our rites. However, if we allow ritual to become mindlessly repetitive and habit forming, it loses its power, and we lose present consciousness.

ROMANCE

2077. True romance is akin to innocence and a belief in goodness, gentleness, the pursuit of beauty, and the connecting of souls through the attracting forces of love. It has nothing to do with an egoic, possessive, sugary sentimentalism.

2078. Wholehearted romantic love primarily worships the beloved's soul. Their ego is seen as the flavouring image adopted by the soul.

2079. In the sacred meeting where romance is born, the relationship of male and female becomes worshipful, and chivalry naturally enters.

2080. We are all here to romance the soul, and our souls are romancing all other souls, and all is to beget union, blessed union.

ROUTINES

2081. Sometimes in the fast pace of work life, we forget that it is people who matter most, rather than things or routines.

RULES

2082. Rules are meant to serve the greater good. They are meant to be servants, not tyrants.

RUSHING

2083. There is no rush required to be more than who and what we are in this moment. For in rushing ourselves in the moment, we lose the moment, and we lose more of ourselves than we gain. When we relax into ourselves, we regain ourselves, and we regain the awareness of the moment.

S

SACRED

2084. Anything that we consecrate to the divine embodies divine virtue and becomes sacred. It then becomes a symbol of the surrendering of our ego, and of our worshipful gratitude. All things can become sacred through conscious reverence.

SACRED CALL

2085. The creator awaits the return call from the pilgrim worshippers in the temple of earth with their ultimate message of reflected love: 'I am that I am.' 'I am that.' 'Thou art that,' ad infinitum.

SACRED MEETING

2086. Because all things are connected, there is an in-built time for the sacred meeting.

SADNESS

2087. Sadness lays bare the weariness of dejection. We emote deprivation and discouragement because we expected things to develop as we wanted. And therefore we were likely too close to being absolutist in wanting our needs to be met.

SAFETY

2088. When we feel the absolute order of the universe, we will naturally place our faith in being inherently safe, regardless of all that appears to the contrary in our own life or in the life of the world. For in such sublime order, there arises the intuitive assurance that there is a place for the fulfilment of all souls.

SCENE

2089. If we have the impression that we are unable to appear in a particular scene, it may be good to ask ourselves who is doing the casting?

SCEPTICISM

2090. There appear to be two kinds of 'sceptic'. One who carefully examines and who has an open mind, and the other who is filled with doubt, refuses to look, and who has a closed mind. The latter is really a cynic.

SCHEDULE

2091. If we live life always according to a schedule, timetable or race, we will miss out on watching ants, speaking to clouds, and listening to rocks, as well as all the infinite, spontaneous, serendipitous and synchronistic delightful byways that life constantly offers.

SCHIZOPHRENIA

2092. We all to a greater or lesser extent experience the schizophrenia of the ego personality versus the conscience of one's soul. The marriage of the two produces a state of individuated conscient-consciousness and beyond.

SCIENCE

2093. During the last few hundred years, science formulated a system of logic and principles that was basically closed to other methods of investigation and perception. This system is no longer appropriate (even according to science, particularly theoretical physics). A new definition could be that 'Science is the art of discovery, of learning, and of wisdom, by whatever means which allows that discovery to take place.'

SEARCHING

2094. If we search for the divine through the ego, we will be searching forever, for the ultimate is beyond the bounds of the ego.

2095. Repetition tends to reinforce the thought, the action, the belief, the emotion, for better or worse. Therefore, if we reinforce what we are searching for, we tend to repeat ourselves as a 'Searcher' and we do not find. Once we become such searchers, the path can go on forever, and we become obsessed by it. If we reinforce and repeat ourselves as the 'Finder' and the 'Experiencer,' then we shall be reinforcing and repeating discoveries.

2096. When we are searching for meaning, it is important that we do not forget that which fuels our journey—our radiance of love to others and to the world.

SEASONS

2097. In all things there is the reflection of its seasonal nature. And to see one aspect is not it in its entirety, the rest of it embraces infinity and eternity.

SECRET

2098. A secret that hides truth is bound sooner or later to be exposed, for the truth is very creative in revealing itself. Any key to opening the door to understanding and meaning must by universal necessity, logic, and compassion, be made available. Truth cannot be exclusive.

SECURITY

2099. Natural security arises when one knows what one's true nature is, and because of this, one has a defined goal of integrity. This creates confidence, and freedom from the confusion of an unknown state and an unknown direction, and therefore one has greater peace of mind.

2100. The pursuit of security—of choosing to associate with those who have only similar views, of striving after paper diplomas of approval, of seeking peer endorsement—are all attempts to secure the insecurable. Life cannot be secured. It is a free-moving, expressive quality of the freedom and spontaneity of the bubbling spirit of creation.

2101. Most of us seem to wrap ourselves in training wires. We seek the conditioning and scaffolding of security. How few step freely and innocently on this world!

SEEKING

2102. All of us have been seeking since time began. The problem is that time begins when we step outside of the present, from where the true 'I' is found, and where time is not.

SELF-ABANDON

2103. We become self-abandoned when we love others from our true self without the egoic awareness of doing so. When we immerse ourselves fully in this love and become this love, the ego tends to be eclipsed.

SELF-ASSURANCE

2104. Genuine self-assurance (or self-determination, esteem, healing, knowledge or will) arises from the security of being aligned with one's soul.

SELF-CENTRED

2105. Self-centredness (or self-deception, denial, reproachful or righteous) occurs when we are centred on the ego; we cannot be self-centred on the soul.

2106. Because most of us see ourselves as being at the centre of our world, of our universe, that is, self-centred, we will not know the world, or the universe, until our consciousness becomes boundless.

SELF-CONSCIOUS

2107. Self-consciousness brings to the surface the latent subconscious fears we harbour, that we may then have awareness of them and begin to heal. Self-consciousness breaks through our normal composure and confidence in order to make apparent our inner residual turmoil. At this point we are more connected to our turmoil than to the source of our being. This is a process of the negative ego, the self that is isolated in the presence of others. The self that wonders is it good enough?

2108. Thc ego is unstable around others because of intense self-focusing and self-preoccupation, for one has forgotten the state of how to be when alone, and how to be with others. When alone we primarily focus on and commune with ourselves, and when with others we primarily focus upon them and the larger picture that surrounds us all.

2109. Self-consciousness seems to be a prerequisite for the development of self-sensitivity.

2110. We become overly self-conscious only in the presence of others. We are more aware of ourselves as having independent existence, and then become subconsciously guilty for our sensations of separateness. This guilt and its ensuing anxiety, cause the fear that the consequences of others seeing or knowing of our separate self will be their disappointment in us.

2111. When we are present around someone who is self-conscious, we too tend to be uncomfortable in our own ego. We want to be free of this sense of being cut off from others, of being divided from the forces of love and harmony. It makes apparent that we want to connect and flow with the joy of life.

2112. If we find ourselves shriveling in intimidation in the presence of another, it is usually because we are directing the heat of internal, often previously unresolved, self-scolding and blame upon ourselves. We can deflect this by breathing deeply of our innermost serenity, paying attention to the other person, and becoming more conscious of our inherent freedom in the present.

2113. We tend to become more self-conscious when we focus on the inward-looking needs of the ego to be loved by others.

SELF-CREATED

2114. Each of us, by the manner in which we live, decides the very world we live in. If we want to live in a world of truth, peace and love, we are obliged to live this way in our daily life, that we may create it. We cannot demand that others give it to us.

2115. We are constantly self-pollinating, self-blossoming; we are self-created, self-made. And we may grow a tendril of ego, or reveal the bloom of the soul.

SELF-DOUBT

2116. The greatest enemy is within the ego and appears as our own self-doubt. And because the ego is not the foundation of our being, or where we come from, it naturally carries doubt if we attempt to place the authenticity of our whole being within it.

SELF-EVIDENCE

2117. The truth is self-evident; beauty and love are self-evident. These contemplations are self-evident. They are known by what they bring; through the opening of a greater vista; through the sense of a larger self-correcting placement of one's feet upon a true path. Self-evidence is a primary key for travelling one's true way.

SELF-FATHERING

2118. If we experience little or no direction, or purpose, we are longing for the inner-light of our soul's guidance, to reveal itself in our self-fathering.

SELF-IMAGE

2119. Primarily we are image-creating beings, but largely pretend that we are beings of the reflections of others, or of something else beyond our control.

When we look into a mirror, are we causative enough to create the image we want or are we passively seeing a reflection? Without a life-enhancing attitude we will likely believe that we are only the reflection, and not the cause. It is preferable we see beyond the reflection of our life to create ourselves in our incomparable image.

2120. We are here to enjoy and to take pleasure in life—to create our own image. We create in our own image regardless of what we do. Why not create ourselves courageously?

2121. Essentially we create the world from within. We create it according to the image we hold, and thus, we are the co-creators of the world.

2122. When we are firmly in the realm of causing the highest of self-images, we constantly see our reflection in the smiling faces of others.

2123. We are made from the accumulation of images from our past, and therefore the past is ever present in our present, even from the very dawn of creation, it too is mirrored in us.

SELF-INTEGRATION

2124. The self-integrating person is one who is gently healing their wounded ego/body. Who is consciously probing their internal mystery in parallel with exploring the mysteries of life, the earth and beyond, in order to integrate their separated sense of selfhood with the divine.

2125. On the self-integrating path one realises that all needs must first be resolved from within, and then the universe responds in kind.

2126. The self-integrating person is also naturally a healer to others.

2127. A self-integrating person speaks more in the present, whereas those unconscious of it, tend to speak from set patterns established in the past.

2128. If we do not radiate our true self, our environment cannot possibly reflect a true self.

2129. The true self does not need to show off. It is impressive all by itself.

2130. Our thoughts and emotions are largely self-controlled, and these determine the integration and direction of our lives.

2131. Many of us are living false-hearted lives and therefore because very few of us are true to ourselves, the world is full of people doing things they do not want to do.

2132. Darkness and ignorance, lightness and enlightenment, are equivalent to being distracted and absent-minded, or attentive and aware.

2133. If one is neither focused on doing or being, then the self-obsessed thought and emotional processes of the ego will tend to dominate. These processes are for the most part destructive both to oneself and to others.

2134. We appear to be primed or already filled with that which we require. If as a boundless being I deeply recognise 'I am health,' 'I am confidence,' 'I am happiness,' 'I am love,' this is already my experience.

2135. The soul appears to operate something like 90% in the heart and 10% in the mind. The ego appears to operate 90% in the mind and 10% in the heart. Therein lies the contradiction of our power and our powerlessness. The most enlightened use would appear to become mindful of the soul's awareness in the heart, which then creates a bridge to the awareness of soul in the mind. The ego in both heart and mind are then aligned in integrity, and balanced to the inner divine.

2136. When we live in the tranquil happiness of the uncorrupted, virginal moment, the outpouring of love from one's heart becomes more subconsciously embedded, and we become consciously/subconsciously aligned with our natural state of being.

2137. To open the way to the internal one requires that the self who normally likes to take charge, steps aside. This stepping aside can occur through conscious breathing, meditation, contemplation, prayer, being mindful, thinking universally, through music, creativity and so on.

2138. It can be very easy to step over the boundaries of the true self to the ego self. From self-acceptance to self-adulation or self-condemnation, we walk a fine line.

2139. To be over mindful of what others think takes away the ability to be oneself.

2140. We all radiate, consciously or unconsciously. We all emanate the life of what we have concluded from our experiences, as well as our hopes, fears, beliefs, pains and desires. If we can still radiate love, we are in balance with our soul and with our reason for being, regardless of what has occurred.

2141. The world contains a multitude of beings in different states. If we are not strong in our own state, then we will likely take on the states of those we associate with.

2142. There is absolutely no cause or reason ever to humiliate ourselves or downgrade ourselves to others, or indeed to ourselves.

2143. How can we separate the body from the soul, or the mind from the heart? What is good for one must promise well in the others. Similarly, those things considered a disservice in one promote disservice in the others.

2144. Our outer self is created from what we have assimilated and what we permit to shine through.

2145. If we are uncomfortable in another's presence, our foremost requirement is to go within and feel the comforting peace of our inner being.

2146. All of our steps to wholeness; our yearnings, relationships, ambition, pleasure seeking, science, exploration, fear, pain, addiction, and disease, are the processes of looking for the divine beloved.

2147. In order to abide in our essential nature and true heart character, we are internally, gently induced to focus on loving and the perceiving of love in others, no matter how deeply hidden it may be. To make this our primary focus regardless of our self-requirements.

2148. It is the child in each of us that wants others to like us, the youth in us that seeks to make this attainable, but the adult in us that fears it is not always possible.

2149. When we begin to practise self-knowing, what this self requires, where this self is going, and consciously know that we help create this reality, our negative patterns, habits and vices begin to be consciously transformed.

2150. It seems very difficult to find happiness, peace and love, outside of ourselves, and yet the ego keeps up the chase. In reality these things are already present inside.

2151. If we see ourselves as being greater or lesser than others, then we are not so closely in communion with our universal self.

2152. Selfishness is a sign of the contracted, fearful ego. Selflessness is a sign of the open, loving soul. Selflessness is our true path.

2153. If we are not in the state of love, we are invariably in the conditions, attitudes, and circumstances of ego.

2154. No one is an absolute saint, including all of the saints. And no one is a complete devil, including all of the devils. If we only identify ourselves with saints and enlightened ones, self-righteously leaving aside care for murderers and thieves, then we have not joined with the universal body.

2155. In order to create the foundation for what we want, perhaps we need to be more the person we plan to be once we have got it.

2156. In the presence of others, many of us look passively for our acceptance in their faces, rather than affirming our own essential nature.

2157. To belittle the self is not being humble; to inflate the self does not make one more important. The central way is to speak mindfully of the truth in one's heart.

2158. The western psychological condition is more concerned with the egocentric, internal-external struggle with life. Whereas the traditional eastern way, was more active with a spirited sense of supplication and gratitude to the divine, or to nature. For both contemporary westerners and easterners, the re-learning of supplication and gratitude will help to dissolve the focus on egocentric struggle, to create a more harmonious way of being, centred and expressed from a macrocosmic reality.

2159. Each and every one of us is a self-illuminating light of the world. We do not need to stand in another's limelight, or hide in the shadows.

2160. Whenever we experience a constricting state, we are experiencing ego-mind. Whenever we experience a guileless state, we are experiencing heart and soul.

2161. If we think we are being holy, or generous, or loving—we are gilding our ego. It is holiness that is holy, generosity that is generous, and love that loves.

2162. Apparently we are here to eat when hungry, drink when thirsty, to listen and speak with mindfulness, to deal with things as they arise, and to love in the love realm of the present.

2163. Coming together and separating are ultimately one and the same, for we learn and experience from both of our divinity. Only when we cover them with ego do we endure suffering.

2164. The graduation of one's selfhood is the taking of responsibility for one's soul projection throughout the ego/mind and body.

2165. Egoic human is a mental creation. Pure human is universal being.

2166. Someone who radiates joy in being in their being, is the sign of one who is integrated.

✳

SELF-MOTHERING

2167. Sometimes we feel the self-mothering of our soul, calling us to enter into the acceptance and nurturing of an all-embracing love, particularly when there is failure, heartache, our needs are not met, or we experience a loss of meaning. Our soul compassionately self-mothers all of our travails.

✳

SELF-REPETITION

2168. If we are prone to repeat ourselves, as though what we are saying is new, we are clearly obsessed and attracted to the particular quality of it. Speaking it to others in order for them to be impressed will only support this obsession. Our primary need is really to hear it for ourselves.

✳

SELF-RIGHTEOUS

2169. When we actively regard another's actions and behaviour as being of little consequence, we increase the qualities of self-righteousness and arrogance within ourselves.

2170. The self-righteous require a good memory. Otherwise they destroy their own ground of self-righteousness when they obliviously carry out the actions they accuse others of doing.

2171. A self-righteous person is primarily practising a communication based in fear, and projected with anger. There is a drive, almost an urgency to convert others to their ego conviction, which rests more firmly in the past than the present, and to which they themselves have been unable to aspire. Hence they are stuck more on the outward form of their conviction and take a false pride in it, which appears hypocritical to others.

SELF-RIGHTNESS

2172. In contrast to self-righteousness, a person who is self-right is one who has delved deeply and found truth, and who is secure in their own state of being within creation. And therefore there is not the egoic need to convert others to their point of view.

SELFISHNESS

2173. Selfishness is the act of the ego cutting itself off from the rest of creation.

2174. Basically selfishness commences the traineeship of the ego in the drama of life, whereby the ego attempts to procure its sustenance from the outside world. However the path of selfishness is eventually discovered to be limited and unfulfilling, whereupon the infinite inner world of selflessness is revealed.

2175. Self-justification of selfishness does not usually create a union of understanding with others, rather it produces more separation from them, as well as a loss of one's inner truth.

2176. The forces of creation cannot be contorted indefinitely to a selfish will.

2177. If another has drawn in their benevolence, their charity, or their contribution, it is appropriate that we become more magnanimous, more open-spirited, more large-hearted, more unselfish and higher minded, rather than react to match them in drawing back also. For in giving we are made free, and in taking away we are imprisoned in selfishness.

SELFLESSNESS

2178. The state of selflessness is the state where there is no small 'I', and no egoic play of thoughts making selfish claims.

2179. When we give selflessly, especially of something we have little of, which may even have a lifesaving capability, then something miraculous seems to occur.

2180. If we let go of our demands through the power of unconditional love, the boundless and the sublime moves into the space that we have vacated.

SENSES

2181. The senses of an individual are the conscious foreground of that individual. The senses of all beings are the subconscious background to that individual.

2182. When we use our senses to look, listen, speak and feel within, we are returning to the inner world from where the constructions of our outer world arise.

2183. It is not a good practice to trust in only one of our senses at a time, particularly during times of haste, confusion or doubt, for we may see or perhaps hear something incorrectly, or add to it with our imaginings. One sense is only a one-dimensional probe into the world. The more senses we use, the more dimensions we have to confirm and corroborate our experience.

2184. If we are using our senses for greater awareness, greater consciousness, for an ever-expanding perception of our spiritual nature, they are leading us home.

2185. In order to internalise our senses; at the same time as consciously using them, if we attempt not to use them, we find ourselves in a midpoint of calm, gentle ecstasy.

2186. All of our senses emanated originally from the centre of the universe. We can use them locally or infinitely.

2187. When we realise that our true nature is the divinity of our soul, we use all our senses as holy instruments of the divine.

2188. If we think, feel, speak and act in order to worship the divine, we create a bridge from the ego of the divine human to the egoless divine. And all becomes a conscious celebration.

SENSITIVITY

2189. Sensitivity is the height and depth and width and colour of the field of our experiences, where the interactions of ego, ideas, morals, judgments, values, loves and so on, are shown.

2190. Balanced sensitivity arises from knowing the self well, while still choosing to live on the cutting edge of ever-greater self/world discovery.

2191. Highly sensitive people are attuned to the inner sensations which they perceive happening in creation to, and in response to their environment. Being highly sensitive allows them to be receptive to many experiences in their inner world, and helps them to redefine themselves.

Though, being overly sensitive exposes the ego to being easily affronted. The ego requires boundaries in order to sustain ego-selfhood. But in the overly sensitive these boundaries are not well defined. Being overly sensitive and open to all things, the ego fears it will be lost in the boundless.

2192. Whichever of our senses are most receptive are also the most refined, and therefore the most easily inspired, as well as the most easily chafed.

2193. Sensitivity marks the keenest response to our impressions, and therefore it requires the height of discernment.

2194. Our level of personal sensitivity defines our individuality. Our collective sensitivity, as the human race.

SEPARATION

2195. Separation can help produce a perspective for understanding. If, however we go further, and isolate, segregate and discriminate, this creates an egoic focus on those things which are regarded as being different, and such differences help create disagreement rather than understanding and unity. The truth is that those things that unite us are always greater, morally and numerically, than those things that divide us.

2196. There can be separation by self-affirmation as well as by self-negation. It is preferable to strive instead for union.

2197. The only thing which creates separation between ourselves and others, other species or the divine, are the beliefs, judgments and opinions of the ego mind. Beyond the ego mind reality is co-extensive.

SEQUENCE

2198. Everything on earth and beyond appears to be part of a sequential chain. It is a consequence of what has gone before, and will help create a successive effect in the future. The point of change, though, exists in the present. It is here where we may alter one sequence for another.

SERENITY

2199. Serenity reflects the state of being clear—the state that arises out of detachment from carrying and obsessing about one's concerns and worries. It is freedom from this self-imposed strife, a gentle joy in one's calm spirit.

2200. When body, mind and spirit are in harmony, serenity spontaneously occurs.

SERIOUS

2201. If we take life too seriously, we will tend to carry the excessive weight of our emotions, in mind and body. Once we realise that this burden is the self-created fantasy of our ego in the drama of life, we are more able to surrender it to divine humour.

2202. Does the state of seriousness really require as much attention as we are inclined to give it? The urgent demands of the anxious ego-mind tend to create an ongoing critical level of stress and sternness in life. Our most solemn obligation is to our soul, and to its absolute joy and vitality for eternal existence.

SERVICE

2203. When we serve someone 'love' is awakened in us and in them; it becomes more conscious in both our hearts and minds.

2204. If we allow ourselves to be a servant, then the world will always require us.

2205. Serving another's ego unconditionally is demanding. We can, however, serve the soul of another, where such devotion serves the boundless love of the divine.

2206. Are we really instrumental, the medium of service we allege to be? Or are we making claims to show how important we are?

2207. If we are to serve others, there is only one way for it to be performed successfully, and that is with joy.

2208. We are here to serve one another. In this way we shall know more fully the multifaceted bliss of the divine.

2209. All things are in service whether they are conscious of it or not.

SEXUALITY

2210. Lovemaking is a physical, mental, spiritual act, of generating the benevolent giving, ecstatic, ego-exploding, union-creating, motivation and inspiration, that opens us to our true state of being—love.

2211. In love and sex, the spirit, mind and body are ennobled and uplifted by the giving and receiving of love and pleasure. However, if one mostly focuses upon gratifying one's own pleasure, the spirit, mind and body are reduced and become contained within the narrow confines of our selfish expression.

2212. Many of us have an overwhelming need and desire for sex, whilst many fear it. We long for the ecstasy of union yet fear the death of our personal ego. There are immense forces operating here—the urge for gathering in towards the illuminated arms of divine embrace, contrasted with the desire to remain apart; both a centripetal and a centrifugal force battling each other, which in itself creates the pleasure, tension, and mystery of our current perception of sex.

2213. When we have an almost uncontrollable urge for sex, we are looking also to be loved, looking to be satisfied by another, looking for happiness from another, looking to have the pain of our aloneness taken away. Perhaps it is an indication that we are not outgoing enough in our love and care for others or ourselves. Certain loves not expressed seem to help create unbalanced hormonal desire.

2214. If we can reduce the sexual conditioning formed by family, peers and society, including such things as emotional possession, withholding and dominance, our innate sexuality will naturally arise and innocently seek and render a passionate pleasure.

2215. The desire for sex can be the desire to feel the electric current of aliveness surging through one's body/mind. We may have become lonely, depressed, bored or burdened by not consciously being alive. Sex brings us powerfully back to the clear emptiness of the moment, from where the vitality and zest of one's generative energy is sourced.

SHAME

2216. Shame primarily ensues from self-rejection; one rejects oneself by considering just how much others might judge and reject us. Having offended the customs of the group that one belongs to, one is disgraced and embarrassed before them and therefore not considered worthy of its benefits or of belonging. It is the ego that is disgraced, though, deep down one's heart and soul has not been recognised by oneself or by the group.

SHARING

2217. It is impossible for us to divide this earth equally among its inhabitants, for how can we apportion the air, the water, or the land? Yet each of us is a shareholder in it, as much as the earth itself is a holder of us. The share we are given is a most flexible one, it is that upon which we walk each day; that from which we breathe; and that from which we eat and drink. And because we are constantly changing shares with one another, our accountability is to make our share wholesomely beneficial, not only for ourselves, but also for those who follow. This is the only way such a share becomes profitable for all.

2218. It seems to be a natural part of human life to learn to share what one has, even as far as sharing the very best we keep for ourselves. For then, knowing the pleasure that others receive from it as well, enhances our own appreciation of what we have.

2219. When we are fully able to share the small things, then undoubtedly we will be ready to step out into the universe and share the greater.

SHORTCOMINGS

2220. Most of us are fairly conscious of our shortcomings as they arise, and appreciate the well-meaning love and advice of others. However, it is difficult to accept the zealous correcting input of some, for this usually places the ego into reaction.

SHYNESS

2221. The lack of confidence, distrust, self-consciousness and timidity of shyness are all a case of mistaken identity. One thinks that one is a limited ego filled with fears and doubts, and that one needs the praise of others in order to behold the good in oneself. However, our true 'I', is the confident, conscious, powerfully radiant, loving soul.

2222. It is difficult to force boldness from the shy, for this would be a contrary force not a supportive one. Rather, we affirm to the shy that they are loved, and allow them to grow in that love until they can assume this responsibility for themselves.

SIGNIFICANCE

2223. Everything in the universe has some significance. If we can give just a fraction of understanding to the existence of something, then our perception of life is enhanced.

SILENCE

2224. Silence is a golden oblivion—the still symphony of peace, where existence itself seems to fade into its pre-genesis state of rest and potential.

SIMILARITY

2225. We are all more similar than different. We all have a body, mind, heart, spirit and soul. It is only in the use of these things that difference is created.

SIMPLICITY

2226. Simplicity cultivates innocence and purity, which then reveal the simple freedom of truth.

2227. There is an in-built natural convention of simplicity in all areas of life, which for the most part is overlooked.

SINCERITY

2228. Sincerity occurs spontaneously (without having to work at being sincere) when we are more aligned with the guilelessness of our true self. Living in this presence, we are naturally open and freer from the pretensions of the inflated or deflated ego.

SINNERS

2229. If we believe that our true identity is the ego, then we will not be able to avoid assuming that we are the misdemeanours of our ego, and calling ourselves sinners.

SITUATION

2230. The outer situation is basically secondary to the primary state of our being. If we live assuming the outer situation is primary and our own state is secondary, we will find it difficult not to live out the role of the victim.

2231. Each situation in the present foreground has a background foundation and a future ground inclination.

SLEEP PREPARE

2232. Just as we prepare in the morning for our day, we can prepare for our sleep journey at night. Shall we wash our face, brush our hair, and wear perfume, to meet friends, lovers and bright destinies?

SMALL

2233. The smallest thing/experience is often considered of no value. But frequently it will yield and point to the greater.

SMILE

2234. When we smile we focus the light of love in our hearts and reawaken others to the light in their hearts.

SOCIETY

2235. The fundamental reason for the grouping together of people in society, is for furthering the fellowship of humanity, rather than giving importance to the divisive, separating trends created by exclusive wealth, fashion, and rank.

2236. Very few of us see ourselves accurately. In society we have learnt to deny ourselves the understanding that would give us self-knowing. And we imagine ourselves to be winners or losers, according to society's expectations.

SOLUTIONS

2237. To find a solution seems to depend on locating the key to the door of the problem, mystery or question. The key resonates more to the solution than to other options. The key usually exists in some form in the field of the one who quests, it basically requires to be noticed. The more keys we discover, the more internal and external connections are made, and the more we discover solutions.

2238. Solutions are best cultivated with a sense of wonder, which helps pierce through our barriers, for the solution may be on the other side of our constricted reality. If we do not have wonder, we cut down the possibilities and deny the joy of discovery.

2239. When a problem is divided into its component parts, then it becomes more soluble, not so fixed, and a solution unravels out of the dissolution.

SOUL

2240. Deep at the core of every human being there is a source of perpetual, boundless, inexhaustible, all-embracing love and happiness, which we have called the soul.

2241. Soul is our original nature of being—the supreme intelligence that creates life. It is the conscious consciousness of eternal love. It is the conscience for truth. And therefore because it is one with love and truth, it is omniscient and innocently holds the ethics of life.

2242. The soul ceaselessly observes whilst inspiring us with love, truth, beauty, and innocence. It is the bottomless well of courage that continually wills us to a conscious nobility. And its unfathomable, mysterious feeling allows us the most profoundly sensitive unity with existence.

2243. It is certain that we have a soul, and that this soul cares and has certainty in us. When we care for our soul we begin to align ourselves with this same certainty, and our presence, confidence and security comes deeply sanctioned from within us.

2244. The soul views with loving subjectivity. When we consciously step into the interior world, we are no longer under the influence of our everyday negative habits, emotions or temptations. Whenever we sense that we are moving away from the soul's subjectivity, it is timely we step inside.

2245. Ordinarily, companionship is necessary for happiness and peace. Yet worldly friendships are often transient. And therefore, at some point, many of us discover that our most lasting company arises from within the infinite.

2246. The soul is in love with the acts and procession of creation.

2247. Foremost we are souls. Our earthly experiences are secondary to this understanding and realisation.

2248. The soul is the unconditional lover who abides in stillness, whilst ministering and guarding the body/mind.

2249. When we observe our doing, feeling, thinking, speaking, and so on, we are more at one with our soul the cause, rather than the outer phenomena of effects.

2250. The soul lives with compassionate detachment. It may do so only because it has a greater presence, a greater vista than the perspective of the egocentric mind.

2251. The pursuit of revelation keeps human souls ongoing.

2252. How much accommodation do we give our souls in our lives? Do we invite them to be with us throughout the day, or can they only find the door open while we sleep?

2253. The soul appears to be a unit of expectant energy of love waiting to be called forth. It is this love that seems to have given us life originally and which now appears to take a background presence.

2254. The continual remembrance of 'I am soul' helps create alignment with our soul. Our cells and creative intelligence become consciously soul-infused.

2255. All souls are divine and therefore timeless. To say that some souls are old, while others are young, is to say some parts of the divine are old and some parts young. The divine is beyond aging.

2256. It is part of our soul's calling, especially when in the presence of others, that we serve, and silently render blessings to them. This fulfils the role of loyalty and reverence amongst heavenly souls on earth.

2257. Constant presence, calmness, joy, beauty, love, abundance, compassion, creativity, gentleness, humour, ecstasy, innocence, truth and nobility, are all inner perceptions of one's state of soul; they are our natural state of being.

2258. In the soul, all is already accomplished. When we act, and pray from the soul, it is already done.

2259. When we bring our ego into the present consciousness of our soul, the ego gently fades and we experience a deepening and enlarging of our presence. We feel a deep stillness, a calm self-assurance that radiates the dignity and majesty of the soul into our actions and our surroundings.

2260. We work consciously with our souls when we recognise the path of love.

2261. Our soul steps before the egoic 'I,' our soul knows the way. And we follow by letting go. The egoic 'I' lets go when we resurrect the natural fidelity originally made by our soul, to our incarnating heart. And deeply, we all desire to live from the authenticity of our hearts.

2262. Naturally the soul has dominion over the heart, which has dominion over the mind, which has dominion over the body. But often in our daily lives it is reversed, so that the body has dominion over the mind, mind over the heart, and heart over the soul.

When we allow the soul its dominion, then our heart, mind and body become spiritualised—that is, our feelings, thoughts and actions become consciously infused with the presence of soul.

2263. When one deeply realises that one has a soul like all others, all the differentiations, inequalities, and separations begin to fall away.

2264. If we only address human beings' skin colour, sex, age, nationality, culture, religion, politics, work, status, and so on, without taking into account the deeper but hidden place of the soul, we have missed the point. We have missed the most fundamental place of insight and union.

2265. The unfettered soul naturally radiates its love upon all it views.

2266. It appears that our essential nature finds its home in the infinite state of existence. This infinite state of existence contains a multitude of experiences through which our soul continually seeks to open us.

2267. Beyond the talkative, surface mind, the attention at the core of one's being is silently nurturing the human seed to a bloom of omniscience.

2268. Each soul has its role as expressed through the numerous and varied incarnations of human beings. In that our soul has a role, with its own attractions and radiations to fulfil that role, it has then its own being, its own traits, and its own nature. And therefore with the quelling of the ego we become one with our true nature, our true role, yet undoubtedly we shall still retain the sense of a particular perspective. This is well expressed in the wild.

Nature is considered one force but contains a multitude of forms and facets.

2269. Supreme sovereign power surges through each of our souls, and thus on the soul level, all is already known, all is in its rightful place. As well, we are also part of an opera of immense proportions occurring in innumerable galactic theatres.

2270. Soul is our true nature. When we step into this nature, we activate our senses to their sublime and ecstatic roles. We enter a deep stillness where calm, peace and knowing naturally arise. And we witness life unfolding before us as an epic poem, in wonder and appreciation.

SPACE CLAIM

2271. We have to be careful when claiming our space, that we do not become fixed on it to the extent that we deny others, and deny loving communication, for then we haven't saved ourselves, we have lost.

SPECIAL

2272. To acknowledge the specialness in all people and all things is to continually practise the presence of love, and therefore the handiwork of the infinite.

SPEECH

2273. We have been given the gift of speech principally so that we may share what is in our inner being, not just mere opinion.

2274. Speaking about ourselves is always a test of self-knowing. Some of us speak meanly, whilst others speak greedily. Very few of us, it seems, are able to find the middle path between these two extremes. When speaking honestly about ourselves, it is naturally accomplished with love and integrity.

SPIRIT

2275. Everyone has a soul, but the spirit is that energy which quickens the body/mind. It is the vital spark that gives fire to the breath of life. And therefore some people are apparently filled with high spirits, and are vital, well motivated, and have a zest for life. Whilst others experience tired or low spirited, depressed energy. Generally, the spirit is responsive to sunlight, conscious breathing, will, enjoyment, and devotion.

2276. The atmosphere contains *prana, chi, life force*, which are all the same spirit. The more we breathe consciously and deeply, the more spirit we embody as life force. The more we experience the benefits of increased energy, motivation, clearness of mind, empty mind, overcoming of obsessive thinking, overcoming of negative emotions, greater joy, increased digestive ability, strength, warmth, healing, and a feeling of co-extensivity with life all around.

2277. Humanity is interdependent with the environment of earth, but also beyond the earth, for the life field of the divine spirit is omnipresently pulsating. The universal spirit is the catalyst for life throughout the universe.

SPIRITUAL

2278. To be spiritual should not mean that we become exclusive and narrow, but rather that we embrace all forms, all life, with a whole view, not a self-righteous or superior one.

2279. To look at the physical condition of ourselves and the world, perhaps with some despair at their seemingly unbalanced state, without taking into account the spiritual context of life, is to ignore the larger, more vital, infinite workings of creation.

2280. A spiritual truth, in order to have earthly value, must be of practical use.

2281. A nation's spiritual health is similar to that of the individual. The spiritual health of a country cannot truly be equated with the number of temples, mosques or churches it possesses. Nor can the number of times an individual visits a place of religious worship measure their spiritual health. The state of spiritual health of both are revealed by such things as their humour, music, arts, love of beauty, truth, tolerance, ability to change towards the positive, benevolence, friendship, joy, vision, and working for the greater good.

SPONTANEITY

2282. The more consciously spontaneous we are, the freer we are to live in the perfect timelessness of now. We carry no baggage of burdens, we do not carry past based emotional tardiness. We are alive to our true being of love and to the infinite possibilities of the present.

2283. If we cannot be spontaneous, we deny our own natural inner energy that arises from the spirit of life, which helps bestow free will and freedom. When we are spontaneous, we allow this natural flow to our energy, which in the process self-empowers us as well as attracts others.

STRENGTH

2284. When we only become outwardly strong in mind and body, we tend to dominate others and our environment. When we become inwardly strong, our outer strength is tempered by compassion.

STRESS

2285. Love is the antidote to stress. Any time we have an excess of stress, is a sign for us to consciously begin to truly love.

2286. The stress of the mind is prepared and created by what the mind focuses upon. It is not prepared by the beholder of the mind. Therefore the mind can become the object of the beholder, which can view it more subjectively, within universal terms.

STUCK

2287. If we are in a stuck situation, then invoking the law of opposites (that is, doing the opposite to what we think, or is expected) can work miracles of change.

2288. The cleansers and movers of standstill and karma are love, truth, gratitude, grace, compassion, and focusing with faith on one's true desire.

STUPIDITY

2289. Nobody was ever born stupid, or born to be stupid. Nobody is dumb, it does not exist. Nobody sets out to be dumb or stupid, these are only terms for prejudiced interpretations of action.

SUBCONSCIOUS

2290. Part of the function of the subconscious appears to be as a reservoir for both the unresolved sublime and the unresolved suppressed. The sublime that we fear is too great to let in, and the suppressed that we fear is too fearful to let out.

2291. The subconscious reflects the conscious mind. Similarly, the force of the divine underlies not only the daily conscious ego mind but also the subconscious ego mind.

2292. We all appear, through the similarity of experiences we go through, to carry a set of subconscious tendencies, which we re-live again and again. Rarely do we deviate very much from these tendencies, except perhaps through sudden, exceptional circumstances. Thus, generally, rich people tend to remain rich or often quickly regain their riches should they suddenly lose their wealth. Similarly, those who are poor tend to remain poor. Some people attempt to train their subconscious in order to force a new set of positive behaviours. Unfortunately, whilst it may work for a few, generally others find that the use of force seems to largely negate the positive beliefs which they are attempting to instil, and the process becomes a battle.

If however, the subconscious is seen as a reservoir of abilities and powers, then perhaps we can readily draw them out by already embracing our beneficial potential.

2293. When we sense unease with another, we are largely tapping into our stored ego subconsciousness.

2294. Whatever is not dealt with in our lives is often suppressed into the subconscious, and then subconsciously recreated in our meetings and interactions with others, so that our internal frustration is then directed at the other's seeming, equally unresolved state.

2295. Frequently when another challenges us, the ego raises out of the subconscious with a childhood reaction of rebellion, blaming, or hurt.

2296. Our subconscious may tend to create haphazardly and negatively from stored subconscious negatives if we do not command our subconscious with a positive image.

2297. Largely it is the subconscious that creates our lives when we are not consciously directing. Many of the thoughts embedded in the subconscious appear to be unresolved thoughts from the daily conscious world, which were not consciously dealt with. These unresolved thoughts help create our experiences. And because the daily conscious mind is often unaware of these subconscious thoughts, the outer situations experienced in the world are often regarded as being quite separate and distinct from oneself, which in turn can heighten the sense of one's own ego towards them.

When we take an inquiring responsibility for our lives, we begin to become more conscious of taking responsibility for the without. And therefore more able to create the without in our own conscious image.

SUBJUGATION

2298. It appears to be the direction of the evolution of our awareness, that all subjugation of others and of other species will one day end.

SUBSTANCE

2299. Substance is the apparently solid phenomenon of existence, but in reality it is a slightly slowed vibration of infinite energy.

SUCCESS

2300. Success in mainstream society is largely dependent upon disregarding one's inner meaning and purpose in return for external material trappings and peer approval.

2301. The sense of success is experienced differently in ego-mind when compared to heart-soul. In ego-mind, success is determined by objective worldly success and usually has a sense of proving oneself and of conquering. In heart-soul, success is determined more by subjective raising of consciousness to know that which we already know in our depths, and has a sense of joy, wonder and rediscovery: 'I have found it!'

2302. What may appear to be successful on earth may be fruitless in heaven. Similarly, that which appears to be failed on earth may be victorious in heaven. Failure or success, judged by the measures of earth, are only half-truths. Heaven's measure must also be taken into account.

SUFFERING

2303. If we cannot come to an understanding that what life is presenting to our personal ego are the challenges necessary to move us beyond it, we shall become trapped in that suffering ego. The suffering ego imposes its dominion upon the body/mind with states of mental, emotional and bodily imbalance that lead to disturbance, disease, and finally death. It appears that we are required to surrender the suffering ego to the greater vista of the lovingly detached soul.

2304. When we see another person suffering and raising an ego defence against our helpful input, the lesson for us is to offer a more objective view, without the involvement of our frustrated ego.

2305. Only the separated, egoic body/mind experiences sickness and emotional deprivation. The soul is perpetually in wellbeing. On the soul level we are already healed, and it is to this that the separated, egoic body/mind is required to aspire.

2306. If we have become long-suffering, we have become resigned to the process. We may be stopping short of what it is attempting to move us to beyond.

SUICIDE

2307. From the sacred viewpoint, we are all eternal, divine beings. And therefore if one decides to commit suicide and kills the body, then the same level of anguish may still exist for the mind in the spiritual realm. For the problem is generally not in the body but in the persecution of the mind. Therefore, the only way to successfully commit suicide is to renew the mind. This is done by changing one's current negative mindset for a new set of thoughts, without the need to destroy the body.

SUPERSTITION

2308. Superstition arises from the naive belief that the subconscious ego is god.

SUPPORT

2309. When falling into the depths of despair, our support will often come to us from the most unexpected sources. Our eyes are opened to the previously unseen care, understanding, and encouragement of others.

SURFACE ISSUES

2310. If deep down our souls are all enlightened, then the surface issues between us are only the act of ego assertion and ego attraction. And therefore to see others as a result of seeing only this play, and to place greater importance on this performance, is to believe more in the ego and less in the soul.

SURRENDER

2311. When we voluntarily surrender, we render our claim to what we are possessing (which for the most part is the giving up of a state of ego mind). In the process, we open, and are softened, and we regain the grace of innocence, compassion and humanity.

2312. Once we have made a choice and we desire its manifestation, at some point prior to its fulfilment, we invariably reach the altar of surrender, where we are given the opportunity to acknowledge the divine, in order that we may recognise the higher powers of unconditional love.

2313. The ego feeds upon shadow, projection and separation. To the ego, the thought of surrender is like death. However when we are bold and we do surrender, ego death melts away and is replaced with the joy of reconnection to life.

2314. Upon reaching the portal of surrender, we pass through abandoning the old driven self, and yield to the light of a new path and a more potent inner power; and often, miraculously, that which we have pursued begins to pursue us.

2315. If we are becoming obsessed with routine, habit, lack of time, being stressed, or anxious about outcomes, it is opportune for us to surrender.

2316. It is far better to surrender a point to someone intent on making it, than to surrender one's true self to the heat of the moment.

2317. We become more self-sufficient and self-supportive when we surrender the ego-self to our loving of others.

2318. Until we surrender ourselves to the benevolence of the divine, we will still be attempting to make our own way in the world. We shall find that the world will create obstructions to our ego, and we will create our own stress to these obstructions, and thus we shall live in fear of not having our needs met.

2319. The one who is self-surrendered can approach any situation, any being, and give their love without fear.

2320. At the altar of surrender, our prior karmas are balanced—and therefore our desire is made more whole, more holy.

SUSPICION

2321. We must not forget that suspicions are also guesses based on beliefs. These beliefs usually arise from a prior conception of loss, which creates a tendency for us to emote doubt and distrust, from where we believe others to be guilty. Truth then becomes a commodity to be fought over and possessed, so that even the truth itself may be regarded suspiciously.

2322. When a suspicion is held, there is a tendency to prejudge and find guilt. In order to approach our suspicions in a balanced way, we need to be equally willing to find innocence.

2323. The expression of suspicion is largely a repugnant act, unless we have directly seen, heard, and truthfully understood the circumstances, in which case it is no longer a suspicion.

SYMBOLS

2324. A potent symbol is an external image that embodies the axiomatic principle of the thing it represents. It becomes the gateway to the core truth, the knowledge of which causes the beholders of this truth to unite.

SYMPATHY

2325. To fully sense and know the pain of another in our own heart and conscience does not seem possible. And yet if we overly identify with commiserations of pity, worry, or anger, we may encourage their anguish whilst also being unable to offer the clarity of an objective discernment. A non-possessive, loving sensitivity allows us to respond with equanimity. Such equanimity not only helps others integrate their suffering, but also helps transform the way we view our own pain and needs.

2326. The deeper our embodiment of love, the more extensively our sympathy and compassion radiates to other human beings, animals, birds, fish, insects, plants, rocks, rivers, oceans, the earth itself, and beyond to the sun, moon, and stars. Through the power of love we feel a greater harmony, understanding, and union with all.

SYMPTOMS

2327. Any kind of symptoms, be they mental, emotional, bodily or environmental, are not created to oppress us; they are not there to be worried about, feared over, or to seek sympathy from in others. They are there as directors to do something, to try again, and to contemplate what it is that our body/mind/earth is attempting to teach us through these symptoms.

SYSTEM

2328. We all live in a system, which is part of the universal system. The solar system appears to operate precisely on the 'As above, so below' principle, and therefore we can see its ramifications on the systems operating on earth, as well as the systems evident in the universe through our observations. These systems are well ordered, efficient, coordinated, and combine to form an ultimate unity.

For a system to operate well requires great will, as is evident in systems devised by humans. And therefore universal systems are also likely to require will. This will is undoubtedly benevolent. Supreme benevolent will is divine. The will of the divine is love. Therefore the ultimate system apparently operates by the power of love. And we as human beings key into this system by our will to love.

2329. The system we live in is an opening system. What we think, say and do affects others, ourselves and vice versa. It is our calling to learn from our actions, what creates harmony and what does not. Inevitably love is the supreme way to open our system.

SYSTEM, THE

2330. The so-called system is not a machine. It is personal faces. It is people.

T

TASTE

2331. When we are ready for a higher taste; customary, established, and habitual tastes fail to satisfy.

2332. The personal taste of each being shows the manifold taste of the divine.

TEACHER

2333. The more noticeable the difference between a spiritual teacher's public presentation, and their normal daily state, the more they are performing and thus overly ego-identified. The less the difference, the more they are self-integrated.

2334. An audience often expects a spiritual teacher to have a particular persona and image, for example to dress in robes of some kind, to be gentle, softly spoken, act humble, to have a permanent smile, and appear to be above the mundane cares of the world. This is for the most part an illusion, which some teachers help to promulgate. This unreal view of spirituality places it far beyond what those in the audience can aspire to in their daily lives.

TEACHING

2335. Everyone has awareness, and therefore if we teach or counsel, we are merely helping to bring forth what is known in the subconscious to the light of consciousness.

2336. To be able to admit to another's teaching is to acknowledge the greater body of which we are all a part. If we allow another to teach and then say 'But I already know this,' often means that we are allowing our ego to cover the gap in our knowledge with a plug of defiant independence. If we cannot accede and bow to others, we will not be able to truly receive or truly serve.

2337. All things, without exception, have the ability to teach us. The day this was written, a dog's unconditional love was the shining example of a true path.

TEMPTATION

2338. Serious temptation urges us onward with the promise of gain (which is never satisfactorily delivered). And after we have given in to temptation, the result is that we sense a loss of our self, of our fundamental innocence.

2339. Temptation is a testing door at a crossroads on our path. If we choose temptation, it can become a revolving door.

2340. Success brings not only a greater capacity for good and joy, but also it seems a greater capacity for temptation.

2341. Temptation is like a coin. On one side we read in dull relief 'Unwise to continue,' and on the other side all shiny and bold 'Why not take a gamble?' But if we take time to examine the shiny side, rub it a little with an inquiring mind and ask 'What are the benefits?', we realise that the shine is only on the surface, and that what we are being tempted by is something which only has the illusion of shininess—its true worth is questionable.

TENDENCY

2342. It appears that the more automatic our tendencies become, both positive and negative, the more unconscious we become. Tendencies, once begun, have the proclivity to become subconsciously embedded and generated.

TENSION

2343. Tension creates dissociation and constriction, as well as tightens our ego towards others, life and ourselves. However the significance and meaning of tension is that it is urging and teaching us to open up, to embrace, and to love.

2344. The more unresolved tension we carry, the more reactive we become to outside stimuli.

TEST

2345. We are all constantly tested by life through our interactions with others and with nature. The standard by which our learning and understanding is measured, is in how willingly aligned we are to the forces of love and truth.

THE FALL

2346. The fall is experienced whenever one believes that one is a self-obsessed ego as opposed to the universal 'I am.'

THE 'I'

2347. Who is this 'I'? Are we the 'I' that thinks? It appears that an 'I' emerges out of a sense of one's separated consciousness. This self-consciousness arises in the mind. But where is the mind and how far does it extend? How far away can our thoughts affect others? Is our sense of self just a series of interlocking thoughts built upon each other over the passing of years? Who initially started these thoughts?—Probably our parents, grandparents and so on. Before these thoughts who were we? Perhaps contemplating this will give an indication of the true I. As soon as this self-consciousness thinks, there appears to be a separating energy sent forth, which creates an active reflection in the mirror of creation. Similarly and most fundamentally, if we experience the state of still presence beyond the realms of self-conscious thought, the universe reflects this also, yet passively with grace. If this separated sense of self is a collection of thoughts and beliefs built since childhood, we realise upon examination that these thoughts were mostly created from the conditioned daily conscious mind of our parents, which are largely made of subconscious thought. If these subconscious thoughts determine our sense of self, regardless of how well we function in the world, we will be living through a limited self. Once we discover this we begin to move beyond the realm of the self-conscious I, and we discover real free will. Inevitably this free will points to the universal I.

2348. If we say 'I know' or 'I do not know,' we are speaking from a false identification of I with ego. The 'I' is a state of being; it is not a state of the conditioned mind.

*

THOUGHT

2349. Thinking is our fundamental ego-creating ability. Primarily we think by conceiving, experimenting, discovering, and reflecting, in order to give life to the particular path that the personal ego desires to create and follow.

2350. When we have thoughts it is advisable to witness them, that is, to bring in the larger perspective of the soul to keep balance.

2351. The internalised monologue we carry is both symbolic of, as well as a yearning for, communion or dialogue with the divine.

2352. Unwitnessed thoughts passing through one's daily conscious mind can become despotic, psychological rulers, directing one's consciousness away from being fully alive in the moment of presence.

2353. Most of the time we spend in obsessive thinking does not provide us with solutions or fulfilment, and denies us a place of inner stillness from where we may love.

2354. Thoughts and ideas are largely useless unless they are acted upon or embraced to further one's understanding.

2355. To see where our reflections arise, by following them to their source, makes clear a deeper reality, and removes surface ripples of confusion.

2356. Whenever we think a new thought which instantly increases our energy and state of well being, so that we feel larger and more boundless, we have located a thought that the body/mind was hungry for. This thought increases our zestful vibration and therefore our ability to access a greater range of possibilities.

THOUGHT ROOM

2357. We all live in rooms, which can be defined by our senses. They can be a bedroom, a lounge room, an office, a car, a shop, a theatre, a beach, a forest, and so on. In other words, whatever our senses can encompass at any one time is the room in which we are currently living. If we were to really live and be present in each room as we journey through life, we would largely be able to quell the discursive mind from nagging, worrying, and fearing what is happening in the other rooms.

THREATS

2358. When threatened, many of us regress to the primitive reactionary mind of our childhood. The fallout of unresolved anger, threats of punishment, and emotions of rejection that we experienced as children come flooding back into our current state, and we become driven and reactive. If we can awaken to the moment, and realise where these emotions mostly arise from, we can respond in a less reactionary way. By breathing deeply and speaking slowly and mindfully, we help regain the present link to our true state.

TIME

2359. On earth our time measures a constant slipping into the past, or a projection into the future. However the present moment seems difficult to measure. If we attempt to measure it, it slips away and our consciousness is lost with it in the past. And therefore our daily conscious mind also has the tendency to slip beyond and behind the moment, where time is—in the beyond and the behind, but full consciousness is not.

2360. Our impressions of time are often dictated by our emotional response. The crossover point from time into timelessness arises from being harmoniously centred in the present.

2361. The perception of time is within us. Ultimately therefore, time cannot lag behind us nor rush ahead, for timelessness appears to be the deeper truth of our soul.

2362. There is a natural flowing spirit in life, that once disturbed, by compartmentalising, regimentation, and over-control, we call time.

2363. Ego time is a constant variable. Soul time is timeless, it is a variable constant.

2364. Time is relative to the degree of consciousness, and therefore the view this consciousness produces. If our consciousness becomes multi-dimensional then the linear view of time will have less importance.

2365. When one has a joyful heart, one's internal clock runs precisely, and finds a harmonious beat with all other things to which it connects. Whether it is catching a bus on time, a chance meeting with a kindred spirit, or revealing moments of serendipity.

2366. In the macrocosmic view, time appears to cease in the unconfined field of the universal eternal now. Whereas in the microcosmic view, time appears to be like the spring of a flowing river, forever running into the past. When we embrace the macrocosmic view, we replace the anxiety causing flow of time consumed, and live in the contentedness of the eternal.

2367. Time is essentially an egoic, separating, limited concept, of oneself and others, existing in a self-delineating system upon the earth. However, against the universal background it loses its significance upon the infinite cascading waves of stillness and timelessness.

2368. If others consistently do not abide by our time schedule, then time is usually teaching us to slow down, and re-enter the rest and stillness of timelessness in the present.

2369. Time apparently creates distance from our ego triumphs as well as our ego misdemeanours, yet to the witnessing soul these are all apparent now. From the soul's view, these things being apparent now, naturally engenders love, understanding and compassion.

2370. Only when time operates do ego desires arise—such as to possess others, material goods, land and so on. Being conscious in the infinite present, there is union with all.

2371. Time can never exist in the now. It was, or may yet be, but it is not present in the present. The moment is now, it is the only place (but neither is it a place) where full consciousness is present.

2372. The equation of time is $\frac{\text{distance}}{\text{speed}} = \text{time}$.

We are told by our science that the earth travels through space at more than 100,000 km per hour, but on the planet's surface there is no sense of this kind of velocity. In other words, time is a background phenomenon, but in the foreground of the present it is not observable. Furthermore, in deep space there is also little sense of the earth's velocity or the velocity of other celestial bodies in the present moment. All stays in harmony and in a state of relativity to each other, so that everything is moving, but also appears to be fairly stable because of this relativity. The energetics of time seem to be much more concerned with the operation of universal dynamics, that is, the movement of celestial bodies to primarily cause energy flows and for the creation of new forms, than with anything so mundane as measuring illusory frames of reference.

2373. Whenever we act without ego consciousness of acting, when we do in the presence of being, the speed and distance of time lose significance.

2374. Quantum physics as well as metaphysics say that time is not just a single linear phenomenon, that all time is present in simultaneously existing lines. Therefore all creation must be present. All so-called pasts and futures exist now. However, because we use only one view of time, one line of time predominates. When we become fully present, we enter the presence of all created and self-created possibilities. Perhaps we need only to begin changing our current beliefs in order to enter a multi-dimensional universe.

2375. If all time is now, eternity is now also. In the present, time dissolves into timelessness. And thus eternity is not something that exists in a distant future.

2376. When I am co-extensively present, time does not occur. If I was always this present, time for me would cease entirely, the ego would not arise, and selfish expression would not appear. If this were extrapolated to all, much of our present civilization would not come to pass.

2377. Time is relative, but souls are absolute.

TIMELESSNESS

2378. If heaven is a place of timelessness, then by the power of 'As above, so below,' we have the possibility of timelessness on earth. The inhabitants of heaven must live in the place where time is not. Perhaps it is the eternally present moment.

2379. Living our lives with a sense of timelessness gives us the freedom to be true to ourselves.

2380. Whenever we live in the moment, we live in the infinite zone of timelessness, and we have as much timeless space as we require.

TIMING

2381. Timing (or coincidence) seems much more important than time. Timing, or the placing of events in sympathy or antipathy, occurs that there may be an acknowledgment of cause, and therefore an understanding of life.

2382. There are times to be still and times to act. If we are still during a time of action, we may lose the opportunity to be a cause. If we act during a time of stillness, we may be acting prematurely.

2383. When we are centred, timing occurs naturally in our lives, and our life experiences and interactions with others are open and relaxed.

TINKERING

2384. If we tinker with things during a negative or blocked emotional state, using this same state, we invariably tinker with results and not causes. We need in some way to transcend in order to make change.

TOLERANCE

2385. Tolerance results from having a greater view. A global view, then a universal view opens our resistance to wider horizons of acceptance.

2386. If we are tolerant beyond the idea that we are being tolerant, we are naturally tolerant.

TOOTHPASTE

2387. In the vast arrangement of the universe, of numberless galaxies, super novae, black holes, pulsars, comets, stellar clouds of suns and moons and planets, the fact that one's lover has left the top off the toothpaste tube—well, it doesn't bear thinking about does it!

TOPICAL

2388. Whatever is topical in our daily consciousness is frequently seen in others and in situations in the outer world. With a conscious use of this knowledge, we can more choose to create the world we wish to live in.

TOUCHING

2389. When we touch our bodies, we are touching the stars. We are touching the centre of the alpha and omega of creation. We are touching the blossom of primordial conception. We are touching the genesis of universal omniscience.

TRADITION

2390. Tradition confers a certain order and stability. Though it is not meant to overly dictate to the present or deny the new.

TRANSACTION

2391. Every transaction contains within it the seasonal flow of the earth and beyond.

TRANSCEND

2392. The universe appears to be in deep stillness but also an ocean of change that is constantly transcending. And therefore it is permanently transcended to a sublime transcending excellence.

2393. When we ascend and step above symptoms, negative states and effects, we are in a state of transcendence to a higher vibration of love.

2394. It appears that all except love and truth can be transcended.

TRAVEL

2395. Through travel to new destinations, we have the opportunity, freedom, and fresh attention to negotiate a particular path by which we may cross to a deeper understanding and meaning of one's role in the world. And one day beyond—of earth's place in the cosmos and of one's part in the universe.

TRIALS

2396. The trials in our lives are not there to oppress us, but to give meaning, that we may contemplate and delve into our inner life, where we find stillness, harmony, deep love, and deep truth. And there to behold the larger picture, so we may continue to mould our lives towards the freedom of our real nature.

TRIVIALITIES

2397. The soul soars infinitely above the trivialities of ego. Whenever we are caught in trivialities we have forgotten our true essence.

2398. If we allow our internal state to be dictated to by dirty dishes and clothes, toothpaste tubes, lateness, burnt food, car trouble, and a myriad other trifles, it is apparent that our internal state is very fragile. Often, our controlling, angry ego is seething just below the surface of a clandestine mask. How will we find deep peace if our internal state is dominated by such trivialities?

TRUST

2399. To trust first requires that we respect, that we appreciate and regard highly. From this comes our confidence, where we confidently expect our deep desire, our will, to be fulfilled. Having such confidence means we can act with self-discerning assurance. This assurance gives loyalty and dependability. And all of this demonstrates our faith.

2400. The one who has trust in life is dearly loved.

2401. When we trust we allow ourselves to deeply know our own truth.

2402. Trust can be blind or conscious. If it is blind, the means as well as the objective are naively unclear. We may be acting out of conditioning, of possessiveness or of social politeness and a sense of duty, in which case it is not really trust, for it lacks the love that comes with conscious trust. When there is conscious trust it is accompanied by an intuitive knowing.

2403. If we trust, regardless of the current external circumstances, our trust will bring us all we need to know for our next step.

2404. When we do not trust in the divine, we give up our essential loyalty to our soul from where our deep will and confidence arise. We compromise our ability to walk our true pathway for one that is doubtful and therefore insecure. And our resultant insecurity is thus founded on our inability to trust.

2405. Whenever we totally trust in the divine, then all is apparent here.

2406. The greatest trust appears to be to trust one's inner, non-possessing, truthful love.

2407. For love to blossom it is necessary to trust in the self-discovery of benevolence in others.

2408. All life is based on trust. When we forget this axiom it becomes replaced with the loneliness of fear.

2409. If we trust and yet are diverted along the way, then our boundaries as to how far we truly trust are likely being revealed. We must remain conscious.

2410. When we trust, it is we who move first, knowing that the components will follow at the appropriate time.

2411. Virtually all states of despair arise because we fail to trust. When it appears that there is nothing left to believe in, that is the most important moment to trust.

2412. To trust in one's inner self, one's abilities, one's pathway, and one's destiny, brings them forward with strength and confidence into the present moment.

2413. In an honourable environment can we allow our ego cover, our pretence, our keep safe attitude, our emotional guard, and our anxious need to defend ourselves, to come down and really trust and allow ourselves to submit and be loved?

2414. The true lover trusts that all is well, because they know that love prevails.

2415. The act of trusting another is an act of the highest respect, for it is placing the same deep confidence in others that we place in ourselves. It is an acknowledgment that the other carries the same blameless innocence that we know ourselves to have also.

2416. If we trust, we move, we flow, and life flows with us. When we do not trust, we are immobilised, and the doors to life appear closed.

2417. When we have constancy in trust, we are in truth, we are living truth.

TRUTH

2418. The truth contains the state of oneness. The state of oneness cannot be negated, though the ego may attempt to do so. Only when duality arises is there separation and the possibility of conflict, and therefore the appearance of untruth.

2419. Truth is the reliable, precisely self-correcting principle that guides and confirms our lives, and the life of the universe.

2420. Whenever truth is experienced firsthand, it is reborn. Thus all truths, though eternal, become pristine, when reborn.

2421. The truth is all around us but for the most part we do not see. We shroud ourselves in tight fitting garments called selfishness, old opinion, generalisations, knee-jerking reactions, follow the so-called tried and true, lose ourselves in dependence and false obligation, are dictated by time, inherited beliefs, mechanical habit, play self-centred games, keep an internally justifying monologue, are led by convention at the cost of our originality, embarrassed by the unconventional, fearful of moving out of our security, become angry when our beliefs are challenged, work for the love of money rather than seek the love of meaningful work, do what is expected of us whilst postponing our own expectations, have minds full of trifles and hearts overshadowed by ignorance and greed, and often place self-righteous judgment upon others whilst thinking ourselves to be perfect. We must ask 'Where do we allow the freedom in our lives to allow truth to shine?'

2422. If the divine is ultimate truth, and the divine is within, then by seeking the divine (i.e. truth) and knowing truth, we will be set free. Free from the constraints that tie us to a conditioned existence.

2423. A truth kept in confidence from one that it would help, is a crime of selfishness and deceit. Truth is not exclusive.

2424. If we think we are getting away with something, we are leaving truth behind.

2425. Truth is spoken and heard more clearly when we speak it with love.

2426. The Truth is beyond our habitualised opinions and views. Habitualised opinions and views are a soporific and a mask.

2427. That which is said from the core of one's truth regularly rings true to both speaker and listener. Whereas that which is said from the realms of avoidance, reaction, confusion, attack or falsehood, has no ring of truth, instead it has a hollow sound of the tightened ego.

2428. At times it is necessary to hold to what we know is our innermost truth, rather than be fooled by the pervasiveness of the seeming external reality.

2429. It does not seem possible to be covetous about truth whilst at the same time able to keep faith with others. There is inevitably a loss of one's honour.

2430. Truth attracts all aspirants.

2431. A truth repeated and repeated has a tendency to lead into unconsciousness and become dogma.

2432. When we act consciously we also act truthfully.

2433. We are here to live our deepest truth as an instrument of heaven.

2434. Truth, as well as being seen for what it is, can also be pointed to by what it is not.

2435. The truth is the most powerful weapon for purifying the earth. Eventually it will cut through all falseness, and prick the conscience of those who perpetrate injustice.

2436. The further removed we are from the truth, the more judgmental we tend to become. It seems to follow the order from supreme truth to high opinion (firmly based in truth), to low opinion (marginally based in truth), to finally judgmentalness (based not on truth at all, but on the holder's prejudice).

We have no right to speak of our judgmentalness or low opinions, for they are far removed from the truth. In speaking a high opinion, it is preferable we own it and not confuse it with the supreme truth. In supreme truth, there is no disunity, all is embraced.

2437. When we vow to truth, the heart unfolds; and when we vow to love, the truth becomes apparent.

2438. Truth appears to be composed of an omnipresent matrix. For if truth is denied in one place, it usually arises somewhere else.

2439. All transitory things are symptoms of a lesser truth. Only the divine is truth everlasting.

2440. We are mutually obliged to live in truth and to speak it, especially if our silence harms others.

2441. The ability to speak truthfully seems to be more an art of listening to the speaker inside; it is a meditative quality.

2442. Truth told for self-gain has a tendency to become untruth.

2443. It appears to be our calling to pursue one's subjective truth, through the mass of collected inner objective untruths, gathered since we arrived here.

2444. Truth causes the feeling, as well as the action of liberation, though sometimes truth is difficult to face. The further removed we are from speaking our personal truth, the more paranoia and disease we seem to embrace.

2445. Whatever anyone believes, is their individual truth, and accordingly it will reveal itself.

2446. The truth of one soul never violates the truth of another.

2447. Truth is sacred and cannot be given into the keeping of unbelievers. Instead it looks for a lover with whom it may unite.

2448. The truth is always the deeper, more meaningful reality. It reaches to the core; it goes beyond any emotion, beyond the ego, to connect to the heart and soul of the matter. And therefore its expression, its language, contains all of the finest states of heart and soul, such as simplicity, beauty and love.

2449. There does not appear to be any pretext or subtext to whole and true love, truth, or innocence.

2450. If we speak our truth unattached to our emotions, it will eventually cut through the forces of ignorance assailed against it.

2451. When the truth is spoken, there is nothing more that we can add. And therefore we may show our appreciation for it by being silent.

2452. Supreme truth must be the background upon which the universe and all else within it are played out, otherwise we would not exist with an ache for, or yearning towards this truth.

2453. Truth has an eternity of time, whereas untruth and illusion are forever hurrying about, for they may not rest in one place too long.

2454. The truth is that which does not contain egoic duality.

2455. Truth is unified, omnipresent subjectivity. It is perceived as light: 'I see.' It is known as: 'I am that I am.'

U

✳

ULTIMATE

2456. In order for the ultimate to be created, there must be an ultimate beginning, for it would appear that the ultimate could not be created from the finite.

✳

UNCERTAINTY

2457. Uncertainty in life does not so much arise from failing to know the external situations of life, but more from not knowing oneself. Surety arises from an interior comprehension.

✳

UNCONDITIONAL

2458. The understanding of the unconditional state cannot be reached through the egoic mind. For the ego mind is finite, whereas the unconditional is absolute and infinite. Our pathway to this understanding is reached through such things as paradox, intuition, surrender, love, and truth.

✳

UNCONSCIOUS

2459. Essentially (whether we are aware of it or not), we are all striving to make conscious the collective unconscious. The more we make conscious the heights and depths of the unconscious, the more we reveal of the divine, the more we realise the heights and depths of our own true mind as being undivided from it.

2460. The state of unconsciousness contains within it the seeds of realisation. Not consciously knowing of these seeds is the transitory state where one's perception is not mindfully directed to the areas of understanding.

UNDERSTANDING

2461. Understanding gives the gift of freedom.

2462. To intimately understand something we need to become one with it. We need to let go of our own thoughts and preoccupations. The understanding then becomes a matter of intuitive knowing, rather than an intellectually based idea of understanding.

2463. The light of understanding usually arises from content and context, the forms are only the wrapper—a symbol of what lies within, a key to unlock, a door to open.

2464. If we wish to understand more, we need to widen our perspective.

2465. Life impresses itself upon us until we have understanding.

2466. It seems that only unless we are attracted to something can we truly understand it.

2467. The forgetting of who we are, why we came here, and the resultant problems this causes, are no less a part of our evolution of understanding.

2468. Things aren't always what they seem—the outer experience provides the means for inner understanding and vice-versa. And therefore the way to this understanding may sometimes be an indirect one.

2469. On the universal level, we feel an innately subjective understanding. Is it then no wonder that sometimes we as individuals do not understand some things? However, if we look from the perspective of we as the universe, we may understand much more.

2470. From the ego view we can only have partial understanding. Things would make more sense if we understood the ultimate reason for their genesis. How often though do we even begin to imagine ultimate reasons?

2471. In attempting to seek understanding with others, we often look for the key to understanding in the other person, forgetting that we already have our own inherent understanding, our own highest truth.

2472. Sometimes it is not possible to have understanding on the level we seek. There are other dimensions from which to view our experience. These dimensions may not give us intellectual understanding, but will give us a deeper understanding through the power of surrender and grace.

2473. Understanding another gives the gift of balm to their mind and heart, and lays a foundation for union with them.

2474. If someone is not ready to hear what we have to say, it is much more difficult for us to speak of it. Understanding more readily occurs between those who have a similar consciousness.

2475. The equation of our understanding, is that which we know now, that is the current (which includes the accumulation from the past), plus the revealing of greater and greater understanding throughout eternity. Therefore it is the current to eternity.

UNEXPECTED

2476. Who amongst us can estimate the mysterious, infinite forces of the unexpected? And for that reason we may keep wonder in our eyes, and will forever underestimate it.

UNFAITHFUL

2477. Everyone lives continuously with faith, either in themselves, someone else, some thing, or the divine. If we are unfaithful in a particular area, we have placed our faith elsewhere.

UNHAPPINESS

2478. Fundamentally unhappiness is a state of ignorance, unawareness, or forgetfulness of the true I.

2479. Unhappiness is at the basis of all emotions. However the cause of unhappiness is a mistaken sense of identity, that one thinks one is primarily an ego.

UNIFIED FIELD

2480. If we see others, things, and ourselves separately, we are not seeing the unified field from where all cause issues, and all integration returns.

2481. When we know where we come from, who we are, what meaning is, and live our true livelihood—our view of others, the universe, and ourselves is immense, and becomes unified into a field of consciousness.

UNION

2482. We are all of the same life mass, individually learning to cohere our part.

2483. The individualisation of union into innumerable egos allows us to step outside of union, that we may observe union and separation. Ego appears to be nature's way of having multiple experiences of an outside perspective. The graceful surrender of ego by embracing it from a perspective of union, allows us to once again merge.

2484. The difference between what we do for ourselves and what we do for others, manifestly shows how close we are to union.

2485. We are all pulling together unconsciously for the most part, on strings of love and truth.

2486. Love and sex both seek union. They are linked in a common cause.

2487. The union we seek with the divine contains the same aspects that we seek with our earthly beloved; they are one and the same.

2488. Our attachment to the conditioned ego-mind restrains us from unfolding to union. However, outside this mind, the fundamental, utmost state of being already exists in omnipresence, without need of becoming.

UNIQUE

2489. The uniqueness of all aspects of creation portrays the unequalled originality and selflessness of the infinite, in that each design has its own place in existence.

2490. When we enhance the gift of our natural uniqueness, we become more confident, more potent, and more magnetic in the world.

UNIVERSARIAN

2491. A universarian is one who has reverence for all life.

UNIVERSE

2492. Every conscious moment in the life of the universe is a moment of victory, a window into the infinite, a light turned on, illuminating and quickening the eternal being.

2493. The universe is in a perpetual state of equilibrium, and therefore all particles arrange themselves accordingly. Thus love is ever present in all places either consciously or quiescently.

2494. Science tells us that there are more stars in the universe than grains of sand on the beaches of earth. Science also says that there are as many synapses in the human brain as there are stars in the universe. In appreciating the immensity of this, one realises that the creator has endowed us with the ability to muse, meditate, dream, and behold an entire universe.

2495. When we begin thinking and speaking in universal terms we are already partaking in the coalescing force of the universe.

2496. We are all instrumental in fulfilling the local and the infinite universe.

2497. Whatever we can conceive of is a shortcoming, compared to what the bounty of the universe can provide.

2498. The calculations of the universe are kept exactly. Every cell and every atom are balanced for their effect from one side of the universe to the other, that all may move accordingly.

2499. If something needs to be done in the universe, it shall be done. The universe is not an experiment—it is a grand design.

2500. It appears that we continue growing into the universe until we realise that we are, and always have been the universe. Then everything becomes personal, we feel and are familiar with all things, people and places.

2501. The universe seems to demand we grow. If we do not, a part of us withers each time we refuse.

2502. Love is the core essence of each of us. This essence appears to abide before and beyond our earthly existence, and to have been the medium through which a spectacular setting that we have come to call a universe was created. Within the realm of this setting nearly all have chosen to forget their essence in order to perform the part of an individual ego-actor in the all-absorbing drama of life. It appears that the creative act of each of us is concerned with remembering our quintessential background of love. And in bringing this essence of love into the foreground, that we may know the universe not only from a creation view, but also experientially, for love opens us to the greatest possibilities of experience.

2503. Behind each thing manifests the universal tide. An incoming and outgoing that has shaped what it is now. All around us has been left by the universal tide.

2504. All of this is a fantasy on a grand scale. Everything is something else . . . a magnificent wrapping over something majestic.

2505. Ultimately the universe shall be seen to be filled only with divine lovers of the divine.

2506. If we perceive with universal mind, sense with universal body, and act with universal spirit, then the heart and soul of the universe becomes apparent. The first cracks of a universal sunrise begin.

UNLOVING

2507. It is not possible to give a reason from the soul point of view for not wanting to love another. Only the ego can manufacture and justify such reasons.

UNRELIABILITY

2508. When we depend upon others but find them to be unreliable, we are put back onto our own resources, and we remember that our primary support comes from within.

UNSURE

2509. There appear to be two ways of being unsure. They are; the one based on a person's lack of confidence, and the second based on suspicion of others. Both are lessons in self-trust.

2510. It is perhaps human to have a sense of the unknown when being in someone else's domain for the first time, but to be unsure of oneself as well, is an indication that we are not as familiar with ourselves as we perhaps thought.

UNTRUTH

2511. Untruths are generally told for self-gain, saving face, or hurting others. All create inner disharmony and have the capacity for creating outer disharmony.

UNWORTHINESS

2512. Unworthiness comes from not seeing the highest truth of oneself. One can only see unworthiness by looking through the illusory eyes of the invalidating ego.

UPLIFT OTHERS

2513. We are here to bring out the very best in each other. What is it that we can do to help those around us make the best of their pathway, in order to bring out the most fruitful of their bodily, mental, and spiritual faculties? In drawing another out, we help increase their confidence and competency not only to their advantage, but also for the benefit of the earth and for others.

URGENCY

2514. The sense of urgency that many of us live our lives by surely arises from a finite view. If we want to live a harmonious life, it is transcendent to believe we live a deeply purposeful forever.

V

VACILLATION

2515. The more vacillating we are, the further removed we are from the harmonising stability of our deep inner presence.

VALUE

2516. The greater the value we put into doing something, positive or negative, the greater it returns this value to us.

2517. Value for money does not always equate with monetary terms, but sometimes to the larger experience surrounding the transaction.

VALUES

2518. Those who establish the rules and the value system, by which they operate, usually have a personal investment in their foundation, which they require others to follow. But nearly every human being has the ability to establish their own value system. We must ask 'Is our value system aligned with love and truth?'

2519. Sometimes the values we hold, the beliefs we cherish, must be sacrificed in order to embrace a wider perspective.

2520. If it is impossible for us to place a $ value on the life of an individual, how is it possible for us to place a value judgment on an entire race or nation?

2521. The automatic, reactive imposition of old subconscious, no longer appropriate values onto new directions, is a loss of consciousness to what may be required to appreciate and help blossom the present.

2522. We have to be vigilant not to let our own tastes and values become the yardstick by which we measure others' tastes and values, but rather to rejoice in the infinite variety throughout the world.

VANDALISM

2523. If something is destroyed maliciously, basically it shows an attempt to remodel outside things in a frustrated effort to make inner change.

VARIATION

2524. There does not appear to be one particular formula for living which is steadfast and unchanging. Rather a kind of creative exploration or open-minded tolerance, which keeps us moving and not stuck, seems to be required of us. Even our so-called good habits tend to lose their power after a while. Apparently we are meant to live with variation in order to experience a greater perception and perhaps a larger involvement, so that we may transform a more comprehensive understanding.

VIBRATION

2525. To raise one's vibration one has to be inspired by ideals, visions, dreams, love, truth, innocence, compassion, beauty, justice, and so on.

2526. Earth life is based on a particular vibratory frequency. Our conditioned thinking and beliefs tend to divide the wholeness of this frequency into unconnected parts. However, our freedom amplifies, through realising the wholeness of earth's frequency.

2527. In raising our vibration, we begin to join with the wavelength of our venerable path, and our essential destination.

VICTIM

2528. The original meaning of victim was that which was offered as a sacrifice to god. We cannot sacrifice the divine to the divine, but as victims who want to move out of victimhood, we realise that we are deepened by trial, and we sacrifice a little of our condemning, persecuted and martyred ego.

2529. Whenever we are victimised, we are also denying our own power and perhaps giving it away. It is this loss of power that we are most reactive to. We help regain our power, our sense of self, by producing an action of love that serves our true nature.

2530. A victim without forgiveness and compassion for their aggressor tends to remain in victimhood.

✳

VIOLENCE

2531. Violence is a forceful denial of the divinity of another and of their needs. Perhaps it fills the aggressor's emptiness with an imitational sense of deity.

✳

VIRTUOSO

2532. If we are to be a virtuoso, an adept who masterfully directs their life from the inner supreme, the place of power, potency, and dominion, we are required to have faith that we are already this, in order that our faith may be made entire. This decision is only possible if one is living a life where one's honour, worth, and innocence are in a state of integrity with one's true state and path, otherwise we lack the power and the sovereignty.

✳

VISIONARY

2533. The visionary conceives a virginal reality and becomes the creator of the first step upon the road to its appearance. The greater the visionary's potency of actualisation, the greater the conscious opportunity of fertilising its conception to give it life into the world. The visionary's potency, or lack of, means that not all visions are to be created on this world. Love has the most potent power for choosing, and bringing forth a vision of excellence.

2534. The reality of those who consider themselves material realists did not suddenly appear out of nowhere; it too was originally conceived by a visionary.

2535. A true visionary tends to be open-handed and therefore extravagantly generous, noble, and lovingly benevolent. Their canvas extends beyond the horizon, with the rubicund promise of a new dawn.

VISUALISATION

2536. Our imaginings, both positive and negative, can also be our visualisation.

2537. If something turns out to be not how we visualised it, then it may not be the vision that is amiss, but the placement and the timing.

2538. If we perform the final act in our visualisation, we help create the most potent blueprint.

VITALITY

2539. Vitality is a sign that one's life vibration is oscillating at a rapid rate. This in turn creates exuberance, wonder, curiosity, creativity, generative ability, and endurance. All of which are determined by the scope of freedom that we give our spirit, to be quickened by life.

VOID

2540. A moment spent in the tranquil void of infinite potential, gives us a glimpse of eternity spent in the infinite.

W

WALKING

2541. When we walk in serenity, we embody the radiance of our soul, and the original, peaceful rapture of mind.

WALLS-BRIDGES

2542. We can build walls or bridges between our divinity and our daily consciousness. We build bridges with awareness, conscience, intuition and love. We build walls only with selfishness.

WASTE

2543. Those who waste have not learned the lessons of love and compassion for other beings, or for the earth.

WEALTH

2544. The pleasure of happiness in abundance is our greatest wealth. Our ability to value and take pleasure creates our fortune.

2545. Wealth is living in happiness and gratitude for what we already have in this moment: our sight, our hearing, our clothes, our housing, this pen that writes . . .

WELFARE

2546. All people, all beings, are the recipients of the welfare of the divine. Governments, multinationals and bureaucrats who think they are in charge are operating under a dense illusion.

WHOLENESS

2547. Wholeness begins when commitment rises to the challenge of the self-inclusive reality of unity.

2548. When we are experiencing wholeness (holiness), we are more able to effectively generate a state of joy, creativity, health, love, truth, happiness and so on. It is an enlarging and focusing of these states which are already present in our wholeness.

WHY

2549. If there is a 'Why' in our lives, why something seems not attainable or available to us at the moment, it is because there is a very good reason for it to be so. And the reason is certainly for our benefit and understanding. This understanding usually comes with hindsight, if we are unable to see it now.

WILL

2550. When we live our true passion, there is no separation between our will and divine will, they are one and the same.

2551. Will operates primarily by awareness or by thought. Awareness is largely a faculty of the soul, while thought is largely a faculty of the ego.

2552. If one's will is more intuitive, and feeling based, it will allow an open understanding and awareness to spontaneously flow through. It is already deeply self-empowered. It is naturally discerning, flexible, and happily determined.

2553. Ego-will tends to be selfishly driven and therefore manipulative, judgmental, prone to attacking, or being upset if its needs are not met, by becoming involved in stubborn battles of (ego) will with others. It desperately wants the self-power to be able to control others, and becomes overly rigid in controlling oneself. Fundamentally it may be unaware of what is really required, because it is so involved with having to prove itself.

2554. When we pray to the divine 'Thy will be done,' we are actually saying: 'Love's will be done.'

2555. In order for our will to be powerful, it needs to be sharpened by being made specific.

2556. A will in purposeful alignment helps pull the earth, its inhabitants, and perhaps even beyond into harmony.

2557. Will can be potent or impotent. The more life and vitality we give to something, the more alive it becomes.

2558. The principal component of an effective will is more than intentional belief, it is a relaxed faith.

2559. The arrow of will points wherever we aim. This primary act determines where we are going, what rules our lives, what we discover, and what we know.

2560. If we are overly using will power to try and discipline ourselves, we do not fully understand the benefits of what we truly desire.

2561. Through little acts of will, we become more will-filled as a matter of course.

2562. A will needs a centre from which to come, and a place for it to act upon. Similarly, the universe in all probability has a central willed intelligence.

2563. If we allow our love, conscience and intuition to direct our will, we shall live and create a more spiritual reality.

2564. The highest will is the commanded will to create through genuine love. Love brings the consciousness of our creation into the present, it is instantaneous, and it already is the outcome. All contrary to love creations are created outside of the full consciousness of the present moment, where fear and frustration dwell.

2565. When our will is for an honourable purpose, then no matter who or what it offends, or what others think of us, we are deeply obliged to pursue it.

2566. The evolved will of creation is to realise the creator.

2567. As human beings that continue to think in terms of the old theology, that is, as children under the guardianship of parental gods, we will be unable to assume the full potency of our will, which comes from maturing into creative gods ourselves.

WILLINGNESS

2568. Willingness is a sign of the adventurer, one who embraces life fully.

WISDOM

2569. The discernment of truth beyond the layers of routine unawareness becomes our wisdom. It is the penetrating insight that causes an illumination of the present and an informed consciousness of what will come.

2570. We cannot have wisdom without embracing the sacred.

2571. Wisdom arises from being able to see, hear, and feel the creative life principle operating everywhere, and an ability to understand this from a boundless viewpoint.

2572. If we desire wisdom, we must have love. For the boundlessness of love will enlarge our vision that we may see above and below, and from all directions. The pervasiveness of truth then begins to become apparent.

2573. When the heart-light of one's soul illumines the mind, then the gnosis of wisdom reveals itself.

2574. In the state of love we are more able to hear the wisdom voice of the inner divine arising through our meditation, contemplation, compassion, imagination and dreams.

2575. Peace, love, innocence, beauty, surrender, compassion, gentleness, stillness, reflection, wonder, joy, sensitivity, understanding and gratitude, are some of the hallmarks of the wise, in that these qualities allow the receptivity for wisdom to arise.

WISH

2576. Our wishes begin the process of invoking. Our will commands it and carries it forward.

WITHDRAWING

2577. If we perceive that another is withdrawing from us, it is likely that we will react unconsciously at first and either overreach ourselves or begin to withdraw also. It is at this point that we need to become conscious, remain in love and therefore remain true to our higher self.

WITHHOLDING

2578. The sense of holding back, of not being bold enough with one's natural inclination to love others joyously and exuberantly, is our pre-eminent challenge.

2579. When we withhold, we tend to constrict, harden, and become inflexible. We become cold, insensitive and more intolerant. We look backwards and we deny ourselves the opportunity to lovingly participate in the present.

When we open we tend to expand, soften and become flexible. We become warm-hearted, sensitive, compassionate and generous. We look with wonder, we engage the present, and have happy expectations of the future.

2580. The place where we withhold is the self-imposed barrier that prevents us uniting with our own love.

2581. If we hold back when life presents the opportunity, we deny the contribution of our unique individuality to the richness of this world.

2582. Whenever we experience the sense of holding back, we are usually denying the expression of a deeper, truer inclination.

WITNESS

2583. When we witness with awareness (the quiescent state of love) without judging whether it is good or bad, we begin to realise our universal state of being. The dichotomy between soul and ego is overcome; the outer world and the inner world are reconciled, and deep peace ensues from where love and joy blossom.

2584. The power of a loving truth witnessed and offered to the divine, fortifies the ability to be true to one's soul, rather than the experience of the loss of power which occurs when this truth is egoically spilled out to others.

2585. We are all eyewitnesses, beholders of this infinite act of revelation. Our lives are the living testimony of an original self-acting, self-witnessing, visionary conception.

2586. If we truly witness, we witness the workings of heaven.

✳

WONDER

2587. Wonder is somehow an expected surprise. It is a re-acquaintance with the fertile delights from the wellspring of creation.

2588. The innocent lover lives in a state of wonder, which is the vast unending margin, where the bounty of heaven enters earth.

2589. What right do we have to draw wonder and delight to ourselves if we do not actively cultivate appreciation for them.

✳

WORDS

2590. When words are more consciously chosen, they contain power. Most of the time we use words automatically—they reveal our state of inattention, and therefore they lack the potency of awareness.

2591. Words tend to objectify and therefore reinforce our ego distance from creation, whilst at the same time enclosing us. When we make our words more subjective, such as found in sublime poetry and prose, or spoken with the love and wisdom of the transcended subjective ego, we personalise creation. We pull creation towards us, we leap off the edge and into the boundless, and we are more able to feel a harmony with all.

WORK

2592. Work without meaning is like life without purpose; both deny our inner nature.

2593. The decision to have a happy heart makes all work lighter.

2594. If there is no sense of ownership (really, a term to denote responsibility, and therefore also the sanction to experience more deeply and to enjoy) it will be difficult for us to put our heart into work when there is no appreciation of these qualities.

Yet from the spiritual view it is claimed that there is no such thing as individual ownership. Therefore, work from this perspective seems to operate on the basis of universal holding, which helps create a pleasure in all aspects of creation.

2595. If we attempt to work faster than our own pace, the resulting stress will make us less productive in the long term. Similarly, if we purposefully work more slowly, especially as part of a team, the resulting stress from emotions of guilt and separateness, is too great a price for the loss of our natural pace, which has an innocent rhythm.

2596. We are all the divine incarnate, and thus we work for the divine whether we are aware of it or not. Some of us may choose work that is not in harmony with our divinity, but eventually, our inherent nature will create divinely.

2597. All of us have solitary work, and work to be done socially. Though inherently all work is social; it reaches out beyond the individual.

2598. If we work for our ego, we are alone, we are in competition with others, and therefore we will experience fear and insecurity, whilst continually attempting to selfishly gain a greater share.

2599. We ennoble the quality of our work as well as ourselves, if we work with love and excellence. We are then more inclined to be fascinated and engrossed with it, and consequently rewarded with greater satisfaction and the peace of fulfilment.

2600. Work done out of habit, work done for the sake of work and not done for the revelation of the human soul, is an avoidance of the soul.

2601. If we believe in a benevolent creator, then the idea that humans are to spend most of their lives in unfulfilling work seems not only illogical but also an avoidance of the deeper meaning of existence. If we do believe in work above love or meaning, in our ignorance, we are making ourselves bonded slaves to the divine.

2602. The worthiness of the work we do can be measured by how much it feeds us physically, mentally, and spiritually. How much our work has a humanitarian/world/universal face to it, can again be measured by how much it feeds others, the world, and the universe, physically, mentally, and spiritually.

WORRY

2603. Worries are the baggage we are carrying now for an imaginary mishap in the future, that if believed in and given enough energy, will oppress and cover over the love and truth at the core of our being. Worries are an avoidance of the present moment.

2604. Our habitual worries, fears, patterns and concerns will continue to recur, unless we consciously transform our reactive ego personality towards these things, by transcending them.

2605. Until we know, we do not know, and our worries and concerns are in vain.

2606. When we are more mindful of our greater good, the circumstances of outer reality become less worrisome.

2607. Our worries and concerns cannot be dealt with by the ego-mind, for it lacks the necessary wisdom. If we persist with attempting to find solutions in the ego-mind, we create an ongoing round of confusion, and burden ourselves.

2608. What is there to worry about? Everything, yes anything and everything!

2609. The ego mind continually sets up a pattern of worries in order of priority. So that whatever is dealt with on top of the list is automatically replaced with the next underlying worry. It is an endless sequence if we attempt to deal with it on the ego level. By surrendering our ego to the divine we become empty, still, and innocent, and from here mindfulness and love begin to flow once more into actions and solutions of grace.

WORSHIP

2610. The act of worship unifies the personal ego in devotion to the soul. It helps create the healing union between soul and ego.

2611. If our worship does not move us, how can we expect the divine to be moved? Hollow words, passionless postures, and habitual rites cannot invoke the benediction of heaven.

2612. True worship springs from the same kind of ardour of the lover to the beloved—in the keen adoration and devotion that burns fiercely in the lover's heart. And likewise, in the zeal and curiosity of the naive and innocent child in awe and wonderment. And all of this done with the faith of one that lovingly glorifies and consecrates, without seeking honour or reward.

2613. Worship is the highest love. The highest love is seeing the transcendence of the divine's sacred beauty incarnated into all things.

WORTHY

2614. Unless we know we are worthy and deserve love, success and honour; unless we already accept ourselves as being valued, just and virtuous, we shall tend to remain fearful of what is good and right for us, and therefore repel it, both consciously and subconsciously.

WOUND

2615. The purpose for the wounds of life seem to be to prod us into a deeper understanding of ourselves, and of our life's pathway.

2616. When we consciously confront any wound from past or present with the unifying power of love, we immediately begin to repair ourselves.

WRONG

2617. We have to be prepared to accept being wrong sometimes in order that some of our boundaries are widened.

X

XENOPHOBIA

2618. Xenophobia is fundamentally the dislike of the unfamiliar, perplexing and exotic in one's own subconscious.

Y

YIELDING

2619. Humanity is yielding a harvest of love pearls, and leaving behind the shells of surrendered ego.

2620. If we can yield while still remembering and being in truth, we will not need to reduce ourselves into enmity, but remain in love.

Z

ZEST

2621. In order to have zest we have to allow ourselves to become hungry for life, so that we can relish and savour the taste and spice of life, and not habitually look for our life's hunger to be continually satisfied with food or addictions. For when we are full, our senses are dulled, and we can no longer taste the zest.

2622. The more we live in the past, the more we close down to the possibilities of the present and the future. The more lifeless, stubborn, bigoted, depressed, serious, ill, bored, unmotivated, self-obsessed and security-minded we become. To live in the present whilst looking forward, confers the gift of zest for life. Such zest is a sign that one is living in close contact with infinite love and power.

The more mindful we become, the more we begin.
Each time we return to mindfulness, we return to the beginning.
Ultimately, there are only infinite upon infinite beginnings.